Columbus, Ohio

T0307100

# Columbus, Ohio

Two Centuries of Business and Environmental Change

*Mansel G. Blackford*

Trillium, an imprint of

The Ohio State University Press • Columbus

Library of Congress Cataloging-in-Publication Data

Names: Blackford, Mansel G., 1944– author.
Title: Columbus, Ohio : two centuries of business and environmental change / Mansel G.
    Blackford.
Description: Columbus : Trillium, an imprint of The Ohio State University Press,
    [2016] | "2016" | Includes bibliographical references and index.
Identifiers: LCCN 2016007847 | ISBN 9780814213148 (cloth ; alk. paper) |
    ISBN 0814213146 (cloth ; alk. paper)
Subjects: LCSH: Industries—Ohio—Columbus—History. | Business enterprises—
    Ohio—Columbus—History. | Columbus (Ohio)—Economic conditions—
    History. | Water-supply—Ohio—Columbus—History. | Water resources
    development—Ohio—Columbus—History. | Land use—Ohio—Columbus—
    History. | Urbanization—Environmental aspects—Ohio—Columbus. | Cities and
    towns—Ohio—Columbus—Growth—History.
Classification: LCC HC108.C77 B53 2016 | DDC 330.9771/57—dc23
LC record available at http://lccn.loc.gov/2016007847

Cover design by James A. Baumann
Text design by Juliet Williams
Type set in Sabon and Alexandria

Cover image: Broad and High streets, 1912. Courtesy of the Columbus Metropolitan
Library.

9  8  7  6  5  4  3  2  1

*For my wife, Victoria*

# CONTENTS

*List of Illustrations*    ix
*Acknowledgments*    xi

Introduction    Columbus throughout Two Hundred Years    1

Chapter 1    Two Centuries of Business Development    8

Chapter 2    The Role of Water in Shaping Columbus    49

Chapter 3    Water and the Development of Columbus    94

Chapter 4    Land Use in a Changing City    116

Chapter 5    Land Use and Urban Development    156

Conclusion    Columbus in 2012    206

Appendix    Populations of Ohio: Columbus and Other Cities, 1800–2010    213

*Bibliographic Essay*    215
*Index*    219

# ILLUSTRATIONS

1.1   The Second Neil House in 1915      25

1.2   Buckeye Steel's Foundry in 1915      35

1.3   One Nationwide Plaza in 1984      46

2.1   Map of Columbus's New Water and Sewer System in 1910      77

2.2   Griggs Dam in 1905      80–81

2.3   Columbus's Water Works in 1908      83

3.1   Flood Damage in Columbus in 1913      96

3.2   O'Shaughnessy Dam in 1926      99

4.1   Joel Wright's Map of Columbus in 1812      120–21

4.2   Goodale Park in 1907      127

4.3   Regulation of Downtown Traffic with a Street Umbrella in 1914      138

4.4   The Proposed Civic Center Looking West in 1908      146

4.5   Safety Poster at Buckeye Steel Castings in 1915      152

4.6   The Industrialized South Side in 1915      154

5.1   Upper Arlington in 1926      170

5.2   The Town and Country Shopping Center around 1948      177

# ACKNOWLEDGMENTS

Many people have helped me in preparing this book. I would especially like to thank staff members of the Ohio Historical Society (recently renamed the Ohio History Connection), the Columbus Metropolitan Library, and the Ohio State University Library for their kind aid. Scott Caputo, in particular, deserves my thanks for helping make images from the collections of the Columbus Metropolitan Library's extensive holdings available for use as illustrations in this volume, as does Rachel Deavers for helping me prepare images from the holdings of the Ohio State University Library. Edward Lentz has earned my gratitude for sharing his encyclopedic knowledge of the history of Columbus on numerous occasions. Similarly, Conrade Hinds has helped me understand the many intricacies of water policies in Columbus. James Bach, L. Diane Barnes, John Burnham, William Childs, Steven Conn, Conrade Hinds, Andrea Lentz, Ed Lentz, Kimberly Neath, Mark Rose, David Stebenne, Tom Weeks, Christian Zacher, and two anonymous readers for the Ohio State University Press read all or parts of earlier versions of this work and offered me valuable suggestions on how to improve it. People at the Ohio State University Press deserve my thanks for turning my manuscript history into this book, especially Tony Sanfilippo, the director of the press, and Tara Cyphers, the managing editor of the press. I would like to thank my wife, who is a librarian by profession, for helping me proofread this study in manuscript form. Some parts of chapter 2 first appeared in an article in *Ohio History,* and I want to thank Will Underwood, the director of Kent State University Press, for permission to reprint that information in this volume.[1] I remain, of course, solely responsible for any errors that may remain in this history of Columbus.

1. Mansel G. Blackford, "Water in the Shaping of Columbus, Ohio, 1812–1912," *Ohio History* 122 (2015), 65–88. Copyright 2015 by Kent State University Press. Reprinted with permission.

# Columbus throughout Two Hundred Years

In 1908 members of a city-planning commission headed by Charles Mulford Robinson, a nationally known urban planner, drafted a design for Columbus. In their introduction they astutely observed, "The city of Columbus represents the mingling of two distinct types of cities." Continuing, they noted, "It is at once a capital city and an industrial city, and, secondarily, it is an educational center."[1] Had they lived another fifty years, they might have added that Columbus had become a major center for insurance and finance. In fact, Columbus has been a multifaceted city throughout its history. The capital of Ohio, Columbus has been a center of commerce, industry, finance, and education at various times, with those roles often overlapping. This history of Columbus examines how and why the city developed as it did economically and what the environmental consequences have been over two centuries of time, 1812 through 2012. It is a complex story, rife with unexpected twists and turns, as well as developments that might have been foreseen in a growing midwestern metropolis. No single factor explains the history of Columbus, but the development and implementation of water-use and land-use policies,

---

1. City Plan Commission, "The Plan of Columbus: Report Made to the Honorable Charles A. Bond, Mayor, to the Honorable Board of Public Service, and to the Honorable City Council," February 1908, p. 9.

1

and interactions among those policies—topics upon which this volume focuses—reveal much about the evolution of the city.

Two major themes run through my work's analysis. One is the tension that was present from the city's earliest days between business growth and environmental change, with the two often at cross-purposes. For instance, industrial development contributed to the pollution of water supplies, which in turn hurt businesses needing supplies of clean water. The second theme is the interaction between private enterprise and public policy in the making of Columbus. There was never a period of laissez-faire in the history of the city. Politics at city, state, and national levels always mattered. This history focuses on interactions among individuals, their many organizations, and their businesses in the evolution of Columbus. Men and women made Columbus what it became. However, they usually did so not as lone individuals but as leaders and members of business firms, business organizations, and various types of civic bodies.

Of course, similar themes run throughout the histories of many, perhaps most, American cities—and, indeed, throughout the history of the United States as a whole. Public and private efforts have often jointly spurred economic development, and there have been frequent conflicts between that development and environmental preservation. In these respects, Columbus's story is America's story, and much of this study is devoted to explaining how and why those stories evolved as they did. Yet Columbus residents were sometimes unusually innovative in their approaches to uses of water and land. Precisely because they lived in a midsize, midwestern city, they could learn from the earlier experiences of their counterparts in larger coastal metropolises and then go beyond them. Not having large sunk costs in preexisting water systems, Columbus residents could, for instance, develop new state-of-the-art methods of treating water and sewage—not always, certainly, but often enough to make their city stand out from many others.

This history is composed of five chapters. Chapter 1 analyzes the business growth of Columbus over the city's two centuries of existence, tracing how residents made important transitions in its business foundations while also describing continuities in them. Chapters 2 and 3 look at how water use and water-use policies helped shape Columbus economically, socially, and spatially. These two chapters examine especially why Columbus became a national leader in water and sewage treatment during the Progressive era of the early twentieth century and what the results of that leadership have been into the twenty-first century. The chapters stress the very important roles that water matters played in the growth of the city and argue, in fact, that water issues largely defined Columbus. Chapters 4 and 5 turn to private and public land-use issues. Like residents in many other American cities, people in Columbus considered a City Beautiful plan in the Progressive era but soon turned instead to public zoning and private-deed covenants to channel urban growth. Downtown, neighborhood, and suburban developments were important parts of the story about land use, as was the spread of a park system. In significance of arguments, those chapters analyzing the development of Columbus up to World War I loom large in this history. By the close of the Progressive era, much of modern Columbus had been built or imagined. In this optimistic time, Columbus's leaders and residents imagined a promising future for their city and took concrete steps to try to make that vision a reality.

Historian Mark Rose has recently observed that there have now been two generations of historians dealing with urban environmentalism. The first generation, he noted, "focused on experts and technology in remediating environmental hazards." The second generation, in contrast, "brought politicians and public policy front and center and made them key actors in shaping urban and environmental change."[2] Urban environmentalism is rapidly coming of age as an important field of study.[3] While a seminal work has looked at Chicago, most studies have focused on large coastal cities—New York, Boston, Philadelphia, Seattle, San Francisco, and Los Angeles.[4] Even examinations of suburbs have taken

---

2. Mark Rose, "Technology and Politics: The Scholarship of Two Generations of Urban-Environmental Historians," *Journal of Urban History* 30 (July 2004), 769–85, esp. 770.

3. Kathleen A. Brosnan, "Effluence, Affluence, and the Maturing of Urban Environmental History," *Journal of Urban History* 31 (January 2004), 115–23; Jonathan J. Keyes, "A Place of Its Own: Urban Environmental History," *Journal of Urban History* 26 (March 2000), 380–90; Martin Melosi, "The Place of the City in Environmental History," *Environmental History Review* 17 (Spring 1993), 1–23; Christine Meisner Rosen and Joel A. Tarr, "The Importance of an Urban Perspective in Environmental History," *Journal of Urban History* 20 (May 1994), 299–310; and Stanley K. Schultz and Clay McShane, "To Engineer the Metropolis: Sewers, Sanitation, and City Planning in Late-Nineteenth-Century America," *Journal of American History* 65 (September 1978), 389–411. For a recent effort to connect infrastructural changes in cities to the evolving ideas of urbanites, see Carl Smith, *City Water, City Life: Water and the Infrastructure of Ideas in Urbanizing Philadelphia, Boston, and Chicago* (Chicago: University of Chicago Press, 2013).

4. On Chicago, see William Cronon, *Nature's Metropolis: Chicago and the Great West* (New York: W. W. Norton & Company, 1991). For a superb environmental study of a coastal city, see Matthew Klingle, *Emerald City: An Environmental History of Seattle* (New Haven: Yale University Press, 2007).

a bicoastal approach.[5] In an attempt to correct this imbalance, my work looks at Columbus, a midsize, midwestern city whose development may have been more typical of that of other American cities.[6] Most generally, this volume contributes to the important, but understudied, field of midwestern history.[7]

The bicentennial of the passage of the Northwest Ordinance in 1787 by Congress stimulated work in midwestern history. In a seminal study published in 1990 historians Andrew R. L. Cayton and Peter S. Onuf correctly observed that other sections of the United States—the South, New England, and the trans-Mississippi West—had long attracted more attention from scholars as regions than had the Midwest, and they set out to change that situation. "The Midwest," they asserted, "was distinctive because it *was* the United States."[8] A flurry of work on the Midwest followed the publication of their study, but it did not last. By the early 2000s much of the burst of research, writing, and teaching about the Midwest as a region had trailed off. In a valuable study published in 2013, historian Jon K. Lauck lamented the "continuing neglect of the region," observing that "midwestern history is a weak and declining field of study."[9]

Scholars who have looked at the Midwest have examined it variously as a geographic region and as a state of mind. As they have pointed

---

5. Carl Abbott, "Jim Rockford or Tony Soprano: Coastal Contrasts in American Suburbia," *Pacific Historical Review* 83 (February 2014), 1–23.

6. Representative works about midwestern cities include Carl Abbott, *Boosters and Businessmen: Popular Economic Thought and Urban Growth in the Antebellum Middle West* (Westport, CT: Greenwood Press, 1981); Timothy R. Mahoney, *River Towns in the Great West: The Structure of Provincial Urbanization in the American Midwest, 1820–1870* (Cambridge: Cambridge University Press, 1990); Jon C. Teaford, *Cities of the Heartland: The Rise and Fall of the Industrial Midwest* (Bloomington: Indiana University Press, 1993); and Richard C. Wade, *The Urban Frontier: Pioneer Life in Early Pittsburgh, Cincinnati, Lexington, Louisville, and St. Louis* (Cambridge, MA: Harvard University Press, 1959). For an early effort to generalize about midwestern cities, see Bayrd Still, "Patterns of Mid-Nineteenth Century Urbanization in the Middle West," *Mississippi Valley Historical Review* 28 (1941), 187–206.

7. On midwestern history as an important, but understudied, field, see *The Identity of the American Midwest: Essays on Regional History*, eds. Andrew R. L. Cayton and Susan E. Gray (Bloomington: Indiana University Press, 2001), a collection of eleven essays. For a recent statement and survey of the historiography, see Jon K. Lauck, *The Lost Region: Toward a Revival of Midwestern History* (Iowa City: University of Iowa Press, 2012). Now-classic studies include Andrew R. L. Cayton and Peter S. Onuf, *The Midwest and the Nation: Rethinking the History of an American Region* (Bloomington: Indiana University Press, 1990); and James R. Shortridge, *The Middle West: Its Meaning in American Culture* (Lawrence: University Press of Kansas, 1989).

8. Cayton and Onuf, *Midwest and the Nation,* xviii.

9. Lauck, *Lost Region,* 4, 73.

out, in recent decades most Americans have come to view Kansas and Nebraska as the heartland of the Middle West, with only a minority of Americans even seeing Ohio as part of the Midwest. Many writers, especially those poets and novelists who have depicted the Midwest in the twentieth century, have pictured it as a land of farms and small towns, ignoring the region's large cities.[10] Writing in 1918, novelist Willa Cather described the land of Nebraska: "There seemed to be nothing to see; no fences, no creeks or trees, no hills or fields. . . . There was nothing but land . . . slightly undulating."[11] Pulitzer Prize–winning poet Theodore Roethke viewed Michigan land in 1953 similarly: "The upland of alder and birchtrees, / Through the swamp alive with quicksand, / The way blocked by the fallen fir-tree, / The thickets darkening, / The ravines ugly."[12] For Cather and Roethke, and for many other writers, nearly uncivilized nature, somewhat hostile to humans, dominated their scenes. No cities and few people intruded.

In looking at Columbus in part as a midwestern city, and by examining the city's relationships with its nearby hinterland, my work addresses important issues in midwestern history. My history argues that in many ways Columbus was a typical midwestern city, but that in other ways, especially the city's continuing economic ascent after World War II, it was atypical. Whether seen as typical or as unusual—and, again, it was some of both—the history of Columbus is well worth studying. Urban historians have recently been emphasizing a number of major themes in examining the development of cities in both the Midwest and the nation: the significance of conflicts among various groups in shaping urban contours, the important roles taken by city governments in influencing the course of urban developments, and the corresponding significance of politics and public policies in determining how cities have grown. This study investigates these matters, along with that of environmental justice and the ways in which decisions about land and water issues have affected different groups in Columbus.

---

10. On this enduring trope, see William Barillas, *The Midwest Pastoral: Place and Landscape in the Literature of the American Heartland* (Athens: Ohio University Press, 2006). For an examination of the realities of the diversity, complexity, and heterogeneity of the Midwest, state-by-state, see the essays by thirteen scholars in *Heartland: Comparative Histories of Midwestern States*, ed. James H. Madison (Bloomington: Indiana University Press, 1988).

11. Willa Cather, *My Ántonia* (Boston: Houghton Mifflin Company, 1954), 7.

12. Theodore Roethke, "Journey to the Interior," in Theodore Roethke, *Last Poems of Theodore Roethke* (Garden City: Doubleday & Company Inc., 1964), 19.

My interest in the history of interactions between business develop-ments and environmental issues reaches back to my first book in 1977. More recently, I have looked at how those interactions have played out in urban settings and what their consequences have been over time.[13] How have Americans reached decisions on developmental issues? How have those decisions shaped regions? What environmental-justice issues have been involved? Who have the winners and losers been? Why? My spe-cific interest in Columbus stems in part from having lived in the city while serving as a member of the history department at the Ohio State University for forty years and, consequently, viewing the many changes occurring in Columbus. In an earlier work, I explored some of the indus-trial development of Columbus.[14] Business historians—and I am one of them—have usually not paid much attention to environmental matters, although that situation is changing. I hope my study of Columbus spurs more research connecting business to environmental alterations.[15]

Over the past decade or so, a growing number of scholars have argued for the value of "deep history," "big history," and "planetary history." These types of history span continents and thousands, even millions, of years. They address nonhuman as well as human matters. Yet even advocates of such approaches to history are uneasy about getting too far away from localities, primary sources, and human agency. My study of

---

13. Mansel G. Blackford, *Politics of Business in California* (Columbus: Ohio State University Press, 1977). But see esp. Mansel G. Blackford, *The Lost Dream: Businessmen and City Planning on the Pacific Coast, 1890–1920* (Columbus: Ohio State University Press, 1993); Mansel G. Blackford, *Fragile Paradise: The Impact of Tourism on Maui, 1959–2000* (Lawrence: University Press of Kansas, 2001); and Mansel G. Blackford. *Pathways to the Present: U.S. Development and Its Consequences in the Pacific* (Hono-lulu: University of Hawai'i Press, 2007).

14. Mansel G. Blackford, *A Portrait Cast in Steel: Buckeye International and Colum-bus, Ohio, 1881–1980* (Westport, CT: JAI Press, 1982). For a look at industrialization in Ohio, see also Mansel G. Blackford, "B. F. Goodrich and the Industrialization of Ohio," *Builders of Ohio,* eds. Warren Van Tine and Michael Pierce (Columbus: Ohio State Uni-versity Press, 2003), 151–63.

15. In 1999 historians Christine Meisner Rosen and Christopher Sellers observed, "Business history has never paid much attention to the environment," and in fact has given "little attention to the effects of resource extraction and use on plants, animals, land, air, or water, much less entire ecosystems and climate." See Christine Meisner Rosen and Christopher C. Sellers, "The Nature of the Firm: Towards an Ecocultural History of Business," *Business History Review* 73 (Winter 1999), 577–600, esp. 577. That situation has begun to change. Articles in the *Business History Review* 73 (Winter 1999) examined relationships between business and the environment, as did those in *Enterprise & Society* 8 (June 2007). See also Christine Meisner Rosen, "The Business-Environment Connection," *Environmental History* 10 (January 2005), 77–79.

Columbus is a microhistory, especially where it examines regions and neighborhoods in the city. However, it also ties development in Columbus to that in the Midwest, elsewhere in the United States, and in Europe to present a larger macrostudy.[16]

My history of Columbus thus lies at intersections between important fields of study: urban history, environmental history (especially urban environmental history), business history, and midwestern history. It adds to and modifies scholarship in those fields, sometimes in small ways, at other times in larger ones, particularly in matters having to do with urban environmental history.

---

16. On the issue of scale in history, see "How Size Matters: The Question of Scale in History," "Conversation" in *American Historical Review* 118 (December 2013), 1431–72. See also John Lewis Gaddis, *The Landscape of History: How Historians Map the Past* (New York: Oxford University Press, 2002), 71–90. On the meaning of big history, see David Christian, *Maps of Time: An Introduction to Big History* (Berkeley: University of California Press, 2004). For a broad-ranging big history, see John L. Brooke, *Climate Change and the Course of Global History: A Rough Journey* (New York: Cambridge University Press, 2014), which looks at more than 200,000 years of history.

CHAPTER 1

# Two Centuries
# of Business Development

Since its founding in 1812, Columbus has been, in turn, a commercial city, an industrial metropolis, and, most recently, a center for finance, higher education, and government services. There has been considerable overlap in these stages in the development of Columbus, which has also served as the capital for the state of Ohio for two centuries. This economic diversity has been an important thread in the fabric of the history of Columbus, giving the city a resilience not shared by Cleveland or Cincinnati, especially during the late twentieth century. In particular, being home to both the state government and the Ohio State University gave the Columbus economy a buoyancy that the economies of many other midwestern cities lacked. Columbus was the only major Ohio city that did not decline in population during either the Great Depression of the 1930s or the severe economic downturn of 2007–10.

As this chapter shows, both public and private actions—the work of governmental officials and that of business leaders—were integral to the development of Columbus. The city had few readily apparent natural advantages: no harbor, no supplies of iron ore, no lodes of gold or silver. Nor was Columbus initially located on well-traveled trade routes. "In the Midwest," urban historian Timothy Mahoney has observed, "most towns began with the decision of some farmer or peddler to specialize as a middleman or merchant among the people in the neighborhood."[1] Not

---

1. Mahoney, *River Towns*, 6.

8

so in the case of Columbus. To the contrary, Columbus came into being only when Ohio's state legislators chose a place in the near-wilderness of central Ohio to build the new state capital. That site became Columbus, at first a fairly isolated locale. Only as time passed and transportation facilities improved did the location of Columbus permit the city to become a center for trade and industry, a crossroads for the United States.[2] As Americans moving west poured across the Appalachian Mountains, Columbus experienced population and spatial expansion. As their city grew, Columbus residents encountered environmental problems and restraints, topics dealt with more fully in succeeding chapters. Clean water needed for drinking and for manufacturing became scarce, threatening city residents with diseases and businesses with stagnation. Similarly, serious issues about land-use matters had to be resolved for Columbus to grow in size and population. This first chapter examines the business growth of Columbus as a way of setting the stage for later chapters, which investigate environmental issues, especially those involving water and land. Chapter 1 looks first at Columbus's political and commercial roots; next it examines the city's growth as a midwestern industrial center; and finally it closes by analyzing the transformation of Columbus into an educational, financial, and governmental metropolis after World War II.

## Economic Development in Ohio

The development of Columbus took place in the context of fundamental economic changes occurring throughout the state of Ohio.[3] In the antebellum years, those before the Civil War of the 1860s, farming was at the center of Ohio's economy. In 1839 the state led the nation in wheat production, and in 1849 in the growing of corn.[4] Ohio's agricultural development was part of that of the Midwest. In 1859 the Old Northwest—Ohio, Indiana, Illinois, Michigan, and Wisconsin—produced nearly one-half of

---

2. Betty Garrett and Edward R. Lentz, *Columbus, America's Crossroads* (Tulsa, OK: Centennial Heritage Press, 1980).

3. For a perceptive essay on Ohio's place in the Midwest, see R. Douglas Hurt, "Ohio: Gateway to the Midwest," in *Heartland,* ed. Madison, 206–25. Hurt has characterized Ohioans as generally "mainstream," "pragmatic," and "conservative" in their outlooks—people long imbued with "Jeffersonian" individualism and the Puritan work ethic.

4. Robert Leslie Jones, *History of Agriculture in Ohio* (Kent, OH: Kent State University Press, 1983), 50, 58.

the wheat and fully one-third of the corn grown in the United States.[5] The speed with which the frontier passed in the region was impressive. Agricultural historian R. Douglas Hurt has observed, "In little more than a century, the portion of the frontier that became the Northwest Territory and the state of Ohio changed dramatically from a region inhabited by newly arrived Indian immigrants to a community of farms, towns, and a few cities settled by white immigrants from New England, Virginia, and Kentucky."[6] Within a few decades, commercial agriculture replaced subsistence agriculture and remained a significant sector of Ohio's economy in the early 2000s.

As early as the 1860s, however, more Ohioans worked in nonfarm than in farm jobs, about twenty years before this was true for the United States as a whole. Ohio's leading industries in 1900 were, in descending order of importance, iron and steel, foundry and machine shops, and flour and grist mills. Ohio ranked second only to Pennsylvania in the production of coal and pig iron, was fourth among the states in the number of manufacturing establishments, and stood fifth in the amount of capital invested in industry. In 1900 laborers in Cincinnati turned out $158 million worth of industrial products, those in Cleveland $140 million, and workers in Columbus about $40 million. Toledo, Youngstown, and Akron also developed strong industrial bases. In short, Ohio was an industrial powerhouse. With industrialization came urbanization. By 1910 more Ohioans lived in towns and cities than on farms or in small villages, about a decade before this pattern was the norm in the United States. Writing in 1919, novelist Sherwood Anderson captured well what industrialization meant to Ohioans and other Midwesterners: "The coming of industrialism," he wrote, "attended by all the roar and rattle of affairs, the shrill cries of millions of new voices that have come among us from overseas, the going and coming of trains, the growth of cities, the building of interurban car lines that weave in and out of towns and past farmhouses, and now in these later days the coming of automobiles has worked a tremendous change in the habits and thoughts of our people in Mid-America."[7]

Deindustrialization took place after World War II, and especially from about 1970 onward, although much less so in Columbus than in

5. Cayton and Onuf, *Midwest and the Nation,* 39.
6. R. Douglas Hurt, *The Ohio Frontier: Crucible of the Old Northwest, 1720–1830* (Bloomington: Indiana University Press, 1996), xiii.
7. Sherwood Anderson, *Winesburg, Ohio* (New York: Penguin Books, 1987), 70–71.

most other major midwestern cities. "Rather than sharing the hardships and economic dislocations of its rustbelt neighbors," urban historian Patricia Burgess has written, "Columbus was a green oasis of economic development—a postindustrial city."[8] In 2015 the largest Ohio-based companies, as measured by revenues, were a mixture of service and industrial firms. The top ten were Kroger (groceries, with $109 billion in revenues), Marathon Petroleum ($91 billion), Cardinal Health ($91 billion), Procter & Gamble ($86 billion), Nationwide Insurance ($36 billion), Macy's ($28 billion), Progressive Insurance ($19 billion), Goodyear Tire & Rubber ($18 billion), American Electric Power ($17 billion), and FirstEnergy ($15 billion). Kroger was the twentieth-largest firm in the United States; FirstEnergy ranked as number 206.[9]

## Columbus as a Commercial City

Columbus—or rather the land that was to become the site of the city, as at first there was not even a village at the site—was chosen as the location for Ohio's new capital by the Ohio General Assembly in early 1812. Located on the eastern bank of the Scioto River, Columbus would be just south of that stream's juncture with the Olentangy River, then called the Whetstone River or Whetstone Branch. The names of the two streams reflected the rural, Native American roots of the Columbus area. "Scioto" meant "hairy river," a reference to hair from shedding deer that coated the stream's surface when deer rubbed their winter coats off on nearby trees. "Olentangy" meant "still river" or "quiet water" in the Wyandot (Huron) language.[10]

Columbus had its immediate origins in the village of Franklinton, established in 1797 just to the west of the Scioto.[11] Founded by Lucas Sullivant, a surveyor for the Virginia Military District, who took much of his pay in the form of land in central Ohio, Franklinton was low-lying

---

8. Patricia Burgess, *Planning for the Private Interest: Land Use Controls and Residential Patterns in Columbus, Ohio, 1900–1970* (Columbus: Ohio State University Press, 1994), 14; and Kevin F. Kern and Gregory S. Wilson, *Ohio: A History of the Buckeye State* (Chichester, UK.: John Wiley & Sons, 2014), 281.

9. *Columbus Dispatch*, 5 June 2015, p. B1, summarizes *Fortune* magazine's top 500 companies.

10. Ed Lentz, *As It Were: Stories of Old Columbus* (Delaware, OH: Red Mountain Press, 1998), 25; and Garrett and Lentz, *Crossroads*, 39.

11. Harold J. Grimms, "The Founding of Franklinton: Its Significance Today," *Ohio Archeological Quarterly* 56 (1947), 323–30, remains valuable, if celebratory.

and suffered from flooding, including an inundation just a year after its founding. A traveler through Franklinton in late 1798 observed that the village consisted of a "number of log cabins, most of which had been recently put up, and were without chinking, daubing, or doors."[12] Franklinton had only about five hundred residents by 1810. Perceiving better prospects for urban growth on the high ground of Wolf's Ridge just across the Scioto River to the east, four landowners—Lyne Starling (Sullivant's brother-in law), James Johnston, Alexander McLaughlin, and John Kerr—pushed state legislators to designate Columbus as the state capital. Starling, Johnston, McLaughlin, and Kerr, often called the "four proprietors," owned land at the proposed site for Columbus and were certain to profit should that location be chosen. Sullivant strongly backed their efforts. The four offered to donate the land they owned there to be the future site of the state capital, and they pledged a large sum for other improvements as well. The promise of land and public buildings, including a statehouse and a penitentiary, combined with the site's central location in Ohio, overshadowed and outbid the other offers from competitors hoping to place the capital at other proposed locations.[13]

Members of the Ohio General Assembly accepted the offer from the Franklinton leaders on 14 February 1812. Ever since Ohio had achieved statehood in 1803, rival political groups in the legislature had moved the capital from place to place, and Columbus seemed to be a workable compromise for its location. Joseph Foos, a Franklinton resident and state senator representing Franklin, Delaware, and Madison counties in central Ohio, probably suggested the name for Columbus. "Ohio City" had been proposed as the name for the capital city, but Foos's lobbying of other legislators led to the acceptance of the name "Columbus." The first meeting

---

12. As quoted in Hurt, *Ohio Frontier*, 220.

13. Ed Lentz, *Columbus: The Story of a City* (Charleston, SC: Arcadia Publishing, 2003), 30–54. See also Charles Cole, Jr., *Fragile Capital: Identity and the Early Years of Columbus, Ohio* (Athens: Ohio University Press, 2001), 1–9; and Chester C. Winter, *A Concise History of Columbus, Ohio and Franklin County* (no place of publication listed: Xlibris Corporation, 2009), 5, 8, 14. The Virginia Military District consisted of 4.5 million acres of land set aside in Ohio to reward veterans of the American Revolutionary War who had been under Virginian command. For more detail on Sullivant and Starling, see Ed Lentz, "Sullivant Fathered Sons and a City," *Worthington News*, 12 June 2014, p. A6; and Charles F. Wooley and Barbara A. Van Brimmer, *The Second Blessing: Columbus Medicine and Health, the Early Years* (South Egremont, MA: Science International Corporation, 2006), 5–6, 18–26. By 1810 Sullivant was the largest landholder in Ohio, possessing 41,459 acres. He sold parcels along the Scioto River and Alum Creek as early as 1800. See Hurt, *Ohio Frontier*, 172–75.

of the General Assembly took place in the new statehouse in Columbus in late 1816.[14]

Columbus resembled other midwestern state capitals—Indianapolis, Indiana, and Springfield, Illinois—in its central geographic location in its state. Columbus was also like Madison, Wisconsin, and Lansing, Michigan, in being close to its state's center of population. As urban historian Jon Teaford has observed, major midwestern cities grew up as river cities, such as St. Louis and Cincinnati; as lake cities, such as Chicago and Cleveland; or as capital cities. Columbus was definitely one of the last type. Nonetheless, doubts remained for several decades about where Ohio's capital should be located, as boosters jockeyed their towns and cities for position in Ohio. Only in 1851 was Columbus permanently designated as the state capital.[15]

Columbus did not develop quickly at first, as diseases and poor access to markets stunted growth. Columbus was initially a small, isolated frontier community. Joel Buttles, an early settler who moved south to Columbus from the town of Worthington about 10 miles to the north, later recalled, "When I first built my house, in which I lived for some years, it was difficult, after the house was finished, to get the large trees around it cut down without falling on and injuring it. It was forest all about it and the country [was] almost in a state of nature." He remembered, "Deer came into what is now, and was then intended to be, the public square, to browse on the tops of trees" during the winter of 1812–13.[16] Another early-day resident living just a few blocks from the statehouse "put some old meat on the ends of the logs of his cabin, and at night the wolves came and carried it off." Yet another recalled that during his first winter in Columbus, "We could plainly hear the wolves howling at night in the east part of town."[17] Columbus was, after all, constructed on Wolf's Ridge.

Uriah Brown, a surveyor and land conveyor who passed through Columbus from Baltimore during the late summer of 1816, recorded

---

14. Cole, *Fragile Capital*, 7, 17; and Garrett and Lentz, *Crossroads*, 27. For more detail, see E. O. Randall, "Location of Ohio Capital," *Ohio Archaeological and Historical Society Publications* 25 (1916), 210–34. On the naming of Columbus, see Ed Lentz, "Local Names Were Rooted in Wrangling," *Worthington News*, 8 January 2015, p. A6; and discussions by the author with Christian Zacher in December 2014.

15. Teaford, *Cities of the Heartland*, 26–30.

16. As quoted in Ed Lentz, "City's Early Days Had Character," *Worthington News*, 6 March 2014, p. A6.

17. As quoted in Ed Lentz, "Early Hunters Saw Deer, Wolves," *Worthington News*, 19 June 2014, p. A6.

a balanced account of the capital. He found Columbus to be "situated among Stumps in abundance of Iron Weeds . . . surrounded with woods" which were inhabited by bares [sic], wolves, bucks, and deer as well as Turkeys and Pheasants in abundance." Still, residents were making their marks upon the wilderness. Brown praised the statehouse as "a magnificent brick building," which had an "Elegant Superb prospect." The Columbus Inn, in which he stayed, had, he thought, "nice, fine accommodations" and "Delightful Liquors." Brown's bill came to $1.62 per night.[18]

However, over the next three or four decades Columbus, which was incorporated as a city in 1834, boomed. Population figures tell part of the story. In 1832 only 2,435 people lived in Columbus. The city had about 6,000 residents in 1840; 18,000 in 1850; 19,000 in 1860; and 31,000 in 1870.[19] Columbus's population increase was part of the surge of people into Ohio and the Midwest. The population of the Old Northwest increased from a few thousand white settlers in 1790 to 6.9 million residents in 1860.[20] Urban historian Carl Abbott has observed in a study of antebellum urban boosterism in the Midwest, "The years 1848 through 1857 were an era of decision for almost every city in the Middle West," and has concluded that in those cities "railroad connections to the East" were prime drivers of growth. Abbott has also more generally found that "city dwellers in the antebellum Middle West lived in the midst of sustained excitement about urban growth."[21]

Columbus residents participated in that growth and excitement, benefiting from state institutions established within its boundaries: the statehouse, state court buildings, the state penitentiary, the state school for the blind, the state deaf and dumb asylum, and the state insane asylum. Building and staffing them created numerous jobs and ancillary businesses. Being designated as the capital of Ohio brought people and economic growth to Columbus. Transportation improvements helped, linking Columbus to the rest of Ohio and the United States and providing

18. Uriah Brown, "Journal, 20 August 1916," two-page typed transcript prepared by Kirk Brown on 10 June 1916, located at the archives and library of the Ohio Historical Society (now named the Ohio History Connection) in Columbus, Ohio. The statehouse Brown described was the first building, not the later neoclassical building constructed a few decades later and used into the twenty-first century.

19. Donald B. Dodd, *Historical Statistics of the United States: Two Centuries of the Census, 1790–1990* (Westport, CT: Greenwood Press, 1993), 446. For the populations of Ohio, Columbus, Cincinnati, and Cleveland, see the appendix at the close of this study.

20. Cayton and Onuf, *Midwest and the Nation*, 29.

21. Abbott, *Boosters and Businessmen*, 3, 31, 198.

access to markets, thereby ending Columbus's isolation. A bridge crossing the Scioto River funded privately by Sullivant joined Columbus to
Franklinton in 1816. In the 1820s and 1830s stagecoach lines fanned
out from Columbus. The National Road reached Columbus from Baltimore in 1831. That thoroughfare across the Appalachians entered the
city from the east along Friend Street (later Main Street), turned north
for four blocks along High Street, and continued west along Broad Street.
A nineteenth-century description of the National Road highlighted its
importance to trade: "The National Road, when completed, appeared
like a white riband meandering over green hills and valleys." "It was sur-
faced," he continued, "with broken limestone, which, when compacted
by the pressure of heavy wagons, became smooth as a floor, and after
a rain almost as clean." "Wagons, stages, pedestrians, and vast droves
of cattle, sheep, horses, and hogs crowded it constantly," he noted, "all
pressing eagerly by the great arterial thoroughfare."[22]

Still, conveyances via roads, even the National Road, were too expensive and too slow for the transportation of most freight, especially heavy,
bulky items such as coal, corn, and wheat. Moreover, most roads were
in poor repair. The journal of Margaret Dwight, who traveled to Warren, Ohio, from Milford, Connecticut, in late 1810, a journey of several
months, is full of comments about poor taverns and bad roads. At one
point, Dwight lamented that she would never see her sister in Milford
again because the roads were in very poor repair, leading her to write,
"I cannot think of traversing this road again." Nonetheless, Dwight also
observed that people were streaming into Ohio. "I think," she concluded,
"Ohio will be filled up before winter, wagons without number."[23]

Canals and railroads proved more effective in moving heavy, bulky
goods. In 1831 a 12-mile-long feeder canal linked Columbus to the Ohio
and Erie Canal at Lockbourne. The entire Ohio and Erie Canal opened
three years later, joining Columbus to Lake Erie and the Ohio River.
Canal barges could carry large amounts of heavy freight long distances
at reasonable rates. Most were pulled by horses or mules driven on tow-
paths at the sides of the canals at about 3 or 4 miles per hour, but faster,
steam-powered packet boats were in use on Columbus's feeder canal by
1859. However, canals had serious drawbacks. They were slow, they

22. As quoted in Opha Moore, *History of Franklin County* (Indianapolis: Historical
Publishing Company, 1930), vol. 1, p. 148. On the National Road, see also Garrett and
Lentz, *Crossroads*, 37.

23. *A Journey to Ohio in 1810*, ed. Max Farrand (Lincoln: University of Nebraska
Press, 1991), 34, 47.

froze in the winter, and they were unusable in times of low water in the summer and fall.[24] Railroads were faster and more flexible. In the 1830s and 1840s, railroads in the United States ran at an average speed of about 15 or 20 miles per hour, and they ran year-round. The first railroad to begin operations in Ohio was the Erie and Kalamazoo, which did so with horse-drawn cars in the fall of 1836.[25] No railroads reached Columbus then. The first railroad to enter Columbus was the Columbus and Xenia, a steam-powered line, which did so in 1850, offering through-connections to Cincinnati.[26]

Railroads were more important to Columbus than they were to Cleveland and Cincinnati, both of which had natural water connections to other sections of the country via Lake Erie and (after 1824) the Erie Canal and the Ohio River, respectively. Writer Lida Rose McCabe, who grew up in Columbus during the 1860s and 1870s, recognized well the significance of canals and railroads to her hometown: "Cut off from the outside world, the home market soon became over run, and the supply being greater than the demand, the farmer was poorly paid for his labor. But later, the canal and railroads opened up facilities, and a ready market was found in the East."[27]

Columbus residents like McCabe were well aware of how essential railroad connections were to their city's future. When cars of the Cleveland, Columbus, and Cincinnati Railroad left Columbus on their maiden trip to Cleveland on Friday, 21 February 1851, they carried 425 passengers, including the governor of Ohio, state legislators, city officials, and members of the press. They were met late on that rainy day by celebratory cannon fire in the northern city. The visitors spent Saturday in celebrations, including a side trip by railroad to Hudson, and church services. The return trip to Columbus was delayed when the locomotive derailed because rain had saturated the ground, separating the tracks. Finally, on Monday, the train returned to Columbus, after hitting a cow, with many of the passengers singing verse: "We hail from the city—the Capital

---

24. On the importance of canals and railroads in spurring economic growth in Ohio, see Harry S. Schreiber, *Ohio Canal Era: A Case Study of Government and the Economy, 1820–1861* (Athens: Ohio University Press, 1968). Francis Phelps Weisenburger, *Columbus during the Civil War* (Columbus: Ohio State University Press, 1963), 4, mentions the steam-powered packet boats.

25. William Rumsey Marvin, "Columbus and the Railroads of Central Ohio before the Civil War," PhD diss., Ohio State University, 1953, 38–39, 49.

26. Ibid, 137.

27. Lida Rose McCabe, *Don't You Remember?* (Columbus: A. H. Smythe, 1884), 68. For a biographical sketch of McCabe, see Garrett and Lentz, *Crossroads*, 36.

city— / We left the storm and rain; / The cannon did thunder, the people did wonder / To see pious folks on a train!"[28]

As the last two lines of the ditty suggest, many Ohioans harbored some doubts about railroads. Members of the school board of Lancaster, Ohio, a town just south of Columbus, forbade using schoolhouses as places in which to sell railroad bonds. The president of the board declared, "Such things as railroads and telegraphs are impossibilities and rank infidelity. If God had intended his creatures travel at the frightful speed of 15 miles per hour, He would have clearly pretold it through his Holy prophets."[29] Such problems as excessive rain and roaming cows grazing along tracks were only temporary. Nor did doubts delay much in the way of construction. By 1853 regular passenger-train service between Columbus and Cleveland took only about four hours.[30]

Transportation improvements affecting Columbus were part of a statewide surge in such developments. From 1835 to 1836 alone, members of the Ohio legislature granted charters to thirty-two railroad companies, five bridge firms, five canal companies, and eleven road and turnpike enterprises. Columbus was a point on six of the thirty-two proposed rail lines, not all of which were built, however. Columbus thus joined other midwestern cities for which rail connections became crucial in the 1850s and 1860s. In fact, "in no area of the nation did railroads assume such prominence during the mid-nineteenth century as in the Old Northwest." The flat terrain of the Midwest, along with the demand to reach eastern markets, almost ensured the construction of numerous railroads. In the 1850s railroad mileage in the Midwest rose from 1,276 to 9,715. By 1860 Ohio and Illinois ranked first and second, respectively, among the states in railroad mileage.[31]

Government bodies paid for many of the transportation improvements. The federal government financed building the National Road, with construction carried out by local contractors. The Ohio state government used revenues from land sales to pay for the building of additional roads. The state government also paid for constructing Ohio's two major north-south canal systems, including the canal used by Columbus merchants. The actual building was carried out by local business contractors. For a while, the state government of Ohio even helped finance the building of

28. As quoted in Cole, *Fragile Capital*, 53.
29. On opposition to railroads in Ohio, see George Rogers Taylor, *The Transportation Revolution, 1815–1860* (New York: Harper & Row, Publishers, 1951), 75.
30. Cayton, *Ohio: The History of a People*, 56.
31. Teaford, *Cities of the Heartland*, 33–34.

railroads chartered in the state. These actions were not unusual. Governmental involvement in transportation improvements was common in antebellum America, with city, state, and national governments providing about 60 percent of the funding for roads, canals, and railroads. Private financing was also important, especially for railroads and some local roads and bridges, including, as we have seen, the first bridge to link Columbus to Franklinton.

Public and private enterprises often joined hands to build up Columbus during the years before the Civil War. A market house was one of the first structures constructed, built in the middle of High Street just south of Rich Street in 1814. Voluntary contributions from property owners whose lots fronted on High Street paid for it. The Columbus borough (later city) council regulated that market. Councilmen—women could not vote or hold public office then—stipulated that a market be held every Wednesday and Saturday from just before sunrise until midmorning. A city ordinance made it illegal to buy or sell articles elsewhere, and buying for resale was also outlawed. A city clerk announced the opening and closing of the market, weighed items if there were complaints, and judged the quality of goods put up for sale.[32] One resident wrote in 1817, "Everything is cheap and plenty, except salt and coffee, and a few other grocery items which come high, owing to the distance they are transported, which is from Philadelphia or Baltimore." A year later, however, she observed that beef was "uncommonly high" in price and that eggs were selling at 6 or 7 cents per dozen. Premium-grade wheat flour went for $2.50 per hundred pounds. Coffee cost $0.62 per pound, and tea sold for $2.25 per pound. These prices came at a time when industrial workers might earn $300 per year—if they could find steady work.[33]

The original market house was replaced by a new one built in the middle of State Street (on the south side of Statehouse Square) about 50 yards west of High Street in 1818. As many as 350 farmers brought their goods for sale to that market, with their wagons often parked on the east side of Statehouse Square. Important for commercial transactions, the market was also a site for social and political events. In 1827 and again in 1828, traveling groups of entertainers put on plays, skits, and dances there.[34] In 1828 Henry Clay, U.S. Senator from Kentucky, made a famous speech about the tariff at the market house. However, the market

32. Cole, *Fragile Capital,* 29.
33. Betsy Deshler, as quoted in Lee, *History of the City,* vol. 1, 267–68.
34. Cole, *Fragile Capital,* 162.

house fell into disrepute when its upper story became a gambling room boasting a billiards table.[35]

City officials then built a new, large combination market house and city hall—which may be seen, perhaps, as a symbolic linking of business with politics—that opened for business as the Central Market at the southwest corner of State and Front streets in 1850. Some 388 feet long and 37 feet wide and built of bricks and limestone, it was made to last. Farmers initially operated sixty-four stands. The second story contained a substantial city council chamber and offices for the city clerk, city marshal, market master, and mayor. McCabe later recalled, "On market days, which occurred three times a week, the place presented a panorama of stirring Western life," full of "song" and "laughter." A centennial celebration in 1950 attracted 10,000 people to the still-functioning market, where about twenty thousand city residents shopped each Saturday. The Central Market was lost in later years to an urban redevelopment project and was replaced by the North Market, just north of the downtown area in Columbus.[36]

Like other people throughout the Midwest, residents of Columbus favored economic development, as can be seen in their embrace of markets and railroads. Yet theirs was not an unconditional acceptance of a market economy. Kinship ties and friendships continued to be important, even as more impersonal market forces came to influence lives. Unfettered markets were not common in Columbus or other American cities in antebellum times. Markets were closely regulated—in Columbus by market masters following the dictates of city ordinances. While it did not slow railroad construction much, the reluctance of people in nearby Lancaster to permit public facilities to be used for railroad fundraising also suggests how ambivalent attitudes toward Ohio's emerging market economy colored developmental efforts.[37]

The Civil War acted as an unexpected stimulus to Columbus's economic development, with Camp Chase, just 5 miles west of the city on the National Road, serving as a major mobilization and training center for the Union Army. About 26,000 Union troops lived and drilled at

---

35. Arter, *Columbus Vignettes*, vol. 1, p. 15; Garrett and Lentz, *Crossroads*, 45; and McCabe, *Don't You Remember?* 61–65.

36. McCabe, *Don't You Remember?* 66, 69. For more detail on markets in Columbus, see Gilbert F. Dodds, "Central Market House" (Columbus: Franklin County Historical Society, 1967), a six-page pamphlet.

37. On this ambivalence toward development throughout the Midwest, see Cayton and Onuf, *Midwest and the Nation*, 25, 43–44.

Camp Chase. The site also became a prison camp for 9,000 Confederate soldiers, where about five thousand of them and their followers perished. Many bodies were repatriated to the South after the close of the conflict, but 2,260 remained buried there in the early twenty-first century. The camp was named after Salmon P. Chase, President Abraham Lincoln's Secretary of the Treasury. Chase had been governor of Ohio between 1856 and 1860 and served as Chief Justice of the United States Supreme Court after the Civil War. Goodale Park, established as one of the nation's first urban parks in 1851 just north of downtown Columbus, acted for a time as another troop-training center.[38] Soldiers on leave spent money in Columbus, and the city also became a supply point for Union armies. In mid-1861 it was reported that Columbus businesses were making everything "from a cannon ball to a camp kettle, from an ammunition wagon to a soldier's overcoat, from grapeshot and shell to a knapsack."[39]

Columbus was mainly a commercial and political city during the antebellum years. Inns, hotels, boardinghouses, restaurants, taverns, banks, real-estate brokerages, and all manner of shops and stores were developed to serve politicians, their families, their entourages, appointees who staffed state institutions, and travelers passing through Columbus. In early 1832, less than a year after the National Road reached Columbus, John Noble, formerly of Lancaster, announced in a newspaper advertisement that he was building the National Hotel in Columbus near the statehouse and that it would be "furnished and attended to in a style equal to the highest expectations." He observed, "The Ohio Stage Company stops at this house and their office is attached to the establishment." Noble's two-story hotel boasted private sleeping rooms, a large eating area, meeting rooms, and a bar; it was a marked improvement over the common eating and sleeping rooms, where guests often slept several to a bed, as had been common in earlier establishments.[40] Similarly, the Eagle Coffee House, "a plain two story brick building," located on the west side of High Street across from the statehouse, also offered refreshments. "Many a goodly company" gathered there in the antebellum years, Lida McCabe wrote, "and over a glass of toddy, mint julep, or slice of rare venison, many a stubborn problem has been magically solved."[41]

38. Lentz, *As It Were*, 68–71; Lentz, *Columbus: The Story*, 77–79; and Wooley and Brimmer, *Second Blessing*, 171–75.

39. Weisenburger, *Columbus during the Civil War*, 17.

40. As quoted in Ed Lentz, "Early Hotels Were Simple Affairs," *Worthington News*, 17 April 2014, p. A6.

41. McCabe, *Don't You Remember?* 101–2.

Much early-day entertainment took place in private homes, not in public venues, however, in the antebellum years. "Large parties," according to one account, "were attended by both young and old people." The gatherings followed a set pattern: "Host and hostesses greeted guests in much the same manner that they do now, although perhaps with more formal and courtly manner. In the dining room was always to be found a table upon which were many delicacies and to which men helped themselves and the women. Wines were generally furnished. . . . Invitations to parties were sent out days beforehand. They were handsomely engraved. After supper, the elders who did not care to dance retired and the young people spent the evening dancing."[42]

Manufacturing in Columbus was initially small-scale, limited by the size of markets. Water-powered mills to grind corn (grist mills) had appeared on the Scioto River at Franklinton and Worthington even before the founding of Columbus.[43] The first mill owned and operated by Columbus residents on the Scioto River was a sawmill erected in 1813, followed by a flour mill three years later.[44] Other manufacturing establishments, many of which used and polluted water, were established over the next five decades: woolen mills, breweries and whisky mills, flax-seed mills, paper mills, slaughterhouses, tanneries, a saddlery factory, soap-making works, candle-making establishments, shoe-making works, and iron foundries.[45] As can be seen from this list, most manufacturers simply processed agricultural goods. Not surprisingly, in 1822 Columbus also housed a maker of plows, Jethro Wood. Wood's plows had interchangeable parts, making them easy to repair when any one part broke or wore out. Changes could be made by farmers in their fields, thereby saving time and expense. By 1858 Columbus possessed fifty-eight manufacturing establishments having a total invested capital of $425,000.[46]

---

42. As quoted in Ed Lentz, "Lavish Parties Marked Social Life," *Worthington News,* 31 July 2014, p. A6.

43. William T. Martin, *History of Franklin County* (Columbus: Follett, Foster, 1858), vol. 1, pp. 5–6, 297–98.

44. Lee, *History of the City,* vol. 1, p. 216; Jacob H. Studer, *Columbus, Ohio: Its History, Resources, and Progress* (Columbus: no publisher listed, 1873), vol. 1, pp. 27–29; and William Alexander Taylor, *Centennial History of Columbus and Franklin County, Ohio* (Chicago and Columbus: S. J. Clarke Publishing, 1909), vol. 1, p. 101.

45. Osman Castle Hooper, *History of the City of Columbus, Ohio: From the Founding of Franklinton in 1797, Through the World War Period, To the Year 1920* (Columbus and Cleveland: Memorial Publishing Company, 1920), vol. 1, pp. 219–24. See also Lyder L. Unstad, "A Survey of the Industrial and Economic Development of Central Ohio with Special Reference to Columbus, 1797–1872," PhD diss., Ohio State University, 1937.

46. Hurt, *Ohio Frontier,* 235; and Taylor, *Centennial History,* vol. 1, pp. 332–38.

Columbus was by the 1850s and 1860s a beehive of business activity.[47] Trade remained much more important than manufacturing, as the city emerged from its economic doldrums of the 1820s.[48] Columbus took part in a general rapid urbanization of the Midwest resulting from the expansion of trade. In the Midwest, "the rate of urbanization was almost four times as great in the 1840s and 1850s as it had been in the 1830s," historian Carl Abbott has written, significantly surpassing the pace of city development for the United States as a whole.[49] However, despite its economic development, Columbus lagged far behind Cincinnati and Cleveland in commercial, industrial, and population growth. Their river and lake connections to the rest of the United States long gave those cities locational advantages over Columbus. Around 1860, when Columbus's industrial output totaled $1.2 million, Cincinnati's came to $47 million.[50]

Columbus remained a compact city centered on Statehouse Square and the Scioto River. People got around town mainly by walking, riding horses, and driving in carriages. Still, the city had begun to spread out north-south along High Street, especially northward, and east-west along Broad Street, especially eastward. Those two major streets intersected at the northwest corner of Statehouse Square, the intersection at the center of much of Columbus's spatial layout. Paved streets remained a rarity, and hogs roamed most thoroughfares, despite city ordinances against them. While log cabins remained along some of its streets, Columbus was no longer a frontier settlement. Wooden-framed structures and brick and stone buildings were becoming common, especially around Statehouse Square. Churches joined saloons on those streets in as-yet-unzoned Columbus. Residences, commercial establishments, and factories were just beginning to sort themselves out into different areas of the city.

Despite all of the activities of its residents, Columbus remained "a small backwater" compared to its larger neighbors to the south and north.[51] Writing in 1963, Ohio historian Francis Weisenburger characterized Columbus as an "easygoing capital city." Franklin County, in which Columbus was located, was still largely rural in 1860. In that year, Franklin

47. Cole, *Fragile Capital*, 211.

48. Henry L. Hunker, *Industrial Evolution of Columbus, Ohio* (Columbus: Bureau of Business Research, College of Commerce and Administration, Ohio State University, 1958), 38. See also Henry L. Hunker, *Columbus, Ohio: A Personal Geography* (Columbus: Ohio State University Press, 2000), 51.

49. Abbott, *Boosters and Businessmen*, 16.

50. Steven J. Ross, *Workers on the Edge: Work, Leisure, and Politics in an Industrializing Cincinnati, 1788–1890* (New York: Columbia University Press, 1985), 76.

51. Burgess, *Planning*, 11.

County was the fourth-most-important grain-producing county in Ohio, the third-most-important producer of corn and horses, and the second-most-important producer of hogs.[52] Cincinnati boasted 161,000 residents, and Cleveland had 93,000, three times more than Columbus's 31,000. For all of its commercial development, Columbus remained as much a site of potentiality as one of accomplishment during the years immediately before and after the Civil War. Still, Columbus had clearly passed through two stages of economic development identified as typical of the antebellum Midwest by historians Andrew R. L. Cayton and Peter Onuf. The first stage was "a period of local economic activity marked by limited production for largely inaccessible markets." Columbus passed that stage in the 1830s and 1840s, moving into the second stage, "a dynamic era of rapid growth." By the 1850s Columbus was, like much of the Midwest, what the two historians have labeled as a bastion of "bourgeois culture."[53] One person who found business advancement in Columbus then was William Neil.

## William Neil, Transportation, and Real Estate

Born in Virginia in 1788, William Neil moved to Kentucky as a young boy with his parents. Later, as a man of twenty-two years of age, he married Hannah Schwing, who had also been born in Virginia. They met in Kentucky and moved together to Ohio at the close of the War of 1812, living for three years in Urbana, a town due west of Columbus. William Neil arrived in Urbana, according to one account, with just "his horse, saddle, and blanket" and his wife. A stone mason by trade, Neil tried to enter the world of banking there without success. The couple moved to Columbus in 1818.[54] Their migration from Virginia and Kentucky to Columbus was a common pattern in the early days of the capital city, for many of the early residents of Columbus came from the Upper South.

Business success did not come easily to Neil in the capital city. He first became involved in a partnership to buy and sell flour. As budding entrepreneurs, he and two partners shipped flour down the Olentangy and the Scioto rivers to the Ohio River by keelboat. The flour then traveled west and south to market in New Orleans via the Ohio and Mississippi rivers. The partners lost money on the sale of their flour. However, Neil

---

52. Weisenburger, *Columbus during the Civil War*, 4–5.
53. Cayton and Onuf, *Midwest and the Nation*, 35, 63.
54. W. A. Taylor, *Centennial History*, vol. 1, pp. 510–15, esp. 513.

made valuable contacts in the venture, engaging in what would later be called *networking*. He built up "social capital," connections that served him well in later business efforts. He got to know other merchants and tradespeople who could help him get ahead. Neil opened a tavern on High Street, opposite Statehouse Square, and this business, in turn, led Neil into transportation enterprises, as he observed people traveling on the National Road in downtown Columbus.[55]

Neil began his stage-coaching business with a line from Columbus to Granville, an emerging town northeast of Columbus. The line was profitable, and Neil reinvested his earnings in the creation of other lines radiating outward from Columbus to Wheeling, Cleveland, Sandusky, Cincinnati, Marietta, and other points, using roads built mainly by the state. Neil's firm went through several name changes to become the Ohio Stage Company, a partnership with other Columbus businessmen. This business controlled most stage coaching in Ohio and throughout the Old Northwest by 1850, and Neil became known as the "stagecoach king." A bit later, Neil became involved in early-day railroading in central Ohio, and he was at one time associated with almost every railroad line leading out of Columbus.[56] In 1833 he even considered running a line of "steam carriages" on the National Road, but nothing came of that idea.[57]

Neil poured the profits from his transportation undertakings into Columbus real estate. In 1828 he purchased the farm of Joseph Vance, just north of Columbus. Vance had been one of his partners in the unprofitable flour-shipping enterprise. This land later became the site of the Ohio State University, and the lane leading to the farm was named Neil Avenue, one of the main streets entering the university. Neil also bought nearly 3,000 acres west of High Street, along with smaller parcels of land in other areas. In fact, he came to own most of the land between High Street and the Olentangy River, from Lane Avenue south to downtown Columbus. When his original tavern burned in 1839, Neil replaced it with a hotel, the first Neil House.

Charles Dickens passed through Columbus in 1842 during a visit to the United States, and the sometimes acerbic British writer had nothing but praise for the Neil House, in which he stayed, and for Columbus more generally. The Neil House was, Dickens wrote, "a very large, unfinished hotel," which was "richly fitted with polished wood of the black

---

55. Ibid; and Lentz, *As It Were*, 29.
56. W. A. Taylor, *Centennial History*, vol. 1, p. 514; and Lentz, *As It Were*, 30.
57. Marvin, "Columbus and the Railroads," 31–32.

Neil House, Columbus, Ohio.

**Figure 1.1.** The Second Neil House in 1915 (Center Building), as seen in a postcard. The Neil House was one of many pubs and hotels that sprang up to serve visitors to the capital of Ohio, a growing commercial center. (Courtesy of the Columbus Metropolitan Library)

walnut." His rooms there "opened on a handsome portico and stone verandah, like rooms in some Italian mansion." Dickens found Columbus to be "clean and pretty, and of course is 'going to be' much larger." The town was still, indeed, very much in the state of becoming.[58]

That hotel was destroyed by fire in 1860, whereupon Neil built a more lavish Neil House Hotel on the same site. It was replaced, in turn, by another new Neil House in 1924. That establishment was torn down to make way for the Huntington Center, a thirty-seven-story office building, in the 1980s. Meanwhile, Neil's wife became very involved in Columbus philanthropic ventures as the founder of the Hannah Neil Mission and Home for the Friendless (families and children), and as one of the organizers of the Columbus Female Benevolent Society. Hannah Neil died in 1868, and her husband died two years later.[59]

The businesses started by William Neil in stage coaching, railroads, and hotels were typical of the many firms that sprang up to serve the

58. Charles Dickens, *American Notes for General Circulation* (New York: Harper Brothers, 1842), 71.

59. W. A. Taylor, *Centennial History,* vol. 1, p. 515; and Lentz, *As It Were,* 30–31.

growing number of residents of and visitors to Columbus. In the antebellum years, commercial businesses generally prospered more than industrial firms in Columbus, which, despite transportation improvements, still faced limited markets and encountered much competition. Like William Neil, many Columbus residents who got ahead in sales and services reinvested their earnings in real estate. Avid boosters, they believed in the future of Columbus. Opportunities, if at times difficult to seize, were available in the capital city, especially after the 1820s. This type of action was not confined to Columbus, as it was typical of what was occurring in cities across the United States. On a much larger scale than the investments of which William Neil was capable, William Vanderbilt plowed back profits earned in steamships and railroads into real estate in New York City.

Pioneering Ohio historian Henry Howe visited Cleveland, Columbus, and Cincinnati in 1846 and 1847. He expressed well what William Neil's Columbus was and was becoming. "The location of the national road and of the Columbus feeder to the Ohio canal, gave an impetus to improvements," Howe observed. He found Columbus to be "beautifully situated on the east bank of the Scioto, about half a mile below its juncture with the Olentangy." In the growing town, "the streets are spacious, the site level, and it has many elegant dwellings." Howe ignored the hogs still found on many avenues. "Columbus has few manufactories only," Howe noted. "It does, however, have a heavy mercantile business, there being many stores of various kinds."[60] That situation was about to change.

## Columbus as an Industrial Metropolis

A reporter for the *Columbus Citizen* vividly described the pouring of the first heat of steel at the foundry of the Buckeye Steel Castings Company in late 1902: "Someone gave the signal and in a minute everyone in the building was on hand to watch the great crane as it lifted the smoking ladle and carried it to the furnace. Then at a touch the furnace itself slowly turned on its axis until the steel came pouring forth in a stream of liquid fire amid a cloud of fiery spray. It was a beautiful sight, indeed."[61] Such reports became frequent, as Columbus became increasingly industrialized.

---

60. Henry Howe, *Historical Collections of Ohio* (Cincinnati: H. Howe & Sons, 1848), 171–72, reprinted in *The Documentary Heritage of Ohio,* eds. Phillip R. Shriver and Clarence E. Wunderlin, Jr. (Athens: Ohio University Press, 2000), 173.

61. "Casting Plant," *Columbus Citizen,* 15 October 1902, as quoted in Blackford, *Portrait,* 21.

Industry became much more important in Columbus after 1860. Industrial growth, as measured by value added by manufacturing per capita, increased faster in Franklin County—Columbus at that time was wholly contained in Franklin County—than in Ohio as a whole or in the United States as a whole. In 1860 the value added by manufacturing per capita for Franklin County stood at $28.51, that for Ohio at $22.18, and that for the United States at $27.10. Thirty years later the corresponding figures were $96.51, $81.87, and $36.40.[62] While small- and medium-size manufacturers, such as machine shops, remained significant, larger companies involved in heavy industry developed for the first time, part of a national trend.[63] The Columbus Buggy Company, located just north of Columbus's downtown, employed hundreds of workers and became the largest buggy-making establishment in the United States and, indeed, the world. Attracted by that firm's success, two dozen other buggy-making companies began operations in Columbus.[64] Although never a Detroit or a Cleveland, Columbus joined other midwestern cities as an industrial center, and by about 1890 midwestern cities were national leaders in manufacturing. In 1860 just two of the nation's top twenty manufacturing centers were in the Midwest, but thirty years later, seven were.[65]

Of course, not all economic growth came from industry. The state government remained a magnet for people interested in relocating to Columbus, and commercial, financial, educational, and governmental institutions were all major employers. As early as 1885 sixty-seven Columbus firms reached out via rail connections to customers in other towns in the wholesale trades of hardware, groceries, boots and shoes, furniture, and the like. By 1909 Columbus boasted of having eight manufacturing establishments, each the largest of its kind in the United States; eighteen railroads; twenty-eight banks; twenty-two savings and loan associations; and a Board of Trade with 1,200 members.[66]

---

62. Eric H. Monkkonen, *The Dangerous Class: Crime and Poverty in Columbus, Ohio, 1860–1885* (Cambridge, MA: Harvard University Press, 1975), 13.

63. On the continuing importance of smaller manufacturers, see Alvin Ketcham, "The Foundry and Machine Shop Industry in Columbus," in *Columbus Manufacturers,* typescript in the Ohio State University Library.

64. Lentz, *Columbus: The Story,* 86, discusses the Columbus Buggy Company. On buggy-making in Columbus, see also W. A. Taylor, *Centennial History,* vol. 1, p. 338.

65. Teaford, *Cities of the Heartland,* 49–50.

66. W. A. Taylor, *Centennial History,* vol. 1, pp. 301–9. The Board of Trade had a rocky start, with four efforts to create such a business organization failing between 1858 and 1884, as Columbus business leaders had difficulty agreeing upon goals and funding. Only in 1884 was a permanent Board of Trade established. It became the Columbus

By the time World War I began, Columbus was home to numerous manufacturing plants, and still more developed in later years. In 1917 there were 38,250 male industrial workers and 8,331 female ones in the city. These laborers included a growing number of African American workers living in a number of predominantly black areas throughout the city. In 1910 about 27 percent of the black workers in Columbus were engaged in industrial work, but a decade later 42 percent were. There was a corresponding drop in the proportion of African Americans employed in personal and domestic service, from 55 percent to just 36 percent. In 1918 Franklin County had 1,557 industrial establishments employing five or more people apiece. Those firms paid $51 million in wages and salaries and produced about $100 million in industrial products that year. Industrial expansion continued throughout the 1920s, with firms in glass-making and manufacturing parts for automobiles joining established businesses in brickmaking, brewing, shoe making, and other fields as part of Columbus's industrial base.[67]

No single reason accounted for the development of industry as a major part of Columbus's economy. People were important. Many of the business leaders who had earned profits in trade invested in (and sometimes ran) manufacturing concerns. Many of them had family or personal connections to business leaders in other parts of Ohio upon which they could draw in times of need. As was the case with William Neil, networking contributed to their business success. In these respects, they resembled the Boston Associates, merchants who invested in textile manufacturing in nearby Waltham and Lowell and who relied in part on family ties to help them get ahead in the early 1800s. Industrial workers to man the factories in Columbus came from numerous sources, as we shall see in more detail later in this study. Substantial numbers of German and Irish immigrants settled in Columbus in the mid-nineteenth century, and immigrants

---

Chamber of Commerce in 1910. See Arter, *Columbus Vignettes,* vol. 1, p. 52; and Ed Lentz, "Board of Trade Took a While to Take Root," *Worthington News,* 5 December 2013, p. A6.

67. Hooper, *Columbus: From the Founding,* vol. 1, pp. 223–24. See also W. B. Jackson, "Industrial Columbus," *Ohio Magazine* 3 (1907), 454–65; and "Chamber of Commerce Plays Important Part in Industrial Development of Columbus," *Ohio State Journal,* 31 December 1918. On glassmaking in Columbus, see Thomas S. Dicke, "The Small Firm and the Associationalist Model: Federal Glass, 1900–1938," in *Essays in Economic and Business History,* ed. Edwin Perkins (Los Angeles: History Department, University of Southern California, 1986), 149–61. On black workers in industry, see J. S. Himes, Jr., "Forty Years of Negro Life in Columbus, Ohio," *Journal of Negro History* 27 (April 1942), 133–54, esp. 142.

from southern and Eastern Europe joined them later in the century. In the twentieth century, northern migrations of African Americans and white Appalachians provided addition supplies of labor. Nearness to raw materials also helped. Railroads brought large amounts of coal from mines in Hocking, Athens, and Perry counties to Columbus in the 1870s and later. Iron came from furnaces in southern and eastern Ohio. Columbus possessed fourteen malleable ironworks as early as 1885.[68]

With considerable boosterism, Columbus's business leaders in 1885 also attributed the development of manufacturing to an "excellent" supply of water suitable for industrial needs and for "the health and comfort of the people." Officers of the Board of Trade observed that Columbus Water Works officials "are continually extending their service pipes, and are especially energetic in meeting the demands of manufacturing establishments locating outside the present radius of water supply." As in transportation developments, public and private efforts to further economic growth were logically seen as being intertwined. However, the Board of Trade members exaggerated the water realities of Columbus. Much of the water was impure and unsuitable for manufacturing and carried diseases to Columbus residents. A typhoid epidemic caused by unclean water swept through Columbus as late as from 1904 to 1906.[69] Members of the Board of Trade became leaders in a campaign to build a new water system for their city in the early twentieth century.

Of great significance were the extensive rail connections from Columbus to much of the rest of the nation. Ohio's canals fell into disrepair after the Civil War and closed in the early twentieth century. The Scioto River, which had been used to float rafts, flatboats, and ships laden with goods to downriver destinations, also descended into disuse. As railroads replaced waterways and highways as the major avenues of commerce, industrialists found that they could locate their plants in Columbus and market their products competitively throughout large parts of the Midwest, East, and South. By 1885 fourteen railroads ran through Columbus, connecting the city's businesses to sources of raw materials and markets. Twenty years later, eighteen railroads linked Columbus to other areas, with 148 passenger trains entering or leaving Columbus daily. Many of the nation's largest urban markets lay within one-day or two-day train trips from Columbus. The first publication of the Columbus Board of

68. Columbus Board of Trade, "The City of Columbus: The Capital of Ohio and the Great Railroad Center of the State" (Columbus: Press of G. L. Manchester, 1885), 10 (source of the quotation), 12.

69. Ibid, 10, 61.

Trade, in 1885, trumpeted loudly in its title, "The City of Columbus: The Capital of Ohio and the Great Railway Center of the State." The booklet claimed that "unsurpassable railway and market facilities" were fast establishing Columbus as "a great manufacturing center."[70]

Transportation developments continued to spur Columbus's economic evolution in later decades. In 1910 air-freight shipments from Dayton to Columbus began, perhaps the first such shipments in the United States. A publicity stunt, the initial shipment carried 200 pounds of silk for the Home Dry Goods Store at a cost of $5,000.[71] In 1929 city officials opened an airport at Port Columbus, which became the transfer point for combined rail-air service across the United States. The Pennsylvania Railroad carried passengers over the Appalachian Mountains to Columbus, where they transferred to airplanes of the Transcontinental Air Transport Company to continue their travel west. A reporter for a Columbus newspaper recognized well the import of the opening day: "Soaring into a murky sky, two Transcontinental Air Transport Inc. planes carrying thirty passengers headed toward Waynoka, Okla., Monday on the inaugural flight of 48-hour coast-to-coast air-train service established by T. A. T. and the Pennsylvania and Santa Fe Railroads." Henry Ford remarked that this arrangement was "the most important railroad event since the first spike was driven in the first rail in America." Charles Lindbergh, who had become famous as the first person to fly solo across the Atlantic Ocean two years earlier, predicted that one-day overnight service between the coasts would be available within a decade.[72]

By the close of the 1920s, manufacturing payrolls and construction work together made up about 40 percent of the payroll of Columbus workers. The top five industries, which accounted for about two-thirds of Columbus's manufacturing output, were, in descending order, iron and steel, food products, leather products, paper and printing, and vehicles.[73] Processing agricultural goods had become less important than in earlier times.

Even as unemployment rose in Columbus during the Great Depression of the 1930s, it remained much lower than that in other major Ohio

---

70. Ibid, 10.

71. Edward J. Roach, *The Wright Company: From Invention to Industry* (Athens: Ohio University Press, 2014), 94.

72. *Ohio State Journal*, 8 July 1929, p. 1.

73. Eugene Van Cleff, "Columbus as an Industrial City," in *Columbus, Ohio: An Analysis of a City's Development,* (Columbus: Chamber of Commerce Industrial Bureau, 1930), ed. Roderick Peattie, p. 32.

and midwestern cities. The unemployment rate for Ohioans reached 37 percent in 1932, slightly higher than the national average of around 33 percent. From 1932 to 1933 the unemployment rate reached 50 percent in Cleveland, 60 percent in Akron and Youngstown, and a staggering 80 percent in Toledo. Columbus's unemployment rate hovered at around 30 percent. In 1939 the 140,000 people who had jobs in Columbus worked in a variety of fields. Some 27 percent were in manufacturing, 22 percent in trades, 17 percent in miscellaneous types of work (including self-employment and professional work), 13 percent in services, 10 percent in government work (including teaching), 8 percent in transportation, and 6 percent in construction.[74]

With a more diverse economic base than its more heavily industrialized northern neighbors, Columbus weathered the Great Depression in better shape. The capital city was the only major city in the state to gain, not lose, population in the 1930s. The population of Columbus rose 15.5 percent during the Depression Decade, because of the growing number of people working for the state government.[75] By way of contrast, five of the twelve largest cities in the Midwest lost population during the 1930s: Cleveland, St. Louis, Toledo, Akron, and Youngstown.[76]

Even so, not all residents thought that Columbus business and civic leaders were progressive enough. Robert Lazarus, head of the city's largest retail establishment, later told a reporter for the *Columbus Citizen-Journal* that he believed city leaders to be very "insular" in their outlooks. More specifically, Lazarus blamed the fear that many members of the city's chamber of commerce had of unions for the failure to attract enough heavy industry to Columbus.[77] Those who have studied Columbus's social and economic development most carefully agree. As one scholar, Gregory S. Jacobs, has recently explained, "Columbus's economic elites sought to maintain close control over a slowly but steadily expanding city, welcoming industrial development only warily."[78] Ironically, the failure of Columbus business leaders to embrace industrialization wholeheartedly probably bolstered their city's economy when

---

74. Peter R. Mansoor, "The Impact of World War II on the Economy of Columbus, Ohio," graduate seminar paper for my offering of History 369B at the Ohio State University, 1992, p. 5. See also Kern and Wilson, *Ohio: A History,* 378.

75. Cayton, *Ohio: The History of a People,* 314.

76. Teaford, *Cities of the Heartland,* 175.

77. As quoted in David Meyers, Beverly Meyers, and Elise Meyers Walker, *Look to Lazarus: The Big Store* (Charleston, SC: The History Press, 2011), 79.

78. Gregory S. Jacobs, *Getting around Brown: Desegregation, Development, and the Columbus Public Schools* (Columbus: Ohio State University Press, 1998), 69.

deindustrialization swept through many midwestern cities after World War II. Not as tied to industry as its neighbors, Columbus's leaders more easily expanded their city's presence in services, finance, and education.

Life in Columbus during the 1930s was difficult. Early 1931 found the Ohio Board of County Commissioners, including commissioners from Franklin County, petitioning their governor and legislators for increased aid, arguing that "the present economic condition" was "an emergency comparable to a catastrophe." They were told no state funds were available.[79] People had to change their lifestyles. They drove less because they did not have money for gasoline to keep their cars running. The birthrate fell, as couples delayed starting families. To escape realities, people went more often to movies shown at large theaters recently opened downtown—the Ohio Theater and the RKO (Radio Keith Orpheum) Palace Theatre. Federal government New Deal projects gave work to thousands and began altering that downtown, most notably through the construction of the Federal District Courthouse and the Post Office Building (later just the Courthouse) in 1937.[80] Various New Deal projects helped put people to work, but the Columbus unemployment rate remained a stubborn 14 percent in 1939.[81]

Federal government spending for World War II ended the Great Depression in Columbus, as elsewhere in the United States. In Ohio, unemployment disappeared as industrial wages rose 65 percent in real terms and farm income soared 200 percent during the conflict. The number of workers in Ohio's basic industries rose from 755,000 to 1,270,000 during the war years. Columbus gained 25,000 industrial jobs during the early and mid-1940s. This growth carried over into the 1950s, as Ohio ranked as fourth or fifth among states in industrial output throughout that decade. In 1953 average per-capita annual income stood at $2,028 in Ohio, tenth-highest among all states, well above the national average of about $1,800.[82]

With economic expansion came explosive population growth in Columbus. The number of people living in Columbus rose from 31,000 in 1870 to 181,000 in 1910; to 291,000 in 1930; and to 376,000 in 1950—an elevenfold increase. By way of comparison, between 1870 and 1950, the population of Cincinnati rose from 161,000 to 504,000, and that of Cleveland

79. "Levy for Poor," *Ohio State Journal*, 3 January 1931.

80. Lentz, *Columbus: The Story*, 116.

81. Mansoor, "World War II," 5.

82. Cayton, *Ohio: The History of a People*, 327; Kern and Wilson, *Ohio: A History*, 389, 398.

soared from 93,000 to 914,000. Ohio's population increased from 2.7 million in 1870 to nearly 8 million in 1950.[83]

Most notable was the construction of a large industrial plant by the Curtiss-Wright Aviation Company on Fifth Avenue near Port Columbus to build warplanes. Curtiss Wright's officers oversaw the building of an aircraft-engine factory in a suburb of Cincinnati in the summer of 1940 and wanted the construction of a major aircraft-manufacturing facility in Philadelphia. However, federal government officials forced them to choose an inland location for their new plant as part of the government's effort to disperse plants from coastal areas, where, they feared, factories might be vulnerable to attack. With land available at Port Columbus, well served by air and rail links, the capital city was a logical choice. In 1940 Columbus received the prized plant, financed by the federal government to the tune of $12 million. It opened in late 1941, with its employment peaking in 1944 at about twenty-five thousand, nearly one-third of Columbus's industrial workforce at the time. At the end of World War II, manufacturing establishments provided 43 percent of all of the jobs in Columbus, but industry soon declined in importance. Employment at the Curtiss-Wright factory fell to fewer than 3,000 workers by late 1945, when no new government contracts took the place of the wartime ones, and the plant soon closed for good. For a short while, North American Aviation leased much the plant to make jet fighters for the United States Air Force, and the Lustron Corporation rented a small part of it, in which its workers produced prefabricated, steel houses. However, neither enterprise compensated fully for the loss of Curtiss-Wright's business and employment.[84]

## Samuel Prescott Bush and Buckeye Steel Castings

The development of the Buckeye Steel Castings Company epitomized many aspects of the capital city's turn to industrialization. Located on the South Side of Columbus in a section of town known as "Steelton,"

---

83. Dodd, *Historical Statistics,* 446.

84. Hunker, *A Personal Geography,* 54; Hunker, *Industrial Evolution,* 58; and Mansoor, "World War II," 9–20. On postwar developments, see Douglas Knerr, *Suburban Steel: The Magnificent Failure of the Lustron Corporation, 1945–1951* (Columbus: Ohio State University Press, 2004).

Buckeye Steel made couplers and other steel parts for railroad cars. The firm employed 400 workers in 1904, and 2,000 twelve years later.[85]

Formed in 1881 as a partnership of several Columbus businessmen who had made their money in trade and early-day industry, Buckeye Steel was established to produce and sell cast-iron products such as stoves and pots and pans. Initially, the company was not a success, for it was simply one of a number of similar firms turning out iron products for the local Columbus market. The partnership faced many competitors and had no specialty product. After Buckeye Steel had lost money for several years, Wilbur Goodspeed, a Cleveland businessman who had invested in the partnership (he had family ties to Columbus residents), moved south to Columbus, reorganized the company as a corporation, assumed its presidency, and invested still more of his money in the firm. Those steps helped, but Buckeye Steel still lacked a specialty product and suffered from competition. By the late 1880s, the corporation was losing substantial sums each year and was teetering on the brink of failure.

Two developments saved Buckeye Steel in the early and mid-1890s. The firm's officers, most of whom had training in engineering, developed a specialty product that set their company apart from its competitors: an automatic coupler to join railroad cars together. First made of iron but soon of steel, automatic couplers quickly replaced the older linch-and-pin couplers, which required that trainmen step between railroad cars to link them, risking physical injury every time they did so should the cars miss the connection. The U.S. Congress passed safety legislation in 1893 mandating that only automatic couplers be employed. Just four or five companies in the United States were prepared to manufacture automatic couplers. Buckeye Steel was one of them. In addition, Wilbur Goodspeed personally knew Frank Rockefeller of the Standard Oil Company, which had its headquarters in Cleveland. The two had been members of a para-military organization, the Cleveland Gatling Gun Regiment, set up by businessmen to deal with labor unrest in the wake of a nationwide railway strike in 1877. Goodspeed and Rockefeller reached a mutually beneficial agreement. In return for receiving free common stock in Buckeye Steel, executives at Standard Oil pressured railroads with which their firm did business (most oil was carried by railroads then, not by pipelines) to buy railcars that used Buckeye Steel's couplers. The railroads did so, almost assuring Buckeye Steel's success. Friendships, networking, and the

---

85. This section of the chapter is based on Blackford, *Portrait*. Except where otherwise noted, the quotations are from pp. 50–51 and 57 of that work.

Figure 1.2. Buckeye Steel's Foundry in 1915. Buckeye Steel's foundry was typical of the size of large industrial businesses in Columbus. Work there was hot, noisy, and dangerous. (From the author's collection)

social capital of its leaders helped Buckeye Steel in every step of the firm's early development.

With a specialty product, important personal connections, and easy access to national markets via Columbus's many railroads, Buckeye Steel found its sales and profits soaring. In the opening decade of the twentieth century the company built an ultramodern, very efficient steel-castings plant in Columbus's South Side (its old iron foundry had been near the downtown). Company officers engaged in good relations with their workers, what scholars call *welfare capitalism,* to try to ensure the harmonious functioning of their plant. Writing in 1918, Samuel Prescott Bush, the firm's president between 1908 and 1927, stated that to improve factory and living conditions, a company should do two things. "First, it should lead and assist in the particular community in which it is situated, in bringing about a wholesome community condition." Continuing, he observed, "Second, within the confines of its own operation and property it must provide all those conditions which make for fair dealing, health, efficiency, and a general outlook on the part of all, of confidence and helpfulness." Buckeye Steel's officers provided washrooms, a cafeteria, medical aid, and even some housing for their workers. They sponsored sports teams and paid for settlement-house workers to help their laborers. They wanted to keep unions out of their factory and to cut down on labor turnover, for recruiting and training new workers was a costly proposition.

By the time of World War I, Buckeye Steel was a very successful business. In 1917 the corporation manufactured nearly 100,000 tons of couplers, made sales of about $10 million from which it derived net profits of $1 million, and possessed assets of over $7 million. At a time when a manufacturing firm with assets of $20 million was considered a big business, Buckeye Steel was a midsize firm. A substantial company by national standards, Buckeye Steel was one of the largest manufacturers in Columbus. It was not, however, in the same league as United States Steel, which had been organized in 1901 with a capitalization of $1.4 billion, or the other eleven major American steel companies known collectively as "Little Steel."

The son of an Episcopal minister, Samuel Bush was concerned about creating a moral society, as he defined it, as can be seen in letters he exchanged with William Oxley Thompson, the president of Ohio State University, in 1922. In mid-August of that year, Bush sent Thompson two newspaper articles about education with an accompanying letter. Bush wrote, "I cannot but feel that there is very much room for improvement in our schools, colleges, and universities." Continuing, he averred, "It would be unfair to attribute so much that is wanting in our citizenship to our educational institutions, as the home exerts a preponderating influence, but I feel that if we are to succeed with our form of government in this country there are some things that must be emphasized in our educational institutions more than they are at the present time." Thompson replied three days later: "I quite agree with the urgency that asserts a religious sanction of morals" and "The fear of God in the minds of many people would be a great corrective." Thompson decried the fact that, as he saw matters, many Americans were becoming "more materialistic," though he did not specify exactly what he meant by that statement. He concluded, "I am profoundly of the opinion that the moral foundation is absolutely essential if we are to continue the best elements of American life," and he wrote that he had "little sympathy with the current notion that everything is all right, if you can only 'get by.'"[86]

86. S. P. Bush to W. O. Thompson, 15 August 1922, and W. O. Thompson to S. P. Bush, 18 August 1922, letters in the W. O. Thompson Papers, Box 3/e/15, Ohio State University

Born in Brick Church, New Jersey, in 1863, Bush attended a public school and then the Stevens Institute of Technology, where he may have known Frederick Taylor, the father of the scientific management movement, an effort to make factories more efficient in the United States. Bush graduated with a degree in mechanical engineering in 1884. He went to work for the Pittsburgh, Cincinnati, and Chicago and St. Louis Railroad (commonly called the Panhandle Route), laboring in the Columbus shops of that line between 1885 and 1888. After working for several other railroads, he moved to Columbus for good as vice president and manager of Buckeye Steel's production works in 1901, becoming the firm's president seven years later.[87]

A powerful man, Bush stood over 6 feet tall and had a loud voice. Sporting hair parted down the center of his head and a bushy mustache, he was formidable. One Buckeye employee later recalled that Bush was "a snorter." That employee observed, "Everyone knew when he was around; when he issued orders, boy it went." There was another side to Bush. He had a dry sense of humor. In 1918 he wrote to his wife, Flora, who was away on one of numerous trips to visit relatives and friends, about the Christmas gift he had purchased for her: "What do you think it is?" Bush asked. "Well, you can guess. A collar with a heavy chain to keep you at home." In a more serious vein, Bush wrote to Flora in the summer of 1908 about how he viewed his business life. Flora was at the time escaping the heat and humidity of Columbus at the Massachusetts seashore. "We have had hard times to bear," he declared, "but surely we should not care to have our lives easy," for "there would be no accomplishment, no development." Like many other businessmen striving to succeed in the capital city, Bush did so in part by hard work and persistence.

However, more was involved, including the astute use of social capital, such as the exploitation of contacts in networking. In Columbus, Bush was a big fish in a relatively small pond. He headed the Arlington Country Club in 1912 and was at various times active in the Automobile Club, the Columbus Club, the Assembly, the Review Club, and the Ohio Club. He was also a member of the Duquesne Club of Pittsburgh

Archives, Columbus, Ohio. For a biographical sketch of Thompson, see Amy Fancelli Zalimas, "William Oxley Thompson on Popular Education, Social Justice, and Social Control in Progressive Era Ohio," in *Builders*, eds. Van Tine and Pierce, 207–17.

87. For a contemporary account of Bush's life, see W. A. Taylor, *Centennial History*, vol. 2, pp. 142–45. Bush was the grandfather of U.S. President George Herbert Walker Bush and great-grandfather of President George W. Bush.

and the Engineers Club of New York City. Flora belonged to women's
organizations for Children's Hospital and the Columbus Gallery of Fine
Arts. During summers she often journeyed to the Massachusetts seashore at Osterville. There she mingled with others of Columbus's social
elite, including Helen Deshler and Daisy Hayden, in luncheons, games
of bridge, and swimming. "The bathing," Flora wrote her husband,
"is very fine indeed, safe and just enough sport for all purposes." The
four Bush children enjoyed crabbing, rowing, playing tennis and baseball,
and swimming. "The children are fine," Flora assured her husband at one
point, "and the change will be of lasting benefit to them. They do look so
much better and vigorous."

Later years brought decline to Buckeye Steel. Tied to the cyclical
and—after World War II—troubled railroad industry for most of their
company's sales, the corporation's officers sought growth and profits in
diversification, first in non-railroad steel products and later in plastics.
When neither effort proved fully successful, they agreed to a friendly
takeover by Worthington Industries, another Columbus manufacturer,
in 1980. Buckeye Steel went out of existence as an independent firm after
nearly a century of existence. Worthington Industries later divested Buckeye Steel. Attempts to revitalize the steelmaker as an independent manufacturer proved only partly successful.

## Columbus as a Financial, Educational, and Service Center

Between 1950 and 1970 the population of Columbus rose from 376,000
to 540,000, and it increased to 787,000 residents by 2010, with about
500,000 additional people living in surrounding suburbs. In contrast, the
population of Cleveland fell from 914,000 to 397,000 between 1950 and
2010, and in the same decades that of Cincinnati dropped from 503,000
to 297,000. In 2013 the city of Columbus boasted a population exceeding
800,000, with 809,798 residents, for the first time. Reaching that mile-
stone prompted humorist Joe Blundo, a columnist for the *Columbus Dispatch,* to remark that his city could be labeled a "big city" only when its
population exceeded the annual attendance of the Ohio State Fair, held in
Columbus each summer. In 2012 fair attendance was 840,000.[88]

---

88. *Columbus Dispatch,* 30 May 2013, p. E1. On the changing populations of
Ohio's major cities between 1970 and 2010, see Kern and Wilson, *Ohio: A History,* 460.

However, these population figures, often proudly trumpeted by Columbus city officials, could be a bit misleading, for they measured only populations within city limits. As mass suburbanization occurred in Columbus and elsewhere after World War II, a growing proportion of people lived outside the city limits. Columbus was the nation's fifteenth-largest city in 2010, but the central Ohio metropolitan area was just the thirty-eighth largest such area in the United States. The population of the Columbus metropolitan area was, however, expected to surpass that of the Cleveland area by 2020 and then grow to 2.4 million by 2040.[89]

From a city based mainly on government, industry, and trade, Columbus became a metropolis whose economy was grounded in financial services, education, and state government services. Even at manufacturing's high point as a part of Columbus's economic picture, trade, finance, and government services had remained important. Industry, which had reached its apogee in Columbus's economy during World War II, fell in relative significance after the conflict. About 30 percent of Columbus workers still labored in industry in 1960, but in 2000 the proportion had plummeted to a scant 11 percent. Already in 1976 Columbus's largest employers were mainly in education, government, and services: the state of Ohio (with 17,300 employees); the Ohio State University (16,200); the federal government (12,500); public schools (7,600); F. & R. Lazarus, a department store (7,400); the city of Columbus (6,800); Western Electric (6,400); Nationwide Insurance (6,000); Ohio Bell (5,000); and the Borden Company (4,600).[90]

These economic shifts occurred as part of the deindustrialization of Ohio and the Midwest. In 1960 some 1.3 million Ohioans had manufacturing jobs, about 41 percent of the state's workforce. Forty years later just 1.1 million Ohioans did—still a large number, showing that manufacturing remained significant in Ohio—but they comprised less than 20 percent of the workforce. Ohio ranked eighth among the nation's states in terms of industrial output in 2010, with only 14 percent of its workers employed in industry. This shift was part of a regional trend. After rising 1 percent in the 1970s, the number of manufacturing jobs in the Midwest fell by 12 percent in the 1980s and continued to decline in later decades,

---

89. Hunker, *A Personal Geography*, 41–44, discusses the changing meanings of metropolitan areas, or metropolitan standard areas.

90. Ibid, 56–59; and U.S. Department of Transportation, Federal Highway Administration, "Interstate 670 Extension: Final Joint Environmental Impact Statement," typescript report, 16 July 1981, pp. 111–48.

as the region gained the unwanted moniker of "Rust Belt."[91] Eight of the region's twelve largest cities lost population between 1950 and 1980.[92]

Columbus largely escaped decline. By 2000 the service sector of the economy, broadly conceived, accounted for 85 percent of employment in the Columbus area.[93] Columbus was home to more than seventy insurance companies. The Columbus region's top seven employers in 2005 were the state government (28,000); the Ohio State University (22,000); the federal government (17,000); the Banc One Corporation (15,500); the Limited Company, a seller of women's apparel (15,000); OhioHealth (15,000); and Nationwide Insurance (12,000).[94] By way of contrast, Honda, the largest industrial firm in central Ohio, employed 13,000 workers. JPMorgan Chase & Company, a financial giant, emerged as a major Columbus business in the early 2000s, with about 12,000 mainly white-collar employees by 2010. Not surprisingly, Columbus bounced back much more strongly from the loss of jobs during the recession beginning in late 2007 than other large cities in Ohio. By 2013 Columbus had regained 113 percent of the jobs lost, while Cincinnati had regained only 33 percent, and Cleveland just 24 percent.[95] It helped that Columbus led large cities of Ohio in the percentage of its residents who had a college degree. In 2010 about 33 percent of those living in Columbus had earned at least a BA or BS, about the same as the average for large American cities. This figure compared to 29 percent in Cincinnati, 28 percent in Akron and Cleveland, 24 percent in Dayton and Toledo, and 19 percent in Youngstown.[96]

---

91. For overviews, see Cayton, *Ohio: The History of a People,* 369–70, 401; and Kern and Wilson, *Ohio: A History,* 458–62.

92. Teaford, *Cities of the Heartland,* 211. On Cleveland's very difficult transition from industrial to service city, see David Stradling and Richard Stradling, *Where the River Burned: Carl Stokes and the Struggle to Save Cleveland* (Ithaca: Cornell University Press, 2015), 16.

93. In 2015 Columbus had about 1 million employed workers. About 36,000 were in construction; 70,000 in manufacturing; 192,000 in trade, transportation, and utilities; 17,000 in information 75,000 in finance; 173,000 in professional and business services; 154,000 in education and health services; 101,000 in leisure and hospitality; and 165,000 in government. See U.S. Bureau of Labor Services, "Columbus, Ohio: Economy at a Glance, 5 June 2015," at http://www.bls.gov/eag.oh_columbus-msa.htm, accessed on 9 June 2015.

94. City Data, "Columbus: Economy," p. 3, at http://www.city-data.com/us-cities/The Midwest/Columbus-Economy.html, accessed on 9 June 2015.

95. *Columbus Dispatch,* 2 June 2013, p. E6. See also Kern and Wilson, *Ohio: A History,* 487, which notes that central Ohio "has remained one of the few areas in the state with relatively strong job growth, wealth, and employment."

96. *Columbus Dispatch,* 3 June 2012, p. G2.

The Ohio State University was, as one observer noted, "largely the elephant not in the room."[97] Indeed, that institution of higher education did not always receive the recognition it deserved for its contributions to the economies of Columbus and Ohio. Established as the Ohio Agricultural and Mechanical College in 1873 (that name was changed to the Ohio State University five years later), the school was Ohio's only land-grant university. It began operation with twenty-four students, including two women. By 1880 the number of students had risen to 302, including 39 women. By 1909 enrollment stood at 1,252, and in 1926 at 12,296. Enrollment continued to rise during the Great Depression, to 17,568 in 1940. Only the exigencies of World War II brought a decline in enrollment, as men and women left to serve in the armed forces. By 1943 enrollment had fallen to fewer than 8,000 students, but it rebounded to 26,000 in 1946, as many attended college on the GI Bill. Enrollment soared to 40,000 students in 1966 and to 63,000 in 1970; it has since remained at about this level.[98] Spending by thousands of university officials, faculty, and staff, and by tens of thousands of students, boosted the economy of central Ohio. So did the millions of dollars paid in city income taxes each year by university employees and students.

University officials also sought to help local businesses develop in a variety of ways. Beginning in the 1990s they maintained an "incubator" for high-technology firms on the university's campus, providing nascent companies with space and services. From late 2008 they maintained the Industry Liaison Office "to foster economic development opportunities in Ohio and beyond by connecting business and industry to Ohio State discoveries." Doing so would, university officials hoped, "result in new ideas for products, improved processes, and an expansion of services." University administrators reached out to Columbus residents in other ways. In 2008 they opened an Urban Arts Space in downtown Columbus in the building of the former Lazarus Department Store, which had closed four years earlier. Perhaps having the greatest immediate impact on Columbus was the opening in 2005 of the South Campus Gateway Center on High Street, "the fruition of a project to improve the OSU campus neighborhood by bringing private residences, restaurants, and small business establishments to the area."[99]

---

97. Anonymous, "Reader 1's Report on [This Manuscript] for Ohio State University Press," June 2015, p. 1, in the author's possession.

98. Raimund E. Goerler, *The Ohio State University: An Illustrated History* (Columbus: Ohio State University Press 2011), 308–36.

99. Ibid, 335; and Industry Liaison Office, Ohio State University, "Building Industry Connections and Partnerships," at http://ilo.osu.edu, accessed on 9 June 2015.

In mid-2015 the Intelligent Community Forum, an international body, selected Columbus from 400 cities worldwide as the "Intelligent Community of the Year," a choice greatly influenced by the presence of Ohio State in the city. Five criteria were used: broadband connectivity, knowledge in the workforce, innovation, digital inclusion, and marketing and advocacy. According to faculty member Jennifer Evans-Cowley in city and regional planning at Ohio State, who was deeply involved in pushing for Columbus's nomination, "Ohio State played a key partnership role in the selection," important as a major center of research.[100]

Two major issues related to growth seemed to develop in Columbus during the early twenty-first century. One was how to retain young professionals. In 2007 the city government sponsored the conference "State of the Young Professionals" to find ways to keep young professional men and women in the city, and Columbus Mayor Michael Coleman soon set up the twenty-five-member Young Professionals Commission to develop strategies to make Columbus more attractive to young people.[101] These efforts bore some fruit. Between 2007 and 2011 many more people who had at least some college education moved into Columbus than out of the city. A report in 2014 looking at the fifty most populous cities in the United States ranked Columbus as the tenth-best place for recent college graduates to get their start, with the cities judged on job markets, median earnings, affordability, and percentage of young people. Columbus was the most affordable of the top twenty cities.[102] One letter writer to the *Columbus Dispatch* observed in mid-2015, "Those of us who have lived in Columbus for decades have often viewed our city as a stodgy sort of place." He thought it was time to change that attitude. Noting that the author Piper Kerman (*Orange Is the New Black*) and the Scottish craft brewer BrewDog had both just moved to Columbus, he concluded that city residents might be "forced to come to terms with Columbus being a truly hip place."[103]

A second, broader issue concerned the identity—or, really, the lack of identity—of Columbus. Business leaders, in particular, thought that their city required a much stronger sense of identity to make a splash on the national scene and frequently talked about the need to create "a stronger brand identity" for Columbus. In early 2014 city officials hired a German consulting firm to help them hone a brand image for Columbus, the third

---

100. Ohio State University, *OnCampus,* 18 June 2015, p. 2.
101. *Worthington News,* 25 April 2007, p. 43.
102. *OnCampus,* 15 May 2014, p. 10.
103. *Columbus Dispatch,* 21 June 2015, p. B14.

such effort in recent years. A year later, Columbus residents still waited for the announcement of recommendations and the rollout of logos and jingles.[104]

## Murray D. Lincoln and Nationwide Insurance

While the development of the Buckeye Steel Castings Company epitomized important aspects of the industrialization of Columbus, the rise of Nationwide Insurance brought to light important elements of the city's transition to a financial-service economy. Throughout its early history, the company was led by Murray D. Lincoln, who managed to combine an idealistic desire to help people—especially farmers—by providing them with the means to earn profits.[105] Later executives played down that idealism.

Nationwide Insurance began its existence as an offshoot of the Ohio Farm Bureau Federation. Established in 1919, the federation's goal, like that of farm bureau federations being established in other states, was to help farmers secure lower prices for supplies such as fertilizer and gasoline and higher prices for farm products. The federations promoted legislation helpful to farmers and encouraged farmers to form cooperatives. Lincoln, who was the executive secretary of the Ohio Federation, later recalled that this type of thinking extended to automobile insurance in the early 1920s: "In trying to serve the farmer, we determined that he wasn't getting a fair break in automobile insurance rates. The rates were geared to the number and kinds of accidents and claims of urban drivers and really bore no relationship to the experience of rural car owners." To address this shortcoming, the Ohio Federation established the Farm Bureau Mutual Insurance Company with $10,000 in capital in 1926, offering a specialty, niche product: car insurance for farmers. Featuring rates considerably lower than those of old-line insurance firms, and strongly backed and advertised by the federation, the fledgling insurance

---

104. Ibid, 27, June 2010, p. D1; 17 February 2014, p. A1; and 18 February 2014, p. D1.

105. This section of the chapter is based mainly on Peter D. Franklin, *On Your Side: The Story of the Nationwide Insurance Enterprise* (Columbus: Nationwide Insurance Enterprise, 1994); and Murray D. Lincoln, *Vice President in Charge of Revolution* (New York: McGraw-Hill Books, 1960). Hard to measure, but probably important in the rise of insurance and banking in Columbus, was the large number of residents of Germanic origin from the mid-1800s. Thrifty and security conscious, they supported banking and insurance institutions.

mutual saw its business take off in the late 1920s. By the close of 1929 it
had 80,000 policies in force and possessed assets of $1.7 million.[106]

Not even the Great Depression and World War II stopped the insurance mutual's growth. Its officers expanded operations into midwestern,
eastern, and southern states, usually sponsored by state farm bureau federations, and also began offering policies to nonfarmers. New products
followed. The Farm Bureau Mutual Fire Insurance Company was set up
to sell fire insurance in Ohio in 1934, and the Farm Bureau Life Insurance Company began offering life insurance a year later. Lincoln assumed
the presidencies of the three insurance mutual companies from 1938 to
1939.[107] He soon took them into noninsurance fields, including the ownership of radio stations and several manufacturing enterprises. A major
change occurred in 1948, when the Insurance Commissioner of the State
of Ohio forced the Ohio Farm Bureau Federation to sever its ties with
the insurance companies to avoid conflicts of interest. By this time, the
mutual companies had 982,000 policies in force and boasted assets of
$51 million.

Lincoln later recalled that he experienced the divorce of the insurance
mutual companies from the Ohio Farm Bureau Federation as "a severe
emotional wrench."[108] He resigned from the federation to devote himself fulltime to the insurance companies. The mutual companies joined
to become the Nationwide Insurance Company in 1955, with Lincoln as
its head. Further growth and many changes took place in the 1950s: the
regional decentralization of sales operations, later partly reversed; the
acquisition of insurance companies in parts of the United States new to
Nationwide; and a tremendous expansion of the sales of mutual funds,
which Nationwide's officers initially saw as an outgrowth of selling insurance, but which they came to recognize as a business in its own right.
Overly rapid expansion hit profits hard, leading to retrenchment in the
1960s, although overseas expansion took place, especially in Germany,
as did expansion into the American West, especially California. In 1964,
for the first time, Nationwide sold stock to the public to raise needed
capital, moving away from its origins as a mutual company. In 1964, too,
Lincoln retired as head of Nationwide Insurance. He died in late 1966 at
the age of seventy-four.

106. Lincoln, *Vice President,* 72. See also Franklin, *On Your Side,* 31–34. In a mutual
company policyholders share in the firm's profits and elect its officers.
107. Franklin, *On Your Side,* 37–47.
108. Lincoln, *Vice President,* 227; and Franklin, *On Your Side,* 69–104.

Born in Massachusetts in 1892, Lincoln later described his home as "a stony little New England farm." However, commerce was always part of Lincoln's upbringing, as his grandfather ran a "small country store." Lincoln recalled that he "enjoyed being on a farm," because he "had the feeling that feeding people was more important than anything else." After attending grammar school and high school, where he met his future wife, Anne S. Hurst, Lincoln went on to the Massachusetts Agricultural College (later the University of Massachusetts) in Amherst. With the help of a faculty member at that institution, he secured a position as a county agricultural agent and then positions as the agricultural officer for several banks. Lincoln came to Columbus to join the Ohio Farm Bureau Federation in 1920 at the age of twenty-nine and, still later, to head Nationwide Insurance.[109]

Lincoln's rural roots and idealism never left him. His office at Nationwide was rustic and Spartan, featuring a simple wood-burning fireplace. He and his wife lived in the countryside outside of Columbus in a dwelling styled after a New England farmhouse. Speaking in 1960, he stated, "I believe the human race was placed on the earth for some purpose. I am not sure what that purpose is, but to accomplish any end at all, we've got to get along with one another. And in the pursuit of life, liberty, and happiness, it seems to me, we ought to be able to live without the strife and war in which we have hereto found ourselves." Continuing, he said that he firmly believed that "science has provided us with the tools . . . to ease—if not literally erase—some of the age-old scourges of man: hunger, disease, improper housing, unemployment—and war."[110] Lincoln came to spend much of his time on national and international cooperative movements and on CARE (a world relief organization), in which he was especially active, as on insurance matters after World War II. This stance placed him at odds with other executives at Nationwide, who often found him to be aloof, distant, cold, and stubborn, leading to management crises in the 1950s and early 1960s. It was lonely at the top. Lincoln once wrote, "In the interests of peace and harmony and good order within an organization, the top executive has to shun close personal relationships with his executives and his staff." Lincoln also found himself partially excluded from the upper reaches of Columbus's fairly conservative business community because of his avid support for cooperatives.[111]

---

109. Lincoln, *Vice President,* 1, 4; and Franklin, *On Your Side,* 13–25.
110. Lincoln, *Vice President,* 290–91.
111. Ibid, 301–2.

**Figure** 1.3. One Nationwide Plaza in 1984. The plaza soared above Columbus, a symbol of the importance of Nationwide Insurance to the city. (Used with permission of the *Columbus Citizen-Journal*, Scripps-Howard Newspapers/Grandview Heights Public Library/Photohio.org)

Nationwide's later presidents partially abandoned Lincoln's idealism to focus more on insurance growth and profits. By 1993 the Nationwide Insurance Enterprise, as the firm had come to be renamed, had over 11 million policies in force, generating premium income of $13 billion. Nationwide had $42 billion in assets and more than 8,000 employees. The firm continued to grow in later decades.[112] In the 1970s and 1980s Nationwide's officers constructed three large headquarters buildings at the north end of downtown Columbus, helping revitalize it; and in the early 2000s they provided most of the financing for a new indoor stadium in the same area, which promptly became known as the "Arena District." They also played more-active roles in local philanthropic ventures. These efforts had the benefit of securing their acceptance in an increasingly open business community in Columbus.

112. Franklin, *On Your Side*, 72, 273.

## Business Development in a Midwestern City

Several elements were important for business success in Columbus: the location of the city astride transportation connections to regional, national, and international markets; the personal connections of business leaders, their "social capital," which helped them expand their firms; and a sometimes overlooked factor in business success, the good luck, sometimes called *vision*, of being at the right place at the right time with the right product or service. As business historian Pamela Walker Laird has conclusively shown, networking, connections, and social capital have *always* been very important elements in the economic successes of American business leaders. Laird has persuasively argued, "Social capital exists in and flows through personal connections and individuals' potential for making connections. Shared expectations and goals bind together networks, which can be made up of groups as informal as golfing buddies or as formal as incorporated institutions." Social capital, Laird has concluded, "operates through such networks, as well as through mentors, gatekeepers, and role models, to inspire as well as advance the ambitious."[113] William Neil, Samuel Bush, Murray Lincoln, and many other Columbus business leaders benefited from all of these advantages.

Columbus shared important characteristics with other midwestern cities, especially in its nineteenth-century growth. Its geographic location and nearness to natural resources spurred the development of industry. Transportation improvements, especially railroads, moved the products of Columbus factories to regional and national markets. As was typical of midwestern cities, heavy industry such as iron making predominated in Columbus, not light industry such as textile spinning. In population too, as we shall see, Columbus resembled other midwestern cities, with German immigrants more numerous than Irish ones, the latter of whom dominated eastern cities such as Boston and New York City. More difficult to measure, but still significant, there long existed a feeling of cultural inferiority among Columbus residents vis-à-vis those of eastern cities, as was typical of the feelings of urban Midwesterners, even those living in Chicago.[114] In other ways Columbus was atypical. It was a state capital, a distinction not shared with any other city in Ohio and shared with only a handful or two in the Midwest. In addition, Columbus was home to a

---

113. Pamela Walker Laird, *Pull: Networking and Success since Benjamin Franklin* (Cambridge, MA: Harvard University Press, 2006), 1–2.

114. Teaford, *Cities of the Heartland,* viii–xii.

major, research-driven state university, which was oriented throughout its history to the needs of agriculture and business.

Columbus thus developed as a dynamic midwestern city, at least after its first decade or two of doldrums. As a midsize city, Columbus did not often possess what economists and business historians often label "first mover advantages" on the national, or even regional, urban scenes. That is, Columbus did not usually get ahead by being the first to do things and then staving off rivals. Boston, Philadelphia, and New York—to name just a few obvious examples—were older, larger, and better-established cities. In the Midwest, Chicago grew much faster. Cincinnati and Cleveland started earlier and long remained ahead of Columbus. Yet not being a first mover had advantages in some ways. Columbus residents could benefit from what was learned about land and water developments in other cities. Then, too, with less capital and knowledge invested in established ways of doing things, Columbus residents sometimes proved more willing to experiment, especially in water policies, than their counterparts in some other larger and older cities.

CHAPTER 2

# The Role of Water
# in Shaping Columbus

In 2012 Conrade C. Hinds, a retired project manager for the city of Columbus Division of Water, stated with great pride, and perhaps a bit of hyperbole, how revolutionary a new water system established in Columbus between 1904 and 1908 was: "The 1908 Columbus Experiment was like the 1969 moon landing to the world's engineering and emerging public health community of that time." It was, Hinds concluded, "the catalyst that helped set a precedent for delivering clean and uncontaminated drinking water on a large scale, not only to the city of Columbus but also to America and the world."[1]

This chapter examines the history of water use and water systems in the making of Columbus to about 1909, placing an emphasis on the construction of state-of-the-art water and sewer systems during the Progressive era of the early 1900s. Those systems grew out of century-long worries that Columbus residents harbored about the inadequacies of their city's earlier water supplies in preventing diseases and combating fires. At times the lack of an adequate supply of clean water retarded Columbus's growth, as waterborne diseases swept through the city, especially in the antebellum years. Columbus's water also had characteristics that made its use in industry problematic. It was "hard" water, which required "softening" for use

---

1. Conrade C. Hinds, *The Great Columbus Experiment of 1908: Waterworks That Changed the World* (Charleston, SC: History Press, 2012), 11, 13.

in steam-generating boilers at a time when steam, not electricity, powered most machinery. Hard water corroded boilers. The Progressive era water and sewer systems nearly eliminated waterborne diseases from Columbus and provided means to soften water for industrial use.[2]

Urban historian Martin Melosi's works have greatly influenced scholarship on urban water developments. His pathbreaking *The Sanitary City: Environmental Services in Urban America from Colonial Times to the Present* focused, in Melosi's words, "on sanitary (or environmental) services—water, sewerage, and solid-waste disposal—because they have been and remain indispensable for the functioning and growth of cities." Melosi emphasized the importance of changing ideas about the origins of diseases in shaping the responses of urbanites to water issues. He stressed especially the significance of the transition from a belief in the miasmic sources of diseases (the concept that vapors arising from decaying organic materials caused diseases) to germ theory (the idea that specific invisible bacteria caused many diseases), which occurred around the 1880s and 1890s.[3]

Melosi's basic approach to water use has informed much of my study, but this chapter and the one to follow extend his work in important ways. Melosi and most other historians who have dealt with urban water matters have looked mainly at developments in large, coastal cities—Philadelphia, New York, Boston, San Francisco, Oakland, and Los Angeles—along with water systems in Chicago.[4] Few have investigated the

---

2. Hardness is a measure of the presence of the minerals calcium and magnesium in water. As water moves through the earth, it can pick up these minerals and become hard. *Hard* refers to the difficulty with which water produces soapsuds, with successively harder water requiring more soap. Softening reduced the magnesium and calcium to 120 parts per million in the water in Columbus, considered moderately hard by national standards but suitable for corrosion control. See City of Columbus, Division of Water and Power, "2007 Water Report," pamphlet, p. 3.

3. Martin V. Melosi, *The Sanitary City: Environmental Services in Urban America from Colonial Times to the Present* (Pittsburgh: University of Pittsburgh Press, 2008), 1. See also Martin V. Melosi, *Precious Commodity: Providing Water for America's Cities* (Pittsburgh: University of Pittsburgh Press, 2011), a collection of eight essays. Daniel Schneider, *Hybrid Nature: Sewage Treatment and the Contradictions of the Industrial Ecosystem* (Cambridge, MA: MIT Press, 2011), is also valuable. Like Melosi, Schneider examines the development of sewage-treatment systems as parts of urban infrastructures. However, he goes further in looking at sewage-treatment plants as human and biological ecosystems that use bacteria to purify sewage, and he depicts sewage treatment as being part of a revolution in industrial processes using microbiology to produce foods, chemicals, and pharmaceuticals.

4. Nelson M. Blake, *Water for the Cities: A History of the Urban Water Supply Problem in the United States* (Syracuse: Syracuse University Press, 1956), which looks

evolution of water works in midsize, inland, midwestern cities. In 1999 historian Maureen Ogle decried the overemphasis on large cities that built centralized, citywide water and sewer systems at early dates. More typical, she suggested, were the experiences of midsize cities in which private systems remained the norm well into the nineteenth and twentieth centuries.[5]

Columbus was just such a metropolis. The city's size and age mattered. Younger and with fewer residents than the large, coastal cities, Columbus long possessed less-well-developed water and sewer systems than they did. At first, there was simply no perceived need for a comprehensive system, and Columbus residents initially did not have the resources to construct one. Developments in Columbus, where comprehensive water and sewer systems were initially slow to be constructed, were typical of the gradual spread of such infrastructures across Ohio and much of the nation. However, in the twentieth century, Columbus came to lead the nation in water and sewer matters. The death in 1904 of Senator Mark Hanna of Ohio from typhoid fever contracted by drinking polluted water in Columbus galvanized city residents to action. Moreover, the rapidly growing size of Columbus and the place its residents wanted their city to take in their nation's urban network demanded building a citywide system. Urban pride was at stake. As a relative latecomer to water issues, those in Columbus could experiment with new treatment methods. They were not held back by the sunk costs of earlier systems.

This chapter and the following one examine how changing conceptions of water use greatly influenced the shape of the city, especially how expert knowledge intertwined with politics to help make Columbus the city it became. Water issues, as much as land-use matters, determined the spatial and social layout of Columbus. Chapters 2 and 3 show that the process of building water systems involved conflicts among groups of Columbus residents. Disagreements raised environmental-justice

---

at developments in Boston, New York, Baltimore, and Philadelphia; Louis P. Cain, *Sanitation Strategy for a Lakefront Metropolis: The Case of Chicago* (DeKalb: Northern Illinois University Press, 1978); Sarah S. Elkind, *Bay Cities and Water Politics: The Battle for Resources in Boston and Oakland* (Lawrence: University Press of Kansas, 1998); David Soll, *Empire of Water: An Environmental and Political History of the New York City Water Supply* (Ithaca: Cornell University Press, 2013); and Joel Tarr, *The Search for the Ultimate Sink: Urban Pollution in Historical Perspective* (Akron, OH: University of Akron Press, 1996).

5. Maureen Ogle, "Water Supply, Waste Disposal, and the Mid-Nineteenth-Century American City," *Journal of Urban History* 25 (March 1999), 321–47. But see also Raja R. Roomann, *Urban Growth and the Development of an Urban Water System: City of Cincinnati, 1800–1915* (Cincinnati: RONNHU Publishers, 2001).

concerns. Who would benefit and who would lose from environmental changes in the use of water? How and why? As Columbus residents grappled with water issues, they showed changing preferences for private and public ownership and operation of water facilities, and they revealed differing opinions over values associated with economic growth and environmental change.

## Local, Fragmented Water Systems

Newlywed Elizabeth ("Betsy") Green Deshler moved to Columbus, Ohio, in the summer of 1817 with her husband David W. Deshler from Easton, Pennsylvania. Betsy was eighteen years of age; David was twenty-five. They were soon living in a house built by David, who was a carpenter, on Broad Street just west of High Street, near the statehouse. From this "plain, wooden building" Betsy penned letters to her parents and brother back in Pennsylvania, describing life in Ohio's newly founded state capital. A constant refrain concerned unhealthy living conditions in Columbus. In late 1821 Betsy wrote to her brother, "The most that appears to occupy the minds of people this year is sickness, taking care of the sick, going to funerals, and hard times." In the fall of 1822 she lamented to him that "there has been much more sickness this season than has ever been known since the settlement of Franklin County. Our burying ground has averaged ten new graves per week." Matters failed to improve in 1823, with Betsy telling her parents in August, "Our town is at present nothing but a scene of trouble, sickness and death." In the spring of 1826 she further informed her brother, "Everyone in this town has been severely afflicted with the influenza."[6] Betsy died in that year at the age of twenty-seven, exhausted.[7]

Betsy's letters make for grim reading indeed, with frequent complaints about "bilious fevers," influenza, and other illnesses. *Bilious fevers* was a catchall term for high fevers of all types. Infectious disease was,

6. Long excerpts from Betsy Deshler's letters may be found in Lee, *History of the City*, vol. 1, pp. 265–71. The original letters are no longer accessible, for they repose in a time capsule buried in a sealed container in the One Columbus Building in downtown Columbus.

7. Garrett and Lentz, *Crossroads*, 29; and Lentz, *As It Were*, 37–40. David Deshler remarried and became one of the leading bankers in Columbus. Like William Neil, Deshler invested his business earnings in Columbus real estate and hotels. Deshler knew Neil well, for the two had been partners in Neil's early flour-shipping enterprise. On the Deshlers, see Cole, *Fragile Capital*, 28–29.

medical historians Charles Wooley and Barbara Van Brimmer have written, "a recurrent threat to life on the frontier and throughout most of the nineteenth century in central Ohio."[8] Like most towns and cities in the antebellum United States, Columbus was a dangerous place in which to live, made unsafe especially by waterborne diseases such as typhoid fever and cholera. A desire to eradicate such diseases and protect themselves from fires lay behind much of the push by Columbus residents to improve their water supplies. As it developed as a center of politics, commerce, and, to a lesser degree, industry, Columbus was an increasingly thirsty city, with a pressing need for water for residential, commercial, and industrial uses. Yet before the 1870s Columbus had no comprehensive water or sewer systems. All arrangements were ad hoc, local, and fragmented.

Copious supplies of water were available. Columbus lay atop a thick layer of glacial till—that is, gravel and sand left behind by retreating glaciers. At the intersection of Front and High streets in the city's downtown, it was 110 feet down to bedrock. A Columbus geologist has described this "area of deep drift" as a "great reservoir for ground water." Bedrock consisted of limestone and shale, with limestone predominating west of High Street. About 39 inches of rain annually percolated into the till and also provided surface runoff for streams flowing north to south in central Ohio: Blacklick Creek, Big Walnut Creek, and Alum Creek, in addition to the Olentangy and Scioto rivers.[9]

Streams, springs, and underground aquifers provided Columbus residents with their first supplies of water. Alfred E. Lee, an early historian of the city observed, "The entire East Broad Street region abounded in springs," and he noted that Spring Street "took its name from numerous natural fountains which issued in its vicinity and fed a brook of clear water known as Doe Run."[10] Another early-day chronicler, Opha Moore, commented on the "marshes, quagmires, and ponds" scattered throughout the landscape of Columbus, along with "slimy bogs."[11] In this soggy situation in the nineteenth century, Lee stated that "wells sunk or driven

8. Wooley and Van Brimmer, Second Blessing, 4. See also Hurt, Ohio Frontier, 269–72. The prevalence of disease increased mortality in frontier Ohio. In the early 1800s about 25 percent of children died before their first birthday, and another 25 percent of children and young adults died by the age of twenty.

9. J. Ernest Carman, "The Geology of the Columbus Region," in Columbus, ed. Peattie, 5. See also Hunker, A Personal Geography, 12–16.

10. Lee, History of the City, vol. 1, pp. 273–74.

11. Moore, Franklin County, vol. 1, p. 139.

to a depth not exceeding thirty feet, and frequently to not more than half this depth, command a generous and unfailing amount of cool and well filtered water."[12] Columbus possessed about 1,700 wells for its 32,600 residents by 1866.[13]

Sewage went into outhouses (called "necessaries") built over underground vaults and cesspools, as was typical of most American cities well into the nineteenth, and even the twentieth, centuries. Privy vaults and cesspools were supposed to be cleaned on a regular basis but often were not, allowing sewage to leak into water supplies. Moreover, while some privy vaults were closed, with mortared systems trapping all waste entering them, most were not. Unmortared brick- or stone-lined privy vaults were cheaper to build than mortared ones and allowed liquids to seep out into the surrounding soil, making room for additional wastes to flow into the vaults. Cesspools were usually simply unlined holes in the ground from which sewage easily spread into the surrounding water table.[14] Water closets, introduced in the early 1800s in some cities, usually emptied into privy vaults or cesspools rather than into sewers, adding to the problem of the disposal of waste. Sewage was composed mainly of water. Only about 0.2 percent of it consisted of solid materials.[15]

As was also typical in American cities, those sewers that did exist in Columbus helped little with sanitation at first.[16] Unconnected local sewer tunnels and pipes carried some sewage into the Scioto River. The first major sewer was a brick one built under part of Broad Street, passing beneath High Street to the river from 1849 to 1850. In 1852 sewers were built under Spring Street between Third and Front streets, and within two more years about 2 miles of sewers underlay Columbus. By 1872 there were major sewers under Fourth Street, South Public Lane (later Livingston Avenue), Centre Alley, Oak Street, Cherry Alley, Broad Street, Mound Street, and West Street. From 1873 to 1874, Peter's Run sewer, whose construction had begun in 1867, was completed; sewage was carried across the feeder canal to the Ohio and Erie Canal in an open wooden trough, a smelly aqueduct about a block in length, to dump into the Scioto River.[17] Sewage was also simply washed away in surface

12. Lee, *History of the City,* vol. 1, p. 686.
13. Hinds, *Experiment,* 29.
14. Ogle, "Water Supply," 340–41.
15. Roomann, *Urban Growth,* vi.
16. Schneider, *Hybrid Nature,* xxi.
17. Hooper, *Columbus: From the Founding,* vol. 1, p. 121; and Lentz, *Columbus: The Story,* 64.

streams, which, in turn, ran into the river. Some of the sewers were built by the city, but many were privately constructed, designed to drain areas for real-estate development. Untreated sewage polluted water supplies, with Columbus's "filth-sodden soil" and water supplies becoming "a prolific source of general and specific disease."[18]

Like residents in most other midsize cities, those in Columbus largely favored private water and sewage solutions. A few American metropolises moved toward municipally owned, centralized municipal water systems in the 1840s and 1850s—New York City, Boston, and Philadelphia—but the vast majority of smaller cities did not. The costs of public citywide systems, a dislike of perceived intrusiveness of government in private affairs, and legal situations that favored individuals over communities militated against centralized water systems for decades.[19] Then, too, in the antebellum years, Columbus residents, like most other Americans, had no knowledge of germ theory and did not fully perceive dangers arising from the intermixture of their water supplies with sewage. Most Americans believed that diseases originated in miasmic airs coming from decaying animal corpses and rotting plant materials. They took these ideas from Europeans, especially as popularized by Edwin Chadwick, a barrister-turned-reformer in Great Britain. Chadwick associated filth with bad airs, and thus with disease, among the "lower classes" in London. Decaying materials, he stated, caused diseases among the poor. The step for reformers seemed simple: remove the filth, and diseases would vanish. A clean city would be free of disease and, perhaps, of poverty as well.[20]

Such thinking did little to address the actual causes of many diseases: invisible bacteria. Waterborne diseases, which often spread in epidemics, resulted, extending well beyond those noted by Betsy Deshler. An international cholera epidemic, which killed 60,000 people in Great Britain during 1831 and 1832, crossed the Atlantic to hit the Columbus area hard in 1832 and 1833, causing the deaths of one-third of the residents of Franklinton. Cholera returned in 1849, killing, in addition to about 200 Columbus residents, 116 prisoners in the state penitentiary just north

---

18. Lee, *History of the City*, vol. 1, p. 691.

19. Ogle, "Water Supply"; and Smith, *City Water*, 57–66.

20. Melosi, *Sanitary City*, 29–31; and Smith, *City Water*, 164–77. See also John Duffy, *The Sanitarians: A History of American Public Health* (Urbana: Illinois University Press, 1990), 93–109. In the 1600s London physicians making home visits wore masks with artificial birds' beaks filled with aromatic herbs to prevent the breathing of foul airs (miasmas). Their masks gave doctors the nickname "quack-snifter," shortened to "quack." See Patrick Taylor, *A Dublin Student Doctor* (New York: Tom Doherty Associates, 2011), 227.

of downtown Columbus. Additional cholera outbreaks occurred in 1850, 1852, and 1854. The 1850 epidemic disrupted the holding of a state constitutional convention in Columbus that year, as convention members fled to Cincinnati. Altogether, some 4,000 Columbus residents moved out of their city to try to escape cholera that year. Typhoid fever was another big killer. In 1867 diphtheria and typhoid fever were so rampant at the State Institution for the Deaf and Dumb in Columbus that the school had to be disbanded and the students sent home. Dysentery (severe diarrhea) was also carried by impure water and often struck those living in Columbus. A fourth water-related disease chronically found in early Columbus was malaria, which was referred to as "the ague," "shakes and fever," and "chills and fever."[21]

Cholera is spread by drinking water and eating food contaminated by fecal matter from infected individuals. It is concentrated in the small intestine and caused by the bacterium *Vibrio cholerae*, resulting in severe dehydration via vomiting and diarrhea and often leading to death. Typhoid fever is spread in the same way, passed on by the bacterium *salmonella Typhi*. Fevers and internal hemorrhaging often resulted in death. Dysentery is an inflammation of the intestine also caused by drinking tainted water or eating contaminated food, resulting in severe diarrhea, dehydration, and often death. Malaria is spread by mosquitoes bred in stagnant water. These diseases were big killers during the Civil War. Of Ohio's nearly 35,000 Civil War deaths of soldiers, about two-thirds resulted from disease. Half of those resulted from typhoid fever, cholera, diarrhea, and dysentery.[22]

Waterborne diseases affected animals as well as people. In 1872 a waterborne epizootic disease, which had first appeared in Columbus in 1858, returned with a vengeance to fell many of the city's horses. Seized with chills and coughing, horses were incapacitated. Stage coaches, horse-drawn streetcars, and omnibuses ceased running. Firemen had to pull

---

21. Early histories of Columbus contain extensive litanies of epidemics, with Lee's account being the most complete. See Martin, *Franklin County*, vol. 1, pp. 6, 305–6, 328–30; Lee, *History of the City*, vol. 1, pp. 716–29; Moore, *Franklin* County, vol. 1, pp. 355–56; Studer, *Columbus*, vol. 1, pp. 36–37, 48–49; and Taylor, *Centennial History*, vol. 1, pp. 52, 103. More recent histories dealing with diseases include Cole, *Fragile Capital*, 24–25; Wooley and Van Brimmer, *Second Blessing*, 97–114; and Winter, *A Concise History*, 42, 117. See also Ed Lentz, "Epidemics Made 1800s Perilous," *Worthington News*, 24 July 2014, p. A6. On the disruption of Ohio's Constitutional Convention in 1850, see Kern and Wilson, *A History of the Buckeye State*, 211.

22. Cayton, *Ohio: The History of a People*, 129; Rosenberg, *The Cholera Years*; and Hinds, *Experiment*, 19–24.

their engines and hose carts by hand. Bakers and grocers delivered their goods on foot, and oxen took over heavy pulling. The city almost shut down temporarily.[23]

Columbus residents sought to prevent and combat these diseases through governmental actions. Borough ordinances aimed to clean up Columbus, thus removing filth, bad air, and disease. An 1828 ordinance specified that outhouses had to be erected at least 20 feet back from any street or alley and stated that they had to have vaults at least 6 feet deep. At about the same time, nuisances were forbidden. Hogs could not roam city streets at large. Loose animals were auctioned by the borough's marshal to the highest bidder. Slaughterhouses were forbidden within borough limits, resulting in their construction just to the south. Ordinances approved in 1820, and again in 1828, required residents to remove decomposing bodies of dead hogs, cows, horses, sheep, dogs, and cats from borough streets within one day or face fines. The repeated passage of this measure suggests, however, that rotting animal bodies were a continuing problem. The 1828 ordinance also forbade leaving manure, lumber, firewood, or "any nuisance of any kind whatever" in the streets; a violation was subject to a hefty fine of $10. An ordinance passed in 1830 provided for the cleaning of High Street. Home and business owners were to "cause to be swept or cleaned so much of High Street as lies in front of the lot or part of the lot they occupies [sic] to the center of the street." There the dirt was to be collected "into convenient heaps on Saturday in each week before 10 Oclock of said day from the 1st day of May to the 1st day of November." Failure to obey this rule resulted in a $1 fine. The borough marshal was ordered to ensure that a city-paid scavenger removed the waste from the center of the High Street to "some proper place of deposit."[24] City employees did not clean Columbus's streets then.[25]

When Columbus was recognized as a city in 1834, its Articles of Incorporation encompassed the borough's earlier ones for street cleaning and the prohibition of animals running at large.[26] City ordinances

23. Lee, *History of the City*, vol. 1, p. 727.

24. The original, handwritten borough ordinances for 1816–30 are available at the library and archives of the Ohio Historical Society (the Ohio History Connection) in Columbus, Ohio, in State Archives Series 5039, Box 18,380. The pages for the book of ordinances in that box for the ordinances referred to above are 55, 94, 148–49, 151, 185.

25. On similar actions in New York City, especially efforts to control the roaming of hogs on city streets, see Catherine McNeur, *Taming Manhattan: Environmental Battles in the Antebellum City* (Cambridge, MA: Harvard University Press, 2014), 6–44.

26. "An Act to Incorporate the City of Columbus in the State of Ohio," in State Archives Series 5039, Box 18,381, vol. 1, pp. 6–10.

approved in 1835 also repeated earlier prohibitions against allowing dead
animals or other nuisances to decompose on city streets. Showing a growing acceptance of the miasmic theory of disease, ordinances also stated,
"Whenever any lot, yard or cellar within the bounds of the city shall contain any stagnant water, filth or offensive matter of any kind which may
be prejudicial to the public health, the same shall be deemed a nuisance
and the owner or owners or occupants of such lot, yard or cellar shall
cause such nuisance to be removed," under the threat of a fine. Likewise,
candlemakers and soap makers were forbidden to use any "stale, stinking
or putrid fat, grease or other offensive matters." Slaughterhouses were
once again outlawed within city limits.[27]

The 1834 Articles of Incorporation permitted Columbus city council members to establish a board of health to "secure said city and its
inhabitants thereof from the costs, distress, and calamities of contagious,
malignant and infectious diseases," and they quickly did so.[28] In the
wake of the cholera epidemic of 1832–33, the council created a temporary seven-member board empowered to take whatever actions were necessary to keep diseases at bay. Only larger metropolises like New York
City had permanent boards of health at this time. Council members also
passed laws that required that the masters of canal boats entering Columbus report to the Columbus Board of Health "any person affected with
cholera or any contagious or infectious disease." Boats carrying infected
travelers were not permitted to land inside the city limits, and infected
people were forbidden to disembark.[29] Officials in Lancaster, just south
of Columbus, also passed ordinances forbidding canal boats carrying
infected passengers from landing in their town.[30] The Columbus Board
of Health had only a temporary existence and soon passed way. Such
was the outcome in a later health crisis. The 1848 outbreak of cholera
prompted the appointment of another temporary board of health. Only
in 1887 was a permanent board of health established, after additional
outbreaks of typhoid fever, diphtheria, and cholera.[31]

---

27. The city of Columbus ordinances may be found in State Archives Series 5039,
Box 18,381, vol. 1, pp. 48–51, 266–70.

28. "Act to Incorporate the City of Columbus," 6.

29. City of Columbus, "Ordinances," 38, 63–64. On the creation of the Board of
Health in 1887, see Wooley and Van Brimmer, *Second Blessing*, 394–97.

30. David R. Contosta, *Lancaster, Ohio, 1800–2000* (Columbus: Ohio State University Press, 1999), 45.

31. Lee, *History of the City*, vol. 1, pp. 725–29; Martin, *Franklin County*, vol. 1,
pp. 328–30; Moore, *Franklin County*, vol. 1, pp. 355–56; and Studer, *Columbus, Ohio:
Its History*, vol. 1, pp. 48–49.

Columbus residents responded to the dangers of fires as they did to those of diseases: through governmental actions. An 1819 ordinance outlawed "the burning of timber, brush shavings or any combustible materials within the Borough of Columbus," without the prior permission of the mayor, subject to a $50 fine. An 1822 ordinance provided for the enrollment in the mayor's office of a hook-and-ax company of fifteen men and a ladder company of twelve men. The mayor could draft men, if necessary. All men were required by law to "act in concert" with the fire companies to extinguish fires. Ordinances of 1822 and 1824 further required that "all houses, stores, and shops" contain their proper "quota of fire buckets," made of "good leather" capable holding 4 quarts of water each.[32]

Columbus's Articles of Incorporation as a city empowered the city council "to secure said City" from "the destructive ravages of fire" by forbidding the construction of any building more than 10 feet tall unless it was made of brick or stone. Any offending structure could be torn down.[33] An ordinance of 1835 laid out detailed specifications for the construction of blacksmith shops, bakeries, and other commercial establishments in ways designed to make them less likely to catch on fire, such was the fear of conflagration. Another 1835 ordinance authorized the city to build 6,000-gallon water cisterns at the intersections of major streets in the downtown area and to connect those cisterns with underground pipes. The council had purchased a hand-pumped fire engine four years before and bought two more in 1835, and the council members recognized the need for water supplies for them. A building to house the three engines and a hook-and-ladder carriage was also built at this time. A third 1835 ordinance laid out plans for the creation of a forty-man hook-and-ladder company and three fifty-man engine companies, along with provisions for the establishment of fire wardens throughout Columbus.[34]

The fire wardens had extensive powers. They could "enter any house or building, lot, yard or other building in this city between sun rising or setting on any week day for the purpose of examining any fire place, stoves, hearths, chimneys, kettles, boilers or other apparatus which may be dangerous in causing or promoting damage by fire." The wardens could order building owners to "remove or amend" any fire dangers "in such manner and within such time as they may deem reasonable,"

32. Borough of Columbus, "Ordinances," 89, 115–16, 129.
33. "Act to Incorporate the City of Columbus," 7.
34. City of Columbus, "Ordinances," 41–42, 56–62, 65–66. An 1848 ordinance further delineated the organization of the fire companies.

with violations subject to a $50 fine. Such was the very considerable police power delegated by city officials to the fire wardens.[35]

Further changes to firefighting soon occurred. After viewing their performance in Cincinnati, Columbus city council members purchased steam-powered, horse-drawn fire engines in the 1850s. At this time, Columbus also began paying members of its fire department, now organized under the leadership of a fire chief, thereby becoming the fourth city in the United States to have paid firemen using steam-powered pumpers. (Cincinnati was the first, having established a professional fire department a few years earlier.) There were controversies in taking these steps. An 1853 ordinance forbidding firemen to run their engines on sidewalks gave offense, leading to the disbanding of several companies. Then, too, the election of the first fire chief by the city council required one hundred seventy ballots, as a result of differences of opinions over how best to organize the fire department.[36] Not all Columbus residents were confident that these steps were enough to prevent fires. One enterprising jeweler built his shop on wheels so that it could easily be moved into the middle of a street in case of fire.[37] He may have been prescient. The Neil House burned to the ground in 1860 due to a lack of water in the cisterns.[38]

## The Use and Abuse of the Scioto River

Looming large in all of Columbus's water matters was the Scioto River, running through the city from north to south. The river came to provide much of the water that residents of central Ohio used for drinking, firefighting, and industry. In the antebellum period, however, the city's inhabitants employed the river mainly for transportation. The Scioto River was considered navigable from Worthington, south to its confluence with the Ohio River. James Kilbourne shipped supplies for Worthington along the Scioto and Olentangy rivers in 1803 upstream by boat from Chillicothe. The availability of river transportation was one of the factors attracting Kilbourne to Worthington's site. In the very early 1800s the Olentangy River also served as the location for a gristmill and sawmill

---

35. Ibid.

36. Hooper, *Columbus: From the Founding*, vol. 1, pp. 18–21; Studer, *Columbus, Ohio: Its History*, vol. 1, pp. 133–34; Teaford, *Cities of the Heartland*, 11–12.

37. Lentz, *As It Were*, 50.

38. Weisenburger, *Columbus during the Civil War*, 6.

for Worthington, and just a bit later waterpower from the river ran the engines of the Worthington Manufacturing Company.[39]

An advertisement for the sale of land in Columbus in 1812 claimed that "the Scioto affords good navigation for about eighty miles, and the Whetstone branch as far as the town of Worthington."[40] Lyne Starling, one of the founders of Franklinton, sent produce south to New Orleans by barge in 1810 and 1811, as did William Neil's flour partnership a few years later. Through legislation passed in 1809, the Ohio General Assembly designated the Scioto River as being among those streams that were navigable. The Scioto River, the measure declared, was navigable "from its confluence with the Ohio River as far up as the Indian Boundary line" just north of Worthington. The legislation specified further that "no person shall be permitted to build a milldam on any of said rivers, or in any manner obstruct navigation on the same."[41] In 1828 the steamboat *Tiosco* departed from Columbus for Portsmouth on the Ohio River "with several small families" onboard. Other boats followed, including the *American,* as late as 1848.[42]

To accommodate traffic on the Scioto River and the feeder canal, the Columbus borough council paid for the building of a wharf on the river in the downtown area. An 1828 ordinance instructed the mayor and council members to hire an engineer "to grade the east side of the river and put in a wharf" at a cost not to exceed $6,000. Another ordinance that was passed seven years later specified exactly how boats and rafts were to use the newly built city wharf. Numerous private wharves and warehouses also came to line the Scioto River.[43]

While employed for commercial purposes, the Scioto River became something of an open sewer, the recipient of waste from streams and sewers draining Columbus. Matters first came to a head on this issue in 1827. What the *Ohio State Journal,* a Columbus newspaper, called "a goodly number of respectable citizens" from Columbus tore down a milldam

39. Goodwin Berquist and Paul C. Bowers, Jr., *The New Eden: James Kilbourne and the Development of Ohio* (Lanham, MD: University Press of America, 1983), 49, 53, 56.

40. The advertisement is reprinted in Martin, *History of Franklin County,* vol. 1, 277–78.

41. Lee, *History of the City,* vol. 1, p. 302, reprints the 1809 legislation. See also Cole, *Fragile Capital,* 28. Even earlier, the Northwest Ordinance of 1787 declared that "waters leading into the Mississippi and Saint Lawrence" were "common highways" that could not be obstructed. See Cayton and Onuf, *Midwest and the Nation,* 12.

42. Lee, *History of the City,* vol. 1, pp. 308–9.

43. Borough of Columbus, "Ordinances," 171–73; and City of Columbus, "Ordinances," 52–53. See also Cole, *Fragile Capital,* 33.

built across the Scioto River by the owners of a gristmill. They did so to
make their river navigable again, but they also wanted to release stagnant waters behind the dam, which they blamed for creating miasmic
airs and spreading diseases. No one was prosecuted for destruction of the
dam.[44] (Milldams obstructing navigation on the Miami River to the west
of Columbus brought threatened vigilante actions by owners of keelboats
and flatboats in 1824.[45]) Columbus city officials outlawed bathing and
swimming in the Scioto River by ordinances passed in 1834 and 1848.
Moral, as well as health, issues may have been at work. The 1834 ordinance levied a $10 fine on anyone "found exposing him or herself naked
or in a lewd or indecent manner."[46] Not coincidentally, perhaps, the first
commercial bathhouse opened in Columbus in 1843.[47]

In their attitudes toward the Scioto River, Columbus residents shared
ideas about rivers with people throughout the antebellum Midwest. They
liked rivers for their utilitarian values, especially as transportation arteries,
but they disliked them and their bottomlands as sources (real and imagined)
of diseases and as places frequented by gangs of criminals, that is, highway-
men. Attitudes toward rivers were thus often quite ambivalent. Rivers were
not seen in totally positive lights. In an 1818 account of his journey from
the East Coast to Illinois, Morris Birkbeck concluded that most American
town builders chose "convenience and profit over salubrity [sic]" in building on rivers and were, therefore, "bad calculators, after all."[48] Even more
vividly, the editor of the Scioto Telegraph observed in early 1820, "The
angel of disease and death, ascending from his oozy bed along the marshy
margin of the bottom grounds . . . floats in his aerial chariot and in seasons
favorable to his prowess spreads mortal desolation as he flies."[49]

The natural environment was not always welcoming to settlers in central Ohio. Even as Columbus residents used the Scioto River for their
own purposes, the river periodically flooded, showing that it had not been
fully tamed. Franklinton was inundated in 1798, prompting its founders to begin looking to the east across the river and leading to the creation of Columbus. Additional floods occurred in 1832, 1834, and 1847.

44. As quoted in Lee, *History of the City*, vol. 1, pp. 717–18.
45. Hurt, *Ohio Frontier*, 371.
46. City of Columbus, "Ordinances," 37, 241–42.
47. Cole, *Fragile Capital*, 87. On the development of bathhouses nationally, see
Smith, *City Water*, 168, 240.
48. As quoted in Mahoney, *River Towns*, 61. While pronounced in the Midwest,
these attitudes were not unique to people in that region.
49. As quoted in Hurt, *Ohio Frontier*, 271–72.

A leading newspaper reported of the 1847 inundation, "So high has [sic] been the waters, and so great the destruction of bridges, that we are almost destitute of the news of this terrific flood." More floods ravaged the Columbus area in 1852, 1859, 1860, 1862, 1866, 1868, 1869, and 1870. Nearly all of the floods broke through levies on the west side of the Scioto River to inundate Franklinton.[50] Such flooding was long the case, even after Franklinton became part of Columbus, annexed in 1864.

## Water Use in American Cities before 1870

Columbus trailed larger Ohio cities in establishing municipal water works. Cincinnati was the first to have one, set up in 1821. Water was pumped from the Ohio River to an elevated storage reservoir from which it was distributed by gravity feed through pipes. The entire works was constructed of wood, including the intake; pumps powered by oxen and horses walking on a circular treadmill; pipes made of logs with 12-foot lengths with 2.5-inch bores drilled lengthwise through them; and the reservoir. At first privately owned and operated under a franchise granted by the city, the water works was taken over by the city in 1839. Iron pipes began replacing wooden ones in 1845. Cleveland installed a municipally owned water works drawing water directly from Lake Erie from an intake crib 300 feet offshore in 1855. By 1870 eleven Ohio towns and cities possessed municipal water works, serving about 380,000 of Ohio's 2.7 million people. At this time, no Ohio cities possessed municipal sewer systems.[51]

None of the water provided to Ohio's urban residents was chemically treated or filtered to remove impurities and prevent diseases. Like residents in Columbus, other Ohioans were innocent of much knowledge of germ theory, and waterborne diseases periodically scourged them. As late as 1885 the annual death rate from typhoid fever in Cincinnati was over 140 per 100,000 people. For the state of Ohio as a whole, the yearly

---

50. *Ohio State Journal*, 4 January 1847, as quoted in Lee, *History of the City*, vol. 1, p. 304. See also Cole, *Fragile Capital*, 26.

51. F. H. Waring, "Public Water Supplies and Control of Water Pollution in Ohio," *Ohio State University Engineering Studies Engineering Series, Engineering Experiment Station Circular No. 57*, vol. 24, no. 4 (September 1955), 1–36, esp. 1–3, 8, 11–12. This report is a revision of earlier ones published in 1941, 1942, and 1955. Waring was the chief sanitary engineer for the Ohio Department of Health. See also J. Douglas Brookhart and Alvin D. Wansing, *History of Ohio's Water Systems* (Columbus: Ohio Section American Water Works Association [AWWA], 2010) 7, 18–20, 78–99, which relies heavily on Waring's report; and Roomann, *Urban Growth*, vi.

death rate from typhoid fever was about 42 per 100,000, with rural residents suffering much less than urban ones.[52]

Large eastern cities led the way in the creation of municipal water works. Philadelphia had an extensive water-pumping and -distribution system from 1801, and Boston and New York possessed such works by the mid-1840s. Smaller, less comprehensive systems were constructed in Chicago, Milwaukee, and St. Louis. Altogether, 244 American cities and towns possessed water works of some sort by 1870. Beyond Richmond, Virginia, however, no American cities filtered their water. Residents of Boston, Cincinnati, and Philadelphia considered establishing "slow-sand" filtration systems, which passed water through beds of sand and gravel to try to eliminate pollutants, but residents rejected these systems as too expensive. Even Richmond's system, established in 1832, proved to be ineffective. Paisley, Scotland, had put in place the world's first effective slow-sand filtration system in 1804, followed by the Chelsea water works of London twenty-three years later. Berlin's water went through slow-sand filtering from 1856. As a consequence of the lack of water treatment, cholera, typhoid fever, and dysentery plagued many American urban dwellers into the twentieth century.[53]

## Changing Ideas and the Movement toward Citywide Water Systems

The diffusion of the germ theory of the origins of diseases combined with the growth of Columbus as an industrial center to spur mightily a demand for clean water. The idea that many diseases are spread by

---

52. Roomann, *Urban Growth,* vi.

53. Melosi, *Precious Commodity,* 37–60. America's experiences compare to markedly different ones in Japan. There, night-soil and urine collectors gathered human feces and urine on a regular basis for use in agriculture and early-day industry. The removal of those products made Japanese cities freer of waterborne diseases than their counterparts in Western Europe and the United States. Cholera came to Japan only in 1858, with the first major epidemic of that disease ravaging parts of that nation in 1877. See David A. Howell, "Fecal Matters: Prolegomenon to a History of Shit in Japan," in *Japan at Nature's Edge: The Environmental Contest of a Global Power,* eds. Ian Jared Miller, Julia Adeney Thomas, and Brett L. Walker (Honolulu: University of Hawai'i Press, 2013), 137–51. However, residents in early-day Nara suffered from diarrhea and dysentery when wells for drinking water were placed too close to sources of fecal contamination. See Tatsunori Kawasumi, "Settlement Patterns and Environment of Heijo-kyo and Ancient Capital City Site in Japan," in *Environment and Society in the Japanese Islands: From Prehistory to the Present,* eds. Bruce L. Batten and Philip C. Brown (Corvallis: Oregon State University Press, 2015), 43–57.

bacteria invisible to the human eye originated in the work of European scientists, chief among them Louis Pasteur, seeking the causes of anthrax and typhoid fever. That concept spread to the United States. Conversion to germ theory in sciences, medicine, and public health (called *sanitation*) took place surprisingly quickly during the 1880s and 1890s. "Starting in the late 1870s," historian Nancy Tomes has observed, "the new scientific discipline of bacteriology scored a succession of dramatic discoveries by rapidly identifying the bacteria responsible for cholera, tuberculosis, gonorrhea, typhoid, and scarlet fever." By 1900 the general principle that microorganisms played a central role in causing communicable diseases was widespread among physicians in Europe and America.[54]

Shifts in thinking about the origins of diseases had consequences for actions. Since few vaccinations against diseases existed then, emphasis was placed on trying to make homes germfree. Early-day home economists sought to instruct all Americans, especially women, on how to make toilets sanitary, how to cook and preserve food safely, and how, more generally, to banish disease-carrying microbes from their homes. Fecal contamination came under special scrutiny as the agents responsible for spreading diseases such as cholera and typhoid. Because disease germs thrived in human sewage, it was assumed that food, water, or air that came in contact with such wastes could become infected.[55]

State and city governments became involved in the fight against bad microbes. In 1887 Massachusetts began the first state program of sanitary chemical analysis and microscopic examination in the United States. A year later, Providence, Rhode Island, set up the first diagnostic laboratory in the nation. The establishment of similar laboratories followed in most large cities.[56] Columbus created a permanent board of health in 1887, joining other Ohio cities that already had one: Mount Vernon (1854), Cleveland (1859), Ironton (1863), Hamilton (1865), Xenia (1866), Dayton (1867), Youngstown (1868), Portsmouth (1869), and Warren (1872).[57] That agency, in addition to employing inspectors to

54. Nancy Tomes, *The Gospel of Germs: Men, Women, and the Microbe in American Life* (Cambridge, MA: Harvard University Press, 1998), 6. For a case study that looks at developments in California's Central Valley, see Linda Nash, *Inescapable Ecologies: A History of Environment, Disease, and Knowledge* (Berkeley: University of California Press, 2006), 49–81. See also Wooley and Van Brimmer, *Second Blessing*, 289–90, 295.

55. Nancy Tomes, "Spreading the Germ Theory: Sanitary Science and Home Economics, 1880–1930," in *Women and Health in America: Historical Readings,* ed. Judith Walzer Leavitt (Madison: University of Wisconsin Press, 1999), 596–611.

56. Melosi, *Sanitary City,* 77, 79, 91.

57. Wooley and Van Brimmer, *Second Blessing,* 375.

examine milk, meat, and bakery products offered for sale in Columbus, had a full-time bacteriologist on its staff by 1908. In that year, the board's chairman asked the city council for more laboratory space to deal with "the rapid increase in the demands on the laboratory service in the Health Department especially in connection with food examinations and contagious disease work," a request soon granted.[58]

New thinking about diseases had mixed consequences for urban water supplies. More emphasis was placed on the individual than on society in explaining the origins of waterborne diseases than before. Microbes, whose existence was now mostly realized, did not come from society-generated filth. Efforts to clean up cities faltered. However, it also became a matter of civic pride to have pure water supplies. "Pure" water came to mean not just water visibly clear and free of turbidity (muddiness) as in earlier times, but also pure in a biological sense, free of disease-causing bacteria. In a widely distributed booster pamphlet, members of the Columbus Board of Trade exclaimed prematurely in 1885 that their city was "blessed with an abundant supply of good healthy water pumped from large wells of spring water." In the same publication they noted, again prematurely, that their city's expanding sewage system provided Columbus with "a practical and thorough drainage."[59]

Urbanites turned to municipal water works for purified water. By 1924 some 9,850 water works had been built in the United States. Most of those water works—70 percent of those in cities with populations of more than 30,000—were publicly owned. Most Americans thought that the new water systems were simply beyond the reach, financially and technologically, of private enterprises. Financing came from combinations of municipal bond sales, property taxes, and user fees. A rising proportion of the plants, though still only a relatively small number of them, filtered their water supplies.[60]

City dwellers also established sewer systems featuring centralized treatment plants. Between 1870 and 1920 the number of cities in the United States with sewer systems rose from about one hundred to roughly

58. "Resolution of the Board of Health with Reference to Additional Space for Use as a Laboratory," 5 May 1908, State Archives Series 5052, Box 2292; and "Health Department Positions & Salaries," 1909, State Archives Series 5052, Box 2293, both at the archives and library of the Ohio Historical Society (Ohio History Connection). The bacteriologist earned $1,500 annually, at a time when a fully employed industrial worker might take home $500 to $1,000 per year.

59. Columbus Board of Trade, "City of Columbus," 8, 61.

60. Melosi, *Sanitary City*, 82–83; Ogle, "Water Supply"; and Schneider, *Hybrid Nature*.

three thousand, serving about 87 percent of the nation's urban population during the later year. Most of the sewer systems released untreated sewage into nearby rivers and lakes. This sewage was increasingly complex in its composition. Sewage contained, in addition to feces, urine, and water, refuse from kitchens; draining from markets; and, increasingly, chemical runoff from factories. Such sewage was hard to deal with, and there was a lot of it. Only in the Progressive era did the same bacterial revolution that changed thinking about the origins of diseases lead to the large-scale purification of sewage by bacteria in treatment facilities. Only in 1940 did more than half of the sewage plants in the United States possess effective treatment capabilities. Most sewage systems, like most water works, were publicly owned and operated, and for the same reasons. Like water works, they were paid for by bonds, taxes, and user fees.[61]

Developments in Ohio mirrored national trends. The number of Ohio's municipalities having water works rose from just 11 in 1870, to 237 in 1920, and to 414 by 1940. By 1920 some 66 percent of Ohio's population benefited from municipal water works, and twenty years later 72 percent did. An increasing proportion of Ohio's water-treatment plants filtered and softened their water supplies. In 1910 some 22 plants serving 952,000 of Ohio's 4.8 million people did so. By 1940 some 167 water works serving 3.9 million of Ohio's 6.9 million residents filtered and softened water.[62] Cincinnati installed new pumps for its water system in 1872 and put in place an experimental "rapid-sand" filtration mechanism in 1907, following an outbreak of typhoid fever that infected 1,930 residents and killed 230 of them in 1906. Rapid-sand filtration was an American innovation that worked faster than the "slow-sand" system developed earlier in Great Britain. In 1908 Cincinnati began operating its River Pump Station, whose pumping machinery, later electrified, and intake piping remained in use in 2010. In 1911 the city began chlorinating its water supply. Cases of typhoid fever nearly disappeared there by 1912. Cleveland extended its water-intake cribs farther out into Lake Erie to try to avoid contamination by sewage and industrial waste carried into the lake's near-shore waters by the Cuyahoga River, especially after a typhoid outbreak similar to Cincinnati's hit the city in 1906. In their actions Clevelanders resembled Chicagoans, who pushed their city's intake cribs farther out in Lake Michigan.[63]

---

61. Melosi, *Sanitary City,* 98, 111; and Schneider, *Hybrid Nature,* xxi.

62. Waring, "Public Water Supplies," 3–5.

63. Waring, "Public Water Supplies," 3–5; Brookhart and Lansing, *Ohio's Water Systems,* 3, 91 98.

Ohio's cities also established more sewage-disposal plants, which partially treated sewage before releasing it. In 1900 only 8 Ohio cities with altogether just 67,000 inhabitants had sewage-treatment plants, but by 1920 some 66 cities with 887,000 residents altogether did. By 1940 the figures had risen to 183 cities with 3.8 million residents.[64] Cincinnati began building sewers, which dumped their untreated loads in the Ohio River, in 1831. By 1904 the city had 186 miles of sewer pipes.[65] Cleveland officials established their city's first sewage-treatment plant in 1922.[66]

Legal requirements imposed on municipalities by the Ohio state government prompted changes. In 1893 the state legislature required that municipalities and private corporations engaging in the water-supply business or building sewer systems obtain approval from the Ohio Department of Health before proceeding with their plans. Ohio's State Board of Health had been founded in 1886 after a decade of debate.[67] State of Ohio laws on water purification and sewage treatment were tightened in 1923 and 1925, following a typhoid-fever outbreak in Salem during 1920. In 1939 Ohio legislators adopted uniform standards, along with their counterparts in other states in the Ohio Valley, for the treatment of sewage and industrial waste before those materials could be released into streams and rivers. The U.S. Congress sanctioned what the states had done in 1940 as the "Ohio Valley Sanitation Compact," which went into effect eight years later. The agreement stated, in part, that all sewage "shall be treated so as to provide at least for the removal of settleable solids and 45 per cent of suspended matter (primary treatment) and that industrial wastes shall be treated to such degree as may be determined to be necessary."[68] Even so, as late as 1948 less than 2 percent of discharge from sewage facilities was treated before it entered the Ohio River.[69]

## A Quest for Clean Water in Columbus

An effort to obtain clean water for Columbus was longstanding. Some Columbus residents felt the need for an improved, citywide water system

64. Waring, "Public Water Supplies," 8, 13.
65. Roomann, *Urban Growth*, 101–15.
66. Stradling and Stradling, *Where the River Burned*, 131.
67. Wooley and Van Brimmer, *Second Blessing*, 374.
68. Waring, "Public Water Supplies," 23–24.
69. Roomann, *Urban Growth*, viii.

as early as the 1850s. In 1853 William Dennison, a member of the city council (and later Governor of Ohio between 1860 and 1862), secured a resolution from his colleagues calling upon Columbus's general improvement committee to look into having the city establish a water works. The council entertained reports from outside engineers over the following decade and in 1863 appointed a committee to examine building a water system. Members of that committee visited water works in several cities and commissioned surveys of stream flows in central Ohio. Yet another council committee reported in 1868 in favor of establishing a water works modeled after systems designed by engineer Birdsill Holly.[70] A resident of Lockport, New York, Holly was responsible for the first "pressure water systems" in America, including a number in Ohio. Holly relied on steam-powered pumps, not just gravity feed, to move water through pipes. He was, according to one account, "known to catch a train out of New York, travel to an Ohio community, and survey the raw water supply." A system of Holly pumps, pipes, and hydrants often resulted.[71]

Such was the case in Columbus. In early 1870 the city council approved a contract with the Holly Manufacturing Company for the purchase of several of Holly's patented rotary pumps, which were guaranteed to throw six 1-inch streams of water simultaneously for firefighting purposes—recent losses to fire of the Neil House and the state insane asylum were very much on the minds of council members—while at the same time supplying Columbus residents with water for business and domestic uses. Auxiliary pumps, pipes, and hydrants were part of the deal. Altogether, the Holly system was to be capable of providing Columbus with at least 4 million gallons of water per day (gpd).[72]

To provide water for the pumps, the city council authorized the digging of a well 20 feet in diameter on the east bank of the Olentangy River just north of its juncture with the Scioto River. Water entered this well through a 256-foot-long brick filtering gallery, where the water settled and lost its turbidity. That gallery was later substantially increased in length. City officials hoped that natural underground filtering, along with the location north of most development in Columbus, would result in pure water for residents of Columbus. The system was supposed to

---

70. Studer, *Columbus, Ohio: Its History*, vol. 1, pp. 136–38.

71. Brookhart and Wansing, *Ohio's Water Systems*, 22. See also Michael Speer, "Urbanization and Reform: Columbus, Ohio, 1870–1900," PhD diss., Ohio State University, 1972, 205–18.

72. For details of the contract and the Holly pumps, see Moore, *Franklin County*, vol. 1, pp. 216–17; and Studer, *Columbus, Ohio: Its History*, vol. 1, pp. 138–40.

create "spring water, well water." To try to ensure that outcome, water police patrolled river banks upstream to eliminate sources of pollution. These efforts proved insufficient, as polluted water flowed downstream from towns such as Worthington and moved laterally through Columbus's underground water table. Earth alone was not enough to filter out all germs. Holly pumps in what became known as the West Side Pumping Station pushed water directly from the well through cast-iron pipes—5 miles of pipes by 1873, 70 miles by 1875, and additional miles in later years—to households, businesses, and hydrants.[73]

Columbus officials soon enlarged this system. In 1889 a 20-foot-wide well and thirty-two tubular wells, each just 6 inches in diameter going 60 feet into the ground, were sunk on the west side of Alum Creek and began providing water to the East Side Pumping Station. This station employed a second set of filtering galleries, Holly pumps, distribution pipes, and hydrants. Major additions were also made to the West Side system in 1897 and 1898, including the sinking of tubular wells, the extension of filtering galleries, and the laying of 3,000 feet of 48-inch-diameter iron pipe. Columbus thus came to possess two systems of wells, pumps, and high-pressure pipes to convey water to homes, businesses, and firefighters. By the late 1890s the West Side wells provided Columbus with 9 million gpd, and the East Side wells distributed another 6 million.[74]

None of these improvements came cheaply. Expenditures on Columbus's water systems totaled $1.7 million between 1871 and 1873, with additional expenses in later years. Tax levies on real estate and personal property, and bond issues totaling $500,000, paid for water-system improvements.[75] Fees that were charged to water customers helped defray operating expenses. By early 1872 some 772 water permits had been issued, with permit holders served from 702 hydrants or stopcocks (spouts or faucets). In some cases, several families or businesses shared hydrants and stopcocks. Hundreds of additional customers signed up over the next decade and a half, until by 1888 Columbus residents consumed about 66 gpd apiece, a figure that, however, also included some water

---

73. John H. Gregory, "The Improved Water and Sewer Systems of Columbus, Ohio," *Transactions of the American Society of Civil Engineers* 67 (June 1910), 206–473, esp. 212–13. Interview by the author with Conrade C. Hinds, 17 January 2014. Engineer Hinds explained that there was "contamination upstream [from] outhouses and the like."

74. Gregory, "Improved Water," pp. 212–13; and Hooper, *Columbus: From the Founding*, vol. 1, p. 117.

75. Studer, *Columbus, Ohio: Its History*, vol. 1, pp. 129–30.

use by businesses.[76] In a typical week in 1889 the operating expenses of the water works included $1,900 for wages and salaries (and $13.90 for shoeing horses), offset by an income of $3,445 in water sales. Cash-on-hand stood at a hefty $143,406. The board of the water works nonetheless found it necessary to petition the city council for financial help in "extending pipe lines and other needed improvements" made necessary by "the rapid growth of our city" in late 1889.[77]

Even as they addressed concerns about water supplies, Columbus residents tackled sewage issues. The city had about 7 miles of sewers by 1870. City workers constructed several trunk-line sewers, with lateral extensions, during the 1870s and 1880s, at an expense of $521,000.[78] By 1890 sewer mileage had increased tenfold to nearly eighty. Dumping their untreated loads into Alum Creek and the Scioto River, the sewers left these bodies of water as polluted as before. This situation satisfied no one. Prodded by the Citizens' Sanitary Association, members of the Columbus city council called on the city engineer to design an intercepting sewer to collect waste from all of the sewers in Columbus and carry it away from the city. The engineer prepared a report in 1887 on routes designed to do exactly that, at an estimated construction cost of between $587,000 and $718,000.[79]

A major intercepting sewer was completed under the east banks of the Olentangy and Scioto rivers in 1892. A smaller intercepting sewer took sewage from the East Side of Columbus to that main intercepting sewer, and a still-smaller intercepting sewer diverted sewage from Franklinton west of the Scioto River to the main interceptor, crossing the river to do so. All three intercepting sewers were linked, and all sewage was pumped to an outlet 2.5 miles south of downtown Columbus, where it was discharged, still untreated, into the Scioto River. The city government spent $4 million on sewer improvements between 1888 and 1893, paid for through a combination of $500,000 in bonds, city tax levies on

76. Columbus City Engineer to Columbus City Council, 16 January 1888, in State Archives Series 5052, Box 2293; and Studer, *Columbus, Ohio: Its History,* vol.1, pp. 141–42. On costs nationally, see Smith, *City Water,* 92–106.

77. Chair of the City Water Works to the City Council of the City of Columbus, 20 October 1889; and Columbus Water Works, "Receipts & Disbursements," March 1889, and July 1893, in State Archives Series 5052, Box 2289.

78. Hooper, *Columbus: From the Founding,* vol. 1, p. 121; and Lee, *History of the City,* vol. 1, p. 662. On sewer-pipe mileage, see Columbus Department of Public Utilities, "Milestones," 1, at http://publicutilities.columbus.gov, accessed on 19 January 2014.

79. Columbus City Engineer to City Council, 16 January 1888, in State Archives Series 5052, Box 2293.

real and personal properties, and user fees. By 1900 Columbus possessed 144 miles of public sewers. The downtown area and much of the rest of Columbus were partially cleaned up, but regions to the south reeked. The overly optimistic idea behind this project was that running water would rapidly diffuse and purify sewage. It did not.[80]

Intercepting sewers like those in Columbus were a common response to sewage problems. In London, local, unconnected sewers carried waste into the Thames River in the early 1800s, grossly polluting that body of water. After a major pollution incident called the "Great Stink" in 1858, London built intercepting sewers that captured the flows of all of the sewers draining into the Thames. Completed by 1865, intercepting sewers dumped their waste into the Thames below London, cleansing the river through London, but continuing to pollute it downstream. Brooklyn had intercepting sewers in 1855, as did Chicago four years later. Cleveland had an intercepting sewer that dumped untreated sewage in Lake Erie from 1905. Such solutions did little, however, to improve water quality beyond the reach of intercepting sewers.[81] Lakes and rivers remained polluted.

Improvements to the Columbus water system, along with the continued modernization of the city's fire department, lessened fire dangers that had been so greatly feared in antebellum years. In 1885 thirty-eight men manned six hose companies throughout the city. They were in charge of twenty horses; four four-wheeled, two-horse hose carriages; two two-wheeled, one-horse hose carriages; three two-tank chemical engines; one hook-and-ladder truck; and two steam-powered pumpers. By 1890 the Columbus fire department possessed six steam-powered pumpers, seven hose companies, and two hook-and-ladder companies. Even so, fires destroyed some buildings. In 1893 the Chittenden Hotel burned to the ground in the downtown. By 1920 Columbus had expanded its fire department to seventeen engine houses sheltering motorized equipment capable of racing to fires at 50 miles per hour. Three hundred firefighters graced the fire department's rolls. Nonetheless, city hall was destroyed by fire in 1921.[82] Still, Columbus suffered from no districtwide or citywide conflagrations like those that destroyed much of Chicago in 1871 and San Francisco in 1906.

---

80. Gregory, "Improved Water," 280; Hooper, *History: From the Founding*, vol.1, p. 121; and Lee, *History of the City*, vol.1, p. 662.

81. Schneider, *Hybrid Nature*, xxi; and Stradling and Stradling, *Where the River Burned*, 131.

82. Board of Trade, "Columbus," 62; and Lentz, *As It Were*, 106.

Water and sewer problems, in fact, defied easy solutions. Even with the construction of intercepting sewers, Columbus was rapidly expanding and still had too few sewers. In 1899 the city's chief civil engineer wrote to the Columbus Director of Public Improvements that he had received "numerous complaints" about "insufficient sewage, and flooding in various parts of the territory north of Broad Street." He urged the director to present these complaints to the city council. The director did so, paving the way for massive improvements in the early 1900s.[83]

It was during the late nineteenth century as well that a sewer issue arose that would vex Columbus residents into the twenty-first century. The question was whether to mix sewage with surface runoff (storm water or rainwater) in the same pipes in combined systems or to construct separate systems for the two, using different pipes. Small-diameter pipes could carry household wastes, and large-diameter pipes could convey storm water. Like many other urbanites across the United States, those in Columbus opted for a combined system as less expensive, at least in the short run.[84] Innovative in many respects with regard to water and sewer matters, Columbus officials followed the pack on this one. The combined system had outfalls through which surface water and sewage could surge into streams and rivers during times of heavy rainfall, polluting them. Once constructed, the combined system, Columbus residents learned to their dismay, was very costly to change. Already in 1892 Columbus historian Alfred Lee observed: "Unquestionably in the author's opinion, the decision would be in favor of the separate system. But the question cannot be approached in this way. Columbus is irrevocably committed to the combined system. Several million dollars have already been spent in the construction of these great lines." Lee concluded, "For better or worse, we must adjust ourselves to the established system."[85] The difficulty in altering the combined system vividly raised the issue of what scholars call *path dependence,* the high degree to which early choices determine later ones. Columbus city engineers did not begin to separate their city's storm-water and sewer pipes until the early 2000s.

---

83. Columbus City Engineer to the Director of Public Services, December, 1899, State Archives Series 5052, Box 2300.

84. Joel A. Tarr, "The Separate vs. Combined Sewer Problem: A Case Study of Urban Technology Design Choice," *Journal of Urban History* 5 (May 1987), 308–39. Cincinnati residents were among the few urbanites to establish separate sewer systems in parts of their city, doing so in 1885. See Roomann, *Urban Growth,* 111. Cleveland residents opted for a combined system. See Stradling and Stradling, *Where the River Burned,* 131–32, 137.

85. Lee, *History of the City,* vol. 1, p. 692.

By far the most worrisome water issue facing Columbus inhabitants was the continuing ravages of waterborne diseases. Cholera killed fifteen prisoners in the state penitentiary in 1873, and another cholera epidemic hit the city in 1892. Malarial fevers proved deadly in 1881, and epizootic outbreaks incapacitated horses again in 1872 and 1875. However, it was typhoid fever that attracted the most attention, when Columbus endured another epidemic of it in 1881.[86] Typhoid fever never really left Columbus until after 1908, when dramatic changes to the city's water infrastructure were completed. John H. Gregory, the engineer most responsible for altering Columbus's water and sewer systems between 1904 and 1908, observed on the first page of a monumental 1910 report on those changes that "typhoid fever had been a constant menace" in Columbus for decades.[87]

Despite advances made in bacteriological knowledge, typhoid fever remained a big killer. As long as sewage from upstream sources, privy vaults and cesspools leaking into the underground water table, and overflowing combined sewers reached Columbus's intake wells and galleries near the Olentangy River and Alum Creek, typhoid fever ended lives. An average of 42 people died of the disease annually in Columbus between 1898 and 1903, about 33 deaths per 100,000 people. The same epidemic that hit Cleveland and Cincinnati raged hard through Columbus between 1904 and 1906. Deaths from typhoid fever spiked to an average of 119 per year, about 78 per 100,000. Between 1898 and 1906 typhoid fever accounted for roughly 3 percent of all deaths in Columbus.[88]

The typhoid fever epidemic was widely reported in Columbus newspapers during 1904, just as the city's citizens were considering bonds to pay for major changes to their city's water system. The *Columbus Evening Dispatch* observed on 4 February 1904, "The subject of the contaminated condition of the water of Columbus is the theme of town talk."[89] Over the next two weeks there was a rising infection count, with deaths passing "the 100 mark for the first time" two weeks later, with "five additional fatalities running the total up to 102, and raising the death rate to seven and four-tenths percent" of those infected.[90] Those afflicted with typhoid fever included well-known Columbus residents, for example, the physical

---

86. Ibid, 727–28; and Wooley and Van Brimmer, *Second Blessing*, 290–94, 379, 386–94.

87. Gregory, "Improved Water," 206.

88. Ibid, 211.

89. *Columbus Evening Dispatch*, 4 February 1904, p. 5.

90. Ibid, 19 February 1904, p. 10.

education director of the YMCA and "one of the reliable members of the All-Columbus Bowling Club." Typhoid reached into the Ohio House of Representatives, as both the porter and the head stenographer came down with the disease.[91]

Senator Mark Hanna was only one of the hundreds of people who fell to typhoid fever contracted in Columbus, but he was by far the most famous. Something of a "king maker," Hanna had been the power behind President William McKinley, also from Ohio. Hanna's doctors announced on 5 February 1904 that the senator, who had been sick for some time, was definitely infected with typhoid fever. On that same day Dr. McKendree Smith, the superintendent of the Columbus Department of Health, stated, "It is to be believed that to Columbus must be ascribed the responsibility for inoculating the great statesman with the disease germs." He concluded, "There is little doubt in my mind that Senator Hanna drank from typhoid bearing water during his visit to Columbus on the occasion of Gov. Herrick's induction into office" in January. "The senator," Smith said, "undoubtedly drank unboiled river water."[92] Hanna died on 15 February 1904 after weeks of illness covered daily by Columbus newspapers, and the senator's death acted as a catalyst for fixing Columbus's water system. On the day Hanna died, the *Columbus Evening Dispatch* editorialized, "It is evident that Columbus, in common with most cities, has paid too little attention proportionately to its sanitary affairs," and it noted that as a result the city was "wrestling with a typhoid fever problem." The editor pledged his full support for plans to improve Columbus's water situation, asserting, "The importance of those plans cannot be overestimated, for upon them depend the safety of the present Columbus and the development of the greater city."[93]

Meanwhile, owners of breweries sought to capitalize on the epidemic. One advertised, "Don't drink water, drink beer, its [sic] better for your health. . . . It don't [sic] need boiling."[94] So did makers of filters for water consumed at home. One advertised, "In these days of sickness and disease, when the ravages of typhoid and other ailments are causing great alarm and consternation, it is of vital importance that water used for all purposes be pure and free from disease-breeding bacilli."[95]

91. Ibid, 4 February 1904, p. 11; and 20 February 1904, pp. 1, 7.
92. Ibid, 5 February 1904, p. 1; and 6 February 1904, p. 2.
93. Ibid, 15 February 1904, p. 4.
94. Ibid, 16 February 1904, p. 13.
95. Ibid, 12 February 1904, p. 8. See also Hinds, *Experiment,* 84–86.

The resulting changes in Columbus's water and sewer systems were massive. Conrade Hinds, the retired project manager for the Columbus Division of Water who has written about this subject, has gone so far as to call the improvements the "Great Columbus Experiment," a term he adopted from engineer Gregory. Hinds was correct, and my study follows his lead in terminology.

## The Great Columbus Experiment

Three interrelated components—a new water supply, a new water-treatment system, and a new way of handling sewage—made up that successful experiment. While some aspects of what Columbus engineers accomplished had already been put in place in other cities, no other American city established all of them at the same time. Moreover, parts of Columbus's systems were brand-new or nearly so. In 1910 civil engineer Gregory explained in technical language the momentous changes he had just overseen: "In 1904 the City of Columbus, Ohio, began the construction of two important sanitary improvements which have recently been completed." Those alterations, he continued, "include works for improving the water supply and for purifying the dry-weather flow of sewage."[96] With those understated remarks, Gregory noted massive alterations made to the water and sewer systems of Ohio's capital city, changes that had repercussions well beyond Columbus.

Columbus leaders began considering new sources of water shortly after workers sank the wells, put in pumps, and extended pipes for water works in the early 1870s. Later in that decade they were starting to think about damming the Scioto River north of its junction with the Olentangy River to create a large storage reservoir. Gregory, a recent engineering graduate of the Massachusetts Institute of Technology, was invited to Columbus in 1886 to devise a plan for a dam on the Scioto River. However, Gregory later recalled, "the cost of the proposed undertaking was so large that the project was laid aside in favor of additional filtering galleries," a reference to extensions adjacent the West and East Side pumping stations.[97] The dam project was revived in 1893, when another engineer reported to the city council on the desirability of a dam and reservoir on

---

96. Gregory, "Improved Water," 206. *Dry-weather flow* meant sewage without storm water.

97. Ibid, 213.

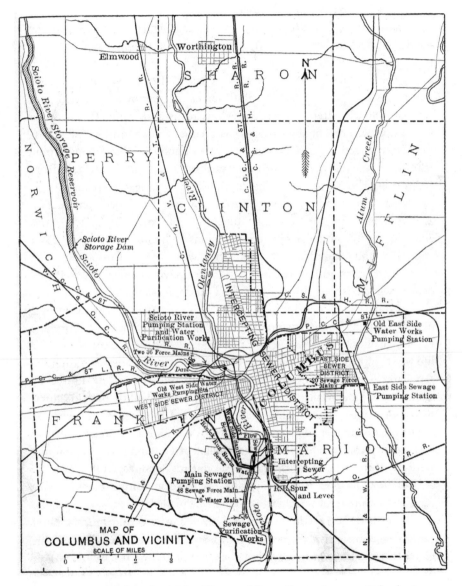

**Figure** 2.1. Map of Columbus's New Water and Sewer System in 1910. Columbus's water and sewer systems had become extensive by the Progressive period of the early 1900s. (From Gregory, "Improved Water," p. 207)

the Scioto River. Three years later Columbus's chief civil engineer estimated that a dam and conduit to convey water to Columbus could be
constructed for $135,000 to $149,000.[98]

Julian Griggs, a professional engineer who had been trained at the
Sheffield Scientific School at Yale University, took the next step to try to
make the dam and reservoir realities. He had come to Columbus in 1880
as an engineer for the Norfolk & Western Railroad, a position he left
when he was appointed as Columbus's chief engineer by Mayor George J.
Karb in 1893.[99] After reviewing previous plans and conducting his own
surveys, Griggs recommended building a concrete dam 30 feet tall across
the Scioto River, 5.5 miles northwest of Columbus's West Side Pumping
Station. His plans were in turn reviewed by a consulting engineer from
California, who urged raising the dam's height to 50 feet to create a larger
reservoir. "Legal and other difficulties," however, precluded construction
at that time,[100] for the necessary funds did not exist. The United States
endured one of the most severe depressions in its history between 1893
and 1896, and Columbus, like most cities, was strapped for money.

More studies followed. Samuel Gray, a civil engineer from Providence, Rhode Island, brought in by Griggs, recommended building a
50-foot-high dam in early 1901. Gray also urged the construction of a
new water-filtration and -softening plant next to the West Side Pumping
Station. Columbus's water was quite "hard," and its use shortened the
life of steam-generating boilers in the city's many businesses. Softening
the water would prolong the lives of boilers and was greatly desired by
Columbus's industrialists. Around this time, members of the Columbus
Board of Trade, "representative of a thousand business men, including
the heaviest taxpayers," began calling for water and sewer improvements.
Gray also recommended the abandonment of Columbus's two pumping
stations, with water from the new reservoir to be conveyed in a gravity-
fed conduit to a new treatment plant downstream. Gray's plans became
the basis for many of the changes soon to be made.[101]

Griggs breathed life into ideas for a dam and reservoir. In early January 1904 he forwarded to the Columbus Board of Public Service cost esti-
mates totaling $569,000, a much higher sum than the 1896 estimate. This

98. Columbus Chief Engineer to Director of Public Improvements, 13 April 1896,
in State Archives Series 5052, Box 2293.

99. Hinds, *Experiment,* 63.

100. Gregory, "Improved Water," 213.

101. Ibid, 214. On the role of the Board of Trade, see City Plan Commission,
"The Plan of the City of Columbus," 1908.

new estimate then went to the city council. A month later, council members, urged on strongly by Mayor Robert Jeffrey, unanimously passed ordinances enabling the construction of a dam (and its reservoir) and for a water-filtration works. In fact, members of the Ohio State Department of Health required the inclusion of building a filtration plant as a condition for their approval of water plans for Columbus. In November 1904 Columbus residents followed up on the passage of the council's enabling ordinances by voting their approval for a bond issue to pay for the dam and water plant. There was little opposition to the measure, which was seen as necessary to rid Columbus of typhoid fever.[102]

Construction of the masonry and concrete dam started in mid-1904 and was completed late in the following year. The dam impounded 1.7 billion gallons of water in a reservoir 5.8 miles in length on the Scioto River, about 5.5 miles northwest of the West Side Pumping Station. Both the dam and the reservoir were named after Julian Griggs. To save money, no conduit was used to convey water to a new treatment station 4.3 miles south of the dam. Instead, water ran freely over the dam and through the Scioto River to that plant. The Griggs Dam was only 30 feet high, not engineer Gray's recommended 50 feet, because people living downstream feared that should a 50-foot-high dam collapse, they would be inundated, and thus they protested its proposed size. Many remembered the 1889 dam failure and resulting flood in Johnstown, Pennsylvania, which had killed thousands, and they pressured Columbus officials for the lower height. However, abutments for Griggs Dam were built strongly enough to support an additional 20 feet of height, should it be added later. Moreover, the dam was constructed in such a way that it could be used to generate electricity if its height were raised. It never was. The cost of the Griggs Dam and Reservoir came to $640,000, with additional sums soon spent to buy land around the reservoir to protect its watershed from pollution. Much of that land is now parkland.[103]

---

102. Chief Engineer Julian Griggs to the Board of Public Service, 8 January 1904, State Archives Series 5052, Box 2289; and Chief Engineer to Board of Public Service, 10 February 1904, State Archives Series 5052, Box 2293. See also *Columbus Evening Dispatch*, 3 February 1904, pp. 1, 8; 4 February 1904, pp. 1, 4; 5 February 1904, pp. 2, 4; 9 February 1904, p. 5; 10 February 1904, p. 2; 16 February 1904, p. 11; 18 February 1904, p. 5; 19 February 1904, p. 4; and 5 April 1904, p. 14.

103. Gregory, "Improved Water," 214–22; Hinds, *Experiment*, 69–73, 97–102; and Columbus Director of Public Service, "Reports as to the Purchase of Land along the Scioto River above Storage Dam," 16 October 1911, in State Archives Series 5052, Box 2300.

Storage Dam, Columbus, Ohio.

Figure 2.2. Griggs Dam in 1905. From 1905, Griggs Dam has provided Columbus residents with a supply of safe water to drink, and its reservoir remains a major source of water for them in the twenty-first century. (Courtesy of the Columbus Metropolitan Library)

As a large body of relatively pure water, Griggs Reservoir was not merely a scenic addition to the Columbus area but, more importantly, a means to dilute any disease germs, rendering them less harmful than they might be in a small container such as a well. The volume of the reservoir, engineer Hinds has opined, was of prime importance. "That, to begin with, would have gotten rid of the typhoid," he observed. Water police patrolled the reservoir on a regular basis to eliminate possible points of pollution.[104]

Professional engineers supervised improvements to Columbus's water and sewer systems in the early twentieth century. Julian Griggs was one. John Gregory joined him in 1904. It was Gregory who designed the new water-purification and sewage-treatment plants for Columbus and oversaw their construction. After doing so, Gregory left Columbus in 1908, only to return for several years in 1918 to serve as consulting engineer.

104. Hinds interview. Hinds observed, in shorthand, "The solution to pollution is dilution."

He joined the faculty of Johns Hopkins University in 1920 and taught there until his death in 1937, but he found time to return to Columbus as a consultant on several additional occasions.[105] Joining him in designing Columbus's new water and sewer systems were two brothers, Clarence and Charles Hoover. Quickly becoming a nationally recognized authority in municipal water purification, Clarence had graduated from the Ohio State University in agriculture in 1903, with training in chemistry and bacteriology. He began work in Columbus at the city's sewage-testing laboratory. Charles graduated from the Ohio State University in chemistry and began working right away as the chemist in charge of the laboratory. He later became the superintendent of the new water- and sewage-treatment facilities, where he was particularly interested in softening industrial water supplies.[106] These men made a strong team.

---

105. Brookhart and Wansing, *Ohio's Water Systems*, 17.

106. Hinds, *Experiment*, 93. Science and engineers were increasingly important in water and sewer plants. Between 1905 and 1925 American municipalities and states

Informing the work of many members of that team was their educator, Ellen Swallow Richards. Born in 1842, she was the first female graduate of the Massachusetts Institute of Technology. In 1880 that university established the first program in sanitary engineering in the United States, with Richards as its director, a position she held until just a few years before her death in 1911. John Gregory studied with her, as did some of the others leading the water and sewage changes in Columbus: Allen Hazen, an engineer who played an important role in advancing water filtration and designing Columbus's new sewage-treatment plant; and Philip Burgess, whose private consulting firm designed a large water-storage dam and reservoir for Columbus in the 1920s—to mention just two of the most significant ones.[107]

With Griggs Dam under construction, Gregory and his assistants moved to consideration of how best to treat water. In early 1904 Griggs obtained funding from the Columbus city council for Gregory to build a pilot facility for water and sewage treatment, where Gregory experimented with ways to soften water and purify sewage. With help from others, Gregory went on to design and construct Columbus's new water-purification and -softening plant. The Columbus installation was the third-largest plant to use rapid-sand filtration methods in the United States at that time and the largest plant to have a water-softening facility.[108]

The treatment of water began with its removal from the Scioto River through an intake conduit to a raw-water well, 13 feet in diameter and 34 feet deep, just off the river near Dublin Road, north of downtown Columbus. Here the water settled, and turbidity was eliminated. Water flowed from that well through pipes to the new Scioto River Pumping Station built on the north bank of the river about 1 mile upstream of its juncture with the Olentangy River. Low-lift service pumps then pushed the water to the purification works, where it was softened and filtered. Once treated, the water went into filtered water reservoirs. From those reservoirs, the water passed on to a filtered-water suction well just north of the pumping station. At that station two huge Holly pumps rammed the water into cast-iron pipes 36 inches in diameter to a point about a mile away, just opposite the old West Side Pumping Station. There the water entered Columbus's existing system of distribution pipes. The plant

spent millions of dollars on sewage research alone. Chicago spent $500,000, and Milwaukee spent $800,000 in those years. See Schneider, *Hybrid Nature*, 66; and Smith, *City Water*, 231.

107. Hinds, *Experiment*, 38–42; and Hinds interview.
108. Hinds, *Experiment*, 89.

Figure 2.3. Columbus's Water Works in 1908. The Columbus Water Works purified and soft-ened water for city residents and businesses. (Courtesy of the Columbus Metropolitan Library)

was designed to treat 20 million gpd, but it could double its capacity fairly easily.[109]

Gregory and his engineers employed state-of-the-art treatment meth-ods. "[The] problem of purifying the water," Gregory averred, "was not simply one of filtration, but softening and filtration combined, and has required, therefore, not only mechanical filtration works, but softening works in addition." Lime, soda, and alum made in a plant devised by Charles Hoover, the "first of its kind ever built at a purification works," were used to purify and soften water in six large tanks. Hoover was the co-discoverer of the sterilizing value of the "excess lime" method of water treatment, which the Columbus plant used to kill disease-causing bacteria. He obtained a patent on this process, and for decades his book describing it, Hoover's Water Supply and Treatment, known colloquially as the "Lime Book," was a bible for sanitary engineers. The volume went through six editions by 1946 and was still in use in the early 2000s.

From the tanks, the water passed through large mechanical filters. Ten filters, using gravel and sand, further purified the water, removing any

109. Gregory, "Improved Water," 225. See also Hinds, Experiment, 106–7; and Hinds interview.

remaining typhoid bacteria. The fully treated water flowed into a clear-water well served by a covered reservoir with a capacity of 10 million gallons. Holly pumps pushed the water from that well into wide cast-iron pipes, which in turn took the water to Columbus's distribution system. The Holly pumps were triple-expansion steam engines, each four stories tall and each capable of handling 25 million gpd. It required thirteen rail-road flat cars to transport the parts for each pump to Columbus, where they were assembled. The massive pumps powered the conveyance of water for sixty-one years. The cost of constructing the water-treatment works totaled $1.3 million.[110]

With the construction of the water-treatment plant begun, city engineer Griggs secured funding for a new sewage-treatment works, whose design and building Gregory oversaw. As we have seen, interceptor sewers carried Columbus's sewage to an outlet on the Scioto River south of downtown Columbus. The sewage was dumped, untreated, into the river. Pollution of the river continued: it was simply moved downstream. Other problems remained. Not all sections of Columbus had adequate sewers. Sewers reached about 80 percent of Columbus residents by 1900. However, privy vaults and cesspools were still common in some parts of the city.[111]

The South Side, in particular, lacked adequate sewer connections. This industrial district was inhabited by immigrants from southern and Eastern Europe, by African Americans who had recently arrived from the South, and by white migrants from Appalachia.[112] Throughout 1904 and 1905, South Side business and civic organizations beseeched Columbus's city government to provide their area with more sewers. In early 1904 the South Side Business and Improvement Association complained to the city council about the "insufficiency of pure water" and the lack of a "proper

---

110. Gregory, "Improved Water," 235–60; Hinds, *Experiment,* 108–16; Brookhart and Wansing, *Ohio's Water Systems,* 34–35; and Hinds interview. Chlorination came a bit later. In 1908, Jersey City, New Jersey, became the first community to chlorinate its drinking water. Cincinnati followed suit in 1911. However, because of fears Americans harbored of introducing chlorine as a chemical into their water supplies, chlorination spread slowly, with filtration long being the preferred method of purification. As late as 1955, only 60 percent of Ohio's water-treatment plants chlorinated their water. Some 34 percent still used lime or lime-soda processes. See Melosi, *Sanitary City,* 94–95; and Waring, "Public Water," 7. When Columbus's water-treatment plant began operations, the West Side and East Side Pumping stations built in the early 1870s were closed and demolished, although thoughts were briefly given to remodeling the East Side Pumping Station for use as a city hospital.

111. Columbus Department of Public Utilities, "Milestones," 1.

112. On the composition of the South Side, see Blackford, *Portrait,* 123.

means of disposing of the city sewage." Its members supported the idea of building a city sewage plant. In the winter of 1905 the body again petitioned the city council, with its members arguing, "The sanitary condition of South Columbus is such that the need for sewers is very great, especially in the extreme South-Eastern section, where the discharge from private sewers and accumulated surface filth is carried into Kian Run to stand in stagnant pools during the greater part of the years, causing this stream to be a hot-bed for the propagation of disease menacing the health of the entire city." The petition called upon council members to take "quick and decisive action in this matter and provide ways and means for relieving us of this dangerous condition with the least possible delay."[113]

The lack of adequate sewers for the South Side raised the issue of what academics and activists call *environmental justice*. As historian Martin Melosi and other scholars have shown, immigrant, African American, and working-class neighborhoods have usually not received city services at the same levels as white, middle-class neighborhoods. They have suffered in comparison. In addition, it has been in such neighborhoods that many city dumps, garbage-disposal plants, sewer works, and the like have been located.[114] The outcries of members of South Side business and civic organizations also show that conflict accompanied some civic improvements; not all was the sweet harmony desired by politicians in the Progressive era.

Help was on the way with regard to sewers in Columbus. In 1898 Griggs urged the city council to improve Columbus's system of sewage pipes and to construct a treatment plant capable of handling 20 million gallons of sewage per day. The city adopted the plan and presented it for approval in late 1900 to the State Department of Health (the now-renamed Ohio Department of Health). The department, however, rejected the scheme "on the grounds that the proposed method of treatment would

---

113. "Communications from the South Side Business and Improvement Association," 4 January 1904 and 8 February 1904; and South Columbus Improvement Association to the Columbus City Council, 30 March 1905, in State Archives Series 5052, Box 2293. See also *Columbus Evening Dispatch*, 5 March 1904, p. 1. Black districts in Columbus generally had subpar toilet facilities. As late as the 1920s, flush toilets were something of a rarity. See Mary Louise Mark, *Negroes in Columbus* (Columbus: Ohio State University Press, 1928), 59–60.

114. Martin Melosi, "Equity, Eco-racism, and Environmental History," in *Out of the Woods: Essays in Environmental History*, eds. Char Miller and Hal Rothman (Pittsburgh: University of Pittsburgh Press, 1987), 194–213. On similar environmental-justice issues in Cleveland a bit later, see Stradling and Stradling, *Where the River Burned*, 59, 118–19, 122, 142.

not modify the sewage to a degree sufficient to prevent the creation of a nuisance." A new plan submitted by the city in mid-1901 won approval. That plan called for sewage treatment in septic tanks and on 80 acres of artificial sand filters, 10 acres of which would be built at first. This more detailed plan for a new sewage-treatment plant secured approval from the State Department of Health in late 1905, and construction began then.[115]

Under Gregory's supervision, engineers designed and built the sewage-treatment plant on the west bank of the Scioto River, 3.5 miles south of Columbus's downtown. All of the sewage of the city went to this plant, carried there in pipes under pressure from pumps at several way stations.[116] Intercepting sewers, powered by pumps, first conveyed sewage to the Main Pumping Station on the west bank of the Scioto River, 2.25 miles south of Columbus's center. Pumps in the Main Pumping Station in turn pushed the sewage through a cast-iron pipe 48 inches in diameter to purification works 1.25 miles farther south. Sewage catchment extended in some cases beyond Columbus's official service district, the area in which sewers ran to carry away household waste. Beginning in 1910, Buckeye Steel Castings paid the city $630,000 annually to handle 80,000 gpd of its industrial waste.[117]

The Columbus plant treated sewage in two steps. First, sewage went into a series of large, open-air septic tanks: four primary tanks, each 56 feet by 150 feet and 12 feet deep; these four tanks were linked to two secondary tanks, each 115 feet by 262 feet and 12 feet deep. Here settling took place. In these two tanks aerobic bacteria (bacteria needing oxygen to function) also began working on the sewage to decompose it. Next, the sewage went to the second, more innovative, purification step. This phase used "sprinkling filters," which were, in Gregory's understated words, "somewhat different from what might be said to be current practice." Sprinkling filters used more aerobic bacteria to purify sewage and were antecedents of "trickling" or "percolating" filters still in use in the early twenty-first century. Rotating sprinklers sprayed sewage drawn from

115. State Department of Health, "Report on Investigation under Section 1249 G. C. of the Pollution of the Scioto River by Sewage from Columbus, September 8, 1927," pp. 2–5, in State Archives Series 5061, Box 2318. For the details of the various sewage-treatment plans, see "Fourth Annual Report of the Division of Sewage Disposal of the City of Columbus, Ohio for the Year Ending December 31, 1911," pp. 3–8, kindly lent to the author by Conrade C. Hinds.

116. Gregory, "Improved Water," 282.

117. "Third Annual Report of the Division of Sewage Disposal, Department of Public Service, Columbus, Ohio, for the Year 1910," pp. 9–13, 18, kindly lent to the author by Conrade C. Hinds.

the secondary tanks onto beds of broken limestone. Bacteria growing on the limestone surfaces completed purification of the sewage as it trickled through the beds, which averaged about 5.5 feet in depth. Initially four, but soon six, sprinkling filters sprayed sewage over 10, and later 15, acres, to purify it. From the limestone beds, purified liquid sewage ran off to settling basins before being released as effluent into the Scioto River.[118]

Sludge, the remaining solid sewage, now purified, was also initially disposed of in the river, usually flushed into the stream when it was at flood stage. However, this method of disposal overwhelmed the river, especially whenever flushing occurred in the summer, when its flow was low. In 1913 the State Department of Health forbade this method. Throughout the twentieth century, the proper disposal of sludge was a contentious issue. Following orders from the State Department of Health, Columbus dried its sludge preparatory to its being incinerated, buried, or sold as fertilizer.[119]

The Columbus sewage-treatment plant had the capacity to handle 20 million gpd of sewage per day, the amount Griggs had suggested in 1898 and a volume that could be boosted fairly easily to 30 million gpd. The cost of building the sewage-treatment plant came to about $1.2 million, paid for by public approval of a bond issue in late 1903.[120]

What made the Columbus experiment most innovative in sewage treatment was the use of sprinkling filters. Sprinkling filters had previously been employed with success in Great Britain, but the Columbus plant was the first one to show that they could work well in very cold climes. Bacterial action slowed a bit in cold months, but heat from decomposing sewage kept the bacteria working. Heat rising from the limestone beds also kept the sprinklers ice-free. The Columbus sprinkling system became a model for sewage plants in the United States, as Gregory noted in 1910: "While, as previously mentioned, somewhat different details [of sprinkling] have been adopted in some of the more recent works, an examination of designs seems to indicate that the details adopted and the experience obtained at Columbus have served as a basis from which to work."

118. Ibid, 293; Schneider, *Hybrid Nature*, xxvi–xxvii, 14. Reading, Pennsylvania, set up a smaller sewage-sprinkling plant at about the same time. See Roomann, *Urban Growth*, 113.

119. Department of Health, "Report, 1927," p. 5. The incineration of sludge was the most common disposal method in Columbus during the early decades of operation of the sewage plant. See Waring, "Water Supplies," 33.

120. Gregory, "Improved Water," 311.

The Columbus plant was, Gregory observed with pride, "the largest of their type now under operation in the United States."[121]

Engineers at the Columbus sewage-treatment plant thus came down decisively on the side of purifying liquid sewage with bacteria. They did not seriously consider farming their city's sewage by piping it to nearby land, where it would (hopefully) be purified by trickling it through soil to fertilize crops. Nothing like what was done in this respect in Japan or China was tried in Ohio. Farming sewage, which was also common in Europe and parts of the United States into the early 1900s, had problems. It required lots of land, 1 acre for every 500 to 1,000 people. Berlin farmed its sewage over 23,000 acres in 1896. Then, too, not all soils were conducive to farming. Much of the soil around Columbus is clayey, a factor that would have prevented adequate seepage of sewage into the ground and thus would have retarded its purification by bacteria in the soil. A few Columbus residents, including local historian Alfred Lee, favored sewage farming as a "natural" way to purify sewage. In 1892 Lee wrote of sewage farming, "By this means a natural agency of decomposition is brought into play. . . . The work is done by one of the great swarms of microscopic life with which we are just becoming acquainted and which, in this case, we know as one form of bacterium." Even though some British and American engineers, and some Columbus residents like Lee, opposed the use of bacteria in treating sewage in liquid form by sprinkling as "unnatural," Columbus engineers opted for that advanced method from the start. Only in 1908 did a royal British commission conclude decisively that both sewage farming and the use of bacteria in tanks and sprinkling mechanisms were "natural" and effective purification methods.[122] Columbus engineers opted for sprinkling before the definitive British endorsement of that method of purification.

Completing efforts to clean up Columbus, and going beyond water matters, was the construction of a new garbage-disposal plant. Under contract with the city, a private businessman built and operated the plant. The plant used incinerators to burn the city's garbage and was called "a reduction works" by the head of the Columbus Department of Public Service. City workers delivered garbage, separated into different categories, to the plant, located just west of the city's South Side on land next to the new sewage-treatment plant.[123] Columbus workers, like those in

---

121. Ibid, 293.

122. Schneider, *Hybrid Nature*, 1–24; and Lee, *History of the City,* vol. 1, p. 693.

123. "Communication from the Board of Public Services as to Contract for Disposal of Garbage," 19 February 1906; and "Communication from the Board of Public Service

Cleveland and some other Ohio cities, used closed steel tank wagons to deliver waste materials to the plant. The wagon tanks dumped their contents without the tanks having to be removed from the wagon bodies.[124]

When it was being planned, the proposed placement of the plant drew howls of protest from the South Side Business Men's Association. In Columbus, prevailing winds blew from the west to the east and threatened to waft odors from the plant over the South Side. This was an issue with the sewer plant as well. The Business Men's Association protested that smells carried by those winds would "injure the south half of the city" and prevent its southward growth. The organization urged that the reduction plant be sited somewhere else, far from their district.[125] Nonetheless, the plant went ahead as planned at a cost of $500,000, raising again the issue of environmental justice. (The plant did not generate electricity. One built after World War II did, but technical problems forced its closing within a few years.)

By the close of 1908, all aspects of Columbus's new water and sewer systems were in operation. The cost came to well over $3 million, including the expense of Griggs Dam, an amount that would be about $83 million in 2010 terms. In 2012 engineer Hinds conservatively estimated that it would require $265 million to replicate the systems following safety and environmental regulations then in force. At even the latter price, the cost of the systems was a bargain, as they removed major health threats from Columbus residents and allowed their city to grow industrially.[126] Not being a first mover in constructing a citywide water and sewer system in the nineteenth century helped Columbus residents build a cutting-edge system in the twentieth century. They had less to lose in abandoning their water-pumping stations on the Olentangy River and Alum Creek than did residents of larger cities in giving up their early water installations. Moreover, Columbus residents benefited from engineering and scientific advances made in treating water and sewage in the late 1800s and early 1900s.

---

in Regard to the Question of the Disposal of Garbage," 16 July 1906, both in State Archives Series 5052, Box 2300. See also Gregory, "Improved Water," 304. More generally, see Martin Melosi, *Garbage in the Cities: Refuse, Reform, and the Environment* (Pittsburgh: University of Pittsburgh Press, 2005).

124. State of Ohio, Board of Health, "Report of a Study of the Collection and Disposal of City Wastes in Ohio, 1910," as reprinted in *Documentary Heritage*, eds. Shriver and Wunderlin, 317.

125. South Side Business Men's Association to the City Council, 26 August 1907, in State Archives Series 5052, Box 2293.

126. Hinds, *Experiment*, 126.

Columbus's water system succeeded in its main goals of providing safe drinking water to the city's inhabitants and soft water to its businesses. Waterborne diseases, which had afflicted those living in Columbus for a century, nearly vanished. Deaths from typhoid fever plummeted from 170 in 1908 to 5 in 1909 and disappeared completely by 1940.[127] Water purification, as carried out in Columbus and other American cities in the Progressive era, was part of what demographers have labeled "the great mortality transition." Called "one of the most remarkable developments in modern history," this transition involved alterations in which diseases killed people. New understandings of microbes "defanged" the older killers of cholera, typhoid, pneumonia, and tuberculosis. People lived longer, falling more commonly to maladies such as cancer and heart disease.[128] Not all escaped cholera and typhoid fever, however. Wilbur Wright—one of the Wright Brothers, pioneers in aviation—died of typhus in Dayton in 1912 after an extended illness. Orville Wright had suffered from typhoid fever in the summer of 1896 but survived, as did one of the brothers' nephews about a decade later.[129]

Not surprisingly, William Taylor unabashedly praised Columbus's water and sewer systems in his history of the city published in 1909: "Columbus, with her immense concrete storage dam . . . establishing a great reservoir or lake over seven miles in length—assured of a water supply, in quantity, meeting any and all contingencies to come, while her 'purification and softening plant' in association therewith, at a cost of one million two hundred thousand dollars, guarantees that the water, so supplied, in its purity, be healthful to drink; and, in its softness 'a thing of joy forever' to both the laundry and the tubes of boilers."[130] As was common in American cities, the possession of modern water and sewer plants aided urban boosters in Columbus. City officials even issued postcards showing off their water and sewer installations, as did their counterparts in Cleveland and Cincinnati.[131]

The water and sewer systems established in the Progressive era remained the basis of those in use in Columbus a century later. That situation was not unusual. The treatment of water to purify it and the use

---

127. Gregory, "Improved Water," 211.

128. Tomes, *Gospel of Germs*, xiii–xiv. For a still-broader look at health and demographic changes, passing through four stages from the Neolithic Age to the present, see Brooke, *Climate Change*, 514–15.

129. David McCullough, *The Wright Brothers* (New York: Simon & Schuster, 2015), 27–28, 176, 256; and Roach, *The Wright Company*, 98.

130. Taylor, *Centennial History*, vol. 1, p. 308.

131. On water works and urban boosterism nationally, see Smith, *City Water*, 204–19.

of bacteria to cleanse sewage remained the norm in the United States and abroad in the opening years of the twentieth-first century. There were important refinements in treatment methods, but the fundamental processes remained surprisingly enduring, dependent on knowledge of the working of bacteria. Biological understandings and processes were still at the center of water matters in the early 2000s. Historian Daniel Schneider has observed of sewage treatment, "A trickling filter built in 1990 would have been entirely recognizable to sanitary scientists of the 1890s."[132] The same could be said of many other water- and sewage-treatment methods.

## Water Improvements during the Progressive Era: The Importance of Public Policy

The construction of new water and sewer systems in Columbus was very much in line with the thoughts and actions of Americans during the Progressive era. In this optimistic period before World War I, many Americans thought that they could control their environments through governmental actions. "There was something especially fresh, ebullient, expectant about life in America during the Progressive era," historian Richard Abrams has written.[133] A harmonious, productive society, Americans believed, could result from governmental actions. All would be well. Historian Michael McGerr, who has written extensively about progressivism, has observed that "expectations were indeed remarkable." "The progressives," he has noted, developed a "stunningly broad agenda" of reforms designed to remake the United States, including the regulation of big business, the amelioration of poverty, the purification of politics, and the transformation of gender relations.[134]

At the city level, progressivism often embraced the improvement of urban infrastructures. In Columbus, the city government placed streetlights on arches across major thoroughfares, leading Columbus to become known for a time as the "Arch City." City officials also modernized streets and their town's electrical system.[135] Some thought bigger. In 1908,

132. Schneider, *Hybrid Nature*, 166.

133. Richard Abrams, *Burdens of Progress, 1900–1929* (Glenville, IL: Scott, Foresman and Company, 1978), 1.

134. Michael McGerr, *A Fierce Discontent: The Rise and the Fall of the Progressive Movement in America* (New York: Oxford University Press, 2003), xiv.

135. For a valuable look at urban infrastructural changes, see Mark H. Rose, *Cities of Heat and Light: Domesticating Gas and Electricity in Urban America* (University Park: Pennsylvania State University Press, 1995).

just as their new water and sewer systems were starting to function, Columbus residents considered adopting a city plan. That plan, among other matters, envisioned majestic new public buildings grouped around a mall fronting a cleaned-up Scioto River in the downtown. The plan called for straightening the Scioto River there, "so obtaining extra length and dignity." Moreover, the scheme proposed building parks and boulevards along rivers and streams throughout Columbus. Low-head dams would impound rivers and streams to create placid, relaxing, romantic vistas. One park, the plan suggested, might be created around the water-filtration plant, which many Columbus residents, planners noted, were already using as picnic area. These concepts represented new ideas about how to use the river.[136]

No longer to be open sewers or transportation arteries, rivers would become, reformers hoped, things of beauty capable of uplifting Columbus residents in their thoughts. Columbus newspapers called on the state legislature to remove a dam across the Scioto River in their city's downtown which had once been used to provide water for the feeder canal. By 1904 the dam was seen as "a menace to the health of the city" because it "holds and retains all of the stagnant water above."[137] State officials decided against removing the dam. Then, too, Columbus citizens, tired of bond issues for urban improvements, failed to fund most of the changes recommended by the city plan. Only after 1970 did many of the parks, including one along the Scioto River in Columbus's downtown, come into existence. However, in the Progressive era Columbus citizens did approve millions of dollars in bonds for sewer and water improvements seen as essential to improve public health, a major achievement of which they were justifiably proud.

Columbus's political leadership paved the way in securing public approval for the water and sewer plants. The city's mayors and city council members almost unanimously pushed for water improvements. Mayor Jeffrey helped get enabling ordinances passed through the city council in 1904, aiding particularly in working out compromises on costs for projects when deadlocks loomed.[138] Between 1912 and 1919 Mayor Karb continued to make changes. Karb had been mayor for awhile in the 1890s, during which time he appointed Julian Griggs as his city's chief engineer. Karb went on to win election as the Sheriff of Franklin County

136. City Plan Commission, "Plan of the City of Columbus," 1908, pp. 35, 52.
137. *Columbus Evening Dispatch,* 6 April 1904, p. 2; and 7 March 1904, p. 4.
138. *Columbus Citizen-Journal,* "Columbus Mayors" (Columbus: Columbus Citizen Journal Publishing, 1975), n. pag.

and as a member of the Columbus city council. Columbus respected their mayors when they and city council members called for the passage of bond issues. Columbus residents showed even more respect for their city's engineers and came to believe in their plans. Expert knowledge meant a lot in the Progressive era, and Columbus had its share, and more, of nationally known engineers in Griggs, Gregory, the Hoover brothers, and others.[139]

However, there were limits to progressivism. Conflict as well as harmony characterized relations among different groups in Columbus during the early 1900s. Conflict was most apparent in the protests of people living in the South Side about sewer and water matters, especially the stench that wafted over their area, a "south side smell," as it became known, which did, indeed, retard growth of that area. Columbus expanded to the north, with water issues greatly influencing that direction of expansion. Environmental-justice concerns about water matters continued into the twenty-first century, reinforcing the northerly growth of Columbus. Such issues were present in land-use as well as in water concerns. As we shall see in later chapters, urban-planning ideas, such as those embodied in the 1908 scheme, won at best partial approval when it came to land-use matters. In fact, violent disagreements separating groups of people in Columbus killed the comprehensive adoption of the 1908 scheme. It would be decades before Columbus residents established new environmental and recreational uses for the Scioto River. Instead, Columbus residents focused on improvements to their water and sewer plants, and to water issues generally, the subjects of the next chapter.

---

139. Columbus engineers were active in the American Water Works Association (AWWA), founded in 1881; the Central States Water Works Association, begun in 189; and the Ohio Chapter of the AWWA, started from 1938 to 1939. See Brookhart and Wansing, *Ohio's Water Systems*, 7, 10–11, 41–48, 269–70. Sewage engineers and sewage-plant operators had their own organizations: a midwestern regional association formed in 1927, and a national organization started a year later—the Federation of Sewage Works Associations (later called the Water Pollution Control Federation, and still later titled the Water Environment Federation). See Schneider, *Hybrid Nature*, 102.

CHAPTER 3

# Water and the Development of Columbus

In a short story published in 1933, humorist James Thurber captured the panic that gripped Columbus residents during a flood of the Scioto River in March 1913. A Columbus resident then, Thurber wrote of fear-stricken behaviors when a rumor spread downtown that Griggs Dam had collapsed. "Suddenly somebody began to run," he explained. "Somebody else began to run, he continued, "perhaps a newsboy in high spirits." Panic was contagious. "Another man, a portly man of affairs, broke into a trot. Inside of ten minutes, everybody on High Street, from the Union Depot to the Courthouse, was running." Concluding, Thurber exclaimed, "Black streams of people flowed eastward down all the streets leading in that direction; these streams, whose headwaters were in the dry goods stores, office buildings, harness shops, movie theaters, were fed by trickles of housewives, children, cripples, servants, dogs, and cats, slipping out of the houses past which the main streams flowed, shouting and screaming. People ran out leaving fires burning and food cooking and doors wide open."[1]

As Thurber's story suggests, water developments continued to shape life in Columbus in important ways after the completion of the Great Columbus Experiment of 1904–8. Alterations to the city's water and

---

1. James Thurber, "The Day the Dam Broke," in James Thurber, *My Life and Hard Times* (New York: HarperCollins, 1999), 21–31, esp. 23.

sewer plants, and the building of new ones south of Columbus, solidified patterns of urban growth established earlier. At the same time, a quest for water as Columbus expanded began running into environmental constraints. Columbus residents, like urbanites across the United States, began espousing new recreational and environmental uses for water and wetlands. This chapter looks at the variety of water matters after 1908 and closes with an assessment of the impacts that water developments had on the history of Columbus over two centuries. Tensions between economic development and environmental change ran through the city's two hundred years of water usage, as did the changing emphases on the roles of private and public contributions to water developments. After 1870, however, Columbus residents saw water developments as mainly the responsibility of their city and state governments.

## The Great Flood of 1913

Even as Columbus residents sought to regulate nature through water and sewer improvements, floods again showed that rivers and streams were not easily mastered. In 1883 the Scioto River flooded after heavy rainfall, with its waters nearly inundating the engines in the West Side Pumping Station. Another flood four years later did minor damage. In 1898 flood-waters "came over the lower levees" and "filled cellars and crept into the first floors" of houses on the West Side. That flood "stopped the [street] cars and factories and paralyzed business for several days." These inundations, and the other twelve times the Scioto River had burst through its banks since 1797, were, however, but preludes to the worst flood in the history of Columbus.[2]

Beginning on 23 March 1913, over 9 inches of rain fell on central Ohio in just three days, including 3 inches during the final twelve hours. On 25 March water began to top river levees, and by noon of that day the West Side of Columbus was "an inland lake." Levee breaks soon sent "torrents" through the "stricken district, tossing lighter buildings to immediate destruction, rending and tearing where it did not demolish." Franklinton found itself under 26 feet of water. On higher ground, the East Side was less affected but was damaged by levee breaks on the "North Side where the Olentangy, out of its banks, threatened for a

---

2. Lee, *History of the City*, vol. 1, pp. 306–9; Moore, *Franklin County*, vol. 1, p. 243 (the source of the quotation); and Lentz, *Columbus: The Story*, 101.

**Figure 3.1.** Flood Damage in Columbus in 1913. Damage from the flood of 1913 was extensive in Columbus, reminding residents that the city's rivers had not been tamed. (Courtesy of the Columbus Metropolitan Library)

time."[3] The flooded area in Columbus totaled 4.2 square miles, and 4,071 private dwellings were destroyed. Direct damage to property in the city came to $5.3 million, with about $9 million in additional indirect damage. In Columbus 93 people lost their lives, and in the immediate flood district from Delaware to Chillicothe, the death toll was 145.[4] Statewide, at least 428 people died, and 20,000 homes were destroyed.[5]

Only partially capable of dealing with the flood, city officials appointed S. P. Bush of Buckeye Steel to head relief activities in its aftermath, in a move similar to that which occurred in Dayton.[6] In that city, where flood damage was even more extensive than that in Columbus, John H. Patterson, the head of National Cash Register Company, took charge. The real

---

3. Moore, *Franklin County*, vol. 1, pp. 243–44.

4. Ibid; George E. Condon, *Yesterday's Columbus: A Pictorial History of Ohio's Capital* (Miami, FL: E. A. Seemann Publishing Company, 1977), 52, 82, 101; and Lentz, *Columbus: The Story*, 101. For more detail, see Conrade C. Hinds, *Columbus and the Great Flood of 1913: The Disaster That Reshaped the Ohio Valley* (Charleston, SC: History Press, 2013).

5. Kern and Wilson, *Ohio: A History*, 348.

6. "S. P. Bush Obituary," *Columbus Dispatch*, 9 February 1948; and *Columbus Citizen*, 9 February 1948.

hero in Columbus was, however, Robert F. Wolfe, one of the founders of the Wolfe Brothers Shoe Company located in Columbus's downtown.[7] Looking out the window of the shoe factory, Robert saw the rising waters and realized that the inundation of Franklinton was imminent. He knew that there were scores of boats at Buckeye Lake to the east of Columbus, along with men who knew how to operate them. Wolfe chartered a train, traveled to the lake, loaded the boats and men, and returned with them to Columbus. A newspaper account reported, "Directed by 'Bob' Wolfe, the boatmen went into the flooded district and began rescuing women and children. By the scores they were taken in boats to places of safety." Wolfe worked at the rescues for several days, "harder and facing more danger than any man in the city." He paid the boatmen and bought food for those dislocated by the flood with his personal funds, later declining state government reimbursement for those expenses. For his efforts during the flood, Governor James A. Cox awarded Wolfe the title of "Commodore of the Ohio Naval Reserves."[8]

Not all Columbus residents were as calm as Robert Wolfe. It was their panic about which Thurber later wrote. As Thurber observed, a rumor developed that Griggs Dam had broken and that the waters of its reservoir were rushing down on Columbus. The *Ohio State Journal* reported the responses of people in Columbus: "Crowds flocked to the State House. Before some officials were aware of the report, they had overrun the place. Many sought to climb the dome." Continuing, the newspaper observed, "In a twinkling the streets became a tangled jam of men and women, who had abandoned desk and counter to seek places of safety. . . . Twelve story buildings in High Street were quickly emptied. . . . In the North Side of the city, crazed residents fled pell-mell in all directions. Many left their houses wide open. Scores of women swooned. . . . Hundreds of volunteer rescue workers fled from the West Side." However, as the newspaper concluded, "It was all a false alarm."[9] In fact, the solidly built dam was never in danger of collapsing.

7. See Webster P. Huntington, *The Men behind the Guns in the Making of a Greater Columbus*, (Columbus: Press of John Pfeifer, 1906), 167–68. Robert and his brother Harry Wolfe acquired the *Ohio State Journal* in 1903 and the *Columbus Dispatch* in 1905. Robert was the publisher of both newspapers until he died in 1927. See Winter, *Columbus*, 193. For more detail on the Wolfe family and its importance to Columbus, see Ray Paprocki, "Inside the Wolfe Empire," *Columbus Monthly,* April 2010, at www.columbusmonthly.com/content/stories/2010/04/inside-the-wolfe-empire.html, accessed 9 April 2016.

8. As quoted in Moore, *Franklin County,* vol. 1, pp. 245–46. Officials at Lazarus Department Store also donated a fleet of canoes from their store's sporting goods department to rescue flood victims. See Meyers, Meyers, and Walker, *Look to Lazarus,* 51.

9. As quoted in Moore, *Franklin County,* vol. 1, pp. 247–49.

State government officials established a commission to study how best
to abate floods in Franklin County. Meanwhile, the Columbus Department of Engineering, impatient with delays, came up with its own solution: widening and improving the channel of the Scioto River from its
junction with the Olentangy River south to the sewage pumping station,
a distance of about 4.5 miles. Levees were improved and strengthened.
Alterations did not go nearly as far as those made to the watershed of
the Great Miami River in the Dayton area, however. A unified water-
management plan replete with dams, storage basins, and planned flood
outlets was quickly adopted.[10]

## Columbus's Water and Sewer Systems
## between the Wars

Improvements to Columbus's water system followed the 1913 flood. The
pumping station and water-purification plant were enlarged and modernized to try to keep up with the city's growth. By 1923 the water plant
could process 54 million gallons of water per day (gpd) or a bit more
in a pinch. Seven years later it could purify 77 million gpd. At this time
residents in Columbus used 78 gpd apiece, about the national average.[11]
The total spent on improvements to the water-treatment plant came to a
hefty $3.6 million between 1920 and 1926.[12] To increase the supply of
water, the city engineers built a new concrete dam—the O'Shaughnessy
Dam, on the Scioto River about 10 miles north of Griggs Dam. The dam
was named after Jerry O'Shaughnessy, who had headed Columbus's water
department at various times in the 1890s and early 1900s. A native of
Delaware, Ohio, O'Shaughnessy had begun working at the Columbus
Water Works as a young man in 1870 digging foundation footers for the
West Side Pumping Station. Intended to both prevent floods and supply

---

10. Ibid, vol. 1, pp. 243, 250. On the 1913 flood statewide, see Judith Sealander,
*Grand Plans: Business Progressivism and Social Change in Ohio's Miami Valley, 1890–
1929* (Lexington: University Press of Kentucky, 1988), 43–84. Arthur Morgan, who
designed the plan for the Great Miami watershed, became the first director of the Tennessee Valley Authority in the 1930s. On improvements to the Scioto River, see Department
of Health, "Report, 1927," 2.

11. Jennings-Lawrence Co., "Water for Columbus," 21 March 1945, report prepared
for the Columbus Chamber of Commerce at the request of the mayor and city council of
Columbus, unpaged; and Waring, "Water Supplies," 24.

12. Department of Health, "Report, 1927," 3; and Hinds, *Experiment*, 43.

Showing O'Shaughnessy Dam on Scioto River, Columbus, Ohio — D-14

**Figure 3.2.** O'Shaughnessy Dam in 1926. Columbus's city officials were proud of O'Shaughnessy Dam, as can be seen in this postcard they issued. (Courtesy of the Columbus Metropolitan Library)

Columbus with water, the new dam impounded 5 billion gallons of water. The cost of its construction was $2.2 million.[13]

The dam and reservoir won praise. The *Ohio State Journal* boasted in 1927, "This mighty reservoir insures an adequate water supply for a city of 500,000 people, a reserve sufficient to carry the city through a 90-day drought, and ample protection against floods." That water supply was "ideal for industrial purposes, and the banks of the huge reservoir form a beautiful park." Beauty and utility could go hand-in-hand. The Columbus city government even issued a postcard of the dam, just as it had of the water and sewer plants. In 1930 a faculty member in geography at the Ohio State University, writing in a promotional brochure published by the Columbus Chamber of Commerce, claimed, "The O'Shaughnessy reservoir will meet the requirements for many years to come" and concluded that "it is obvious that the present supply of water is adequate for the needs of the city even if the population is doubled."

---

13. Moore, *Franklin County*, vol. 1, p. 295. In 1987 a hydroelectric plant was added to the dam to provide power for Columbus's municipal buildings and streetlights. Winter, *A Concise History*, 51.

The *Columbus Evening Dispatch* proudly featured the dam on its front page on 11 August 1934, boasting that water impounded by the dam was sufficient for the needs of city residents even in dry times.[14] Such optimists would soon be proven wrong, as the rapid growth of Columbus, even during the Depression decade, led to renewed searches for water for city residents and businesses.

Some of the same type of very optimistic thinking underlay the rationale behind the building of big "high" dams in the American West during the 1930s and 1940s, such as Hoover Dam (later Boulder Dam) on the Colorado River and the Grand Coulee Dam on the Columbia River. The desire to control floods, provide water for irrigation, and generate electricity, thereby building up regional economies and creating jobs, lay behind the construction of the high dams. The basic assumption was that nature could and should be put to use for the benefit of people. The dams were also seen as things of beauty. Woody Guthrie went so far as to celebrate the building of the Grand Coulee Dam in a number of his songs. Nonetheless, not all benefited from the high dams. Native Americans found their fishing sites inundated, especially along the banks of the Columbia River, and salmon could no longer swim upstream to spawn. At the time, few people thought much about how dams disrupted webs of nature—out West or in Ohio. Development almost always trumped environmental preservation before World War II.[15]

Changes also came to sewage treatment in Columbus. A major refinement was the use of the activated-sludge process in purifying sewage. Developed in Great Britain around 1914, this method forced oxygen through ponds of liquid sewage to speed up bacterial action. The process quickly spread to the United States. By 1940 sewage from over half of the nation's population that received secondary sewage treatment obtained that treatment through the activated-sludge process.[16] Columbus was one of the cities adopting it.

As pathbreaking as Columbus's sewer-treatment system had been in the Progressive era, significant problems developed as the city grew in

14. *Columbus Evening Dispatch,* 11 August 1934, p. 1; Guy-Howard Smith, "The Human Resources of Columbus and Environs," in *Columbus,* ed. Peattie, 31; and *Ohio State Journal,* 22 September 1927, p. 1.

15. Guthrie composed over twenty songs about the Grand Coulee Dam and the Columbia River. On Woody Guthrie and high dams on the Columbia River, see Richard White, *The Organic Machine: The Remaking of the Columbia River* (New York: Hill and Wang, 1995), 62–63.

16. Schneider, *Hybrid Nature,* 30–34.

the 1920s and 1930s. Columbus's continuing economic and population development exacerbated environmental problems. In times of heavy rain, enormous quantities of raw sewage, including large amounts of industrial waste, poured from sewer overflows into Alum Creek, the Olentangy River, and the Scioto River. Any hope of using the rivers as pleasure grounds, as proposed by the 1908 city plan, was decades away. The intercepting sewers were just not up to the task of removing all of the storm water and sewage from the expanding city. Then, too, the sewer plant could not handle the growing amount of sewage coming from Columbus, and the plant sometimes released untreated sewage into the Scioto River.

As early as 1910 the director of the city's new sewer plant decried "the inability of the septic tanks to properly perform their functions over an extended period of dry weather," a complaint repeated many times in later years.[17] In 1915 city officials converted the plant's open septic tanks to closed, two-story Imhoff septic tanks. Designed by German sanitary engineer Karl Imhoff, these tanks separated the settling of sewage from its purification by anaerobic bacteria (bacteria that did not need oxygen to function). Because of efficiencies in their operations and their lower operating costs, many sewage plants switched to Imhoff tanks, whose construction in Columbus was completed in 1917. Columbus engineers also built larger intercepting sewers. Voters approved a 1-mil property levy in late 1925 to raise $3 million to pay for continuing sewage improvements.[18]

These steps helped some, but releases of raw sewage continued. Residents in cities downstream from Columbus complained to the State Department of Health about the pollution of the Scioto River. An investigation by the department in 1927 found Columbus's intercepting sewers to be "totally inadequate." The city maintained twenty-one overflow points into the Olentangy and Scioto rivers and three into Alum Creek, all of which were often in use, even in times of dry weather. The department's investigation also found that at the sewer plant, "untreated sewage escapes into the river through a relief overflow." That situation occurred especially during winter and spring months. During that time of high water in the river, city officials frequently shut down the sewer plant to save money, hoping that the dilution of raw sewage in the flowing river water would purify it. Dilution did not work well, much to the distress

---

17. "Third Annual Report of the Division of Sewage Disposal," 16.

18. Department of Health, "Report, 1927," 1–12; and "Milestones," 3. See also Schneider, *Hybrid Nature*, 73.

and disgust of Ohioans living downstream. State Department of Health investigators reported that there were "floating sludge masses in the stream and sludge deposits along the banks" of the Scioto River. The river was "discolored and odors can be detected." Investigators concluded that the Scioto River south of Columbus had "every appearance of a septic tank." In 1927 State Department of Health officials mandated that Columbus officials remedy the situation.[19]

Columbus officials responded by building a new sewage plant designed by John Gregory and several other sanitary engineers using the activated-sludge process. City officials considered several sites and plans. They thought of building the installation at a new location on the Scioto River several miles south of the Progressive era sewer plant. Members of South Side business and civic organizations had been petitioning city officials to do so, for South Side residents disliked the sewer odors spreading over their section of Columbus. The South Side Protective Association petitioned the city council in early 1933 to "implore our City Fathers to duly consider the interests and welfare of the South Side." A few months later, the South Side Civic and Industrial Association called upon the city council "to protect the citizens and property owners of south-side Columbus against obnoxious odors."[20] Other business and civic organizations in Columbus backed the requests of the South Side groups at numerous, very acrimonious public hearings held by the city council. The list was long: the North Side Civic Association, the West Side Board of Trade, the Beechwold Community Center, the Linden Community Center, the Allied Council of Central Civic Associations, the Northside Improvement Association, the Parsons Avenue Business Men's Association, the Southwest Advancement League, and many others. All agreed that it was desirable to build the new plant as far south as possible.[21]

---

19. Department of Health, "Report, 1927," 10–16. A separate report issued at the same time decried the pollution of Alum Creek and mandated that stream's cleanup. See State of Ohio Department of Health, "Report on Investigation under Section 1249 G. C. of the Pollution of Alum Creek by Sewage from the City of Columbus and the Village of Bexley, September 8, 1927," in State Archive Series 5061, Box 2318. A municipality of 5,500 residents, Bexley had a sewage-treatment plant using Imhoff septic tanks constructed from 1913 to 1914. Bexley secured its drinking water from Columbus's water system.

20. South Side Protective Association to Columbus City Council, 27 February 1933; and South Side Civic and Industrial Association to Columbus City Council, 4 June 1933, both in State Archives Series 5061, Box 2318.

21. "Minutes of Public Hearing on Proposed New Sewage Disposal Plant Site," 28 February 1930, in State Archives Series 5061, Box 2318.

Columbus's mayor and city council members, after first agreeing to construct the new plant far south of the South Side, reversed themselves and built the new plant on land right next to the older sewer plant, once again going against the requests of South Side residents. Conflict characterized site selection. Columbus already owned the land there, making construction at that site easier and less expensive than at a more southerly location. It was estimated that a new plant built adjacent to the old one would cost about $4 million, while a new plant at a more southerly site would cost over $6 million. As the Great Depression worsened, cost considerations became decisive factors in site selection.[22] Construction of the plant began in 1934, and the facility, known as the Jackson Pike Plant, came online three years later with the capacity to handle 50 million gpd of sewage. It was financed by a combination of city bond issues and New Deal funds from the federal government.[23]

With improvements to their water and sewer systems, Columbus residents looked to the future of their city's infrastructure with some confidence. That confidence, however, eroded with industrial and population growth during World War II, which strained Columbus's water system. Columbus's per capita consumption of water increased to 102 gpd from 1941 to 1944, and on 24 January 1945 city residents faced a water crisis. The emergency on that cold winter day was caused by the temporary blockage of water-outlet gates at the Griggs and O'Shaughnessy dams by ice, debris, and frozen fish. Once the gates were cleared, the immediate crisis passed. However, the water shortage brought home to Columbus residents their vulnerability to interruptions in their water supply. Columbus's mayor and city council members asked their city's chamber of commerce to look into present and future water situations for Columbus. The chamber delegated that task to the private civil and municipal engineering firm of the Jennings-Lawrence Company.[24]

The engineers for that Columbus firm issued their report in March 1945. After praising members of the Columbus Water Works Department for handling the water emergency well, they noted that long-term challenges remained. The filtering capacity of the water-treatment plant was once again being exceeded at times and needed to be increased, and standby pumps were required to ensure that enough water could always be pushed into Columbus's distribution system. Most critical, the

---

22. Columbus Director of Public Service to Columbus City Council, 29 January 1930, in State Archives Series 5061, Box 2318.

23. "Milestones," 4, at http://publicutilities.columbus.gov.

24. Jennings-Lawrence, "Water for Columbus."

engineers averred, "Additional water storage capacity is necessary now if the waterworks is to continue to provide adequate services in the future." That water could come, they thought, from a number of sources. Dams on the Scioto River upstream of the O'Shaughnessy reservoir could impound more water, as might dams on Darby Creek and Big Walnut Creek. Then, too, underground water from the Deep Stage aquifer, a remnant of the preglacial Newark River, might be tapped. The Olentangy River might also "be developed to add to the public water supply," but the engineers thought that doing so was "not advisable for aesthetic reasons."[25]

Adding urgency to the report of the consulting engineers was a drought that struck Columbus and much of the rest of the Midwest hard in the summer of 1945. Water levels in the Scioto River dropped so low that city engineers pumped water from an abandoned quarry in Delaware County just north of Columbus into the stream to try to compensate for the evaporation of its water. The 1945 engineering report and the drought set the stage for dealing with water issues well into the years after World War II. Columbus political leaders would continue their quest for water for their city's burgeoning population, but that search would become increasingly complicated. As Columbus officials sought above-ground and below-ground sources of water ever farther from home, they would find themselves in competition for that water with their counterparts in other cities and towns.[26] Moreover, environmental issues and demands that water be put to recreational use would make their quest even more difficult.

## The Continuing Search for Water after World War II

Heading an expansive city, Columbus's political and business leaders continued the quest for water begun in earlier times. The average daily consumption of water in the city soared from 66 million gpd in 1960, to 94 million gpd in 1970, to 104 million gpd in 1980, and to 131 million gpd in 1990. Columbus was not an especially thirsty city, compared to others. Most American cities needed new water sources after World War II. In 1990 Columbus's water sources produced 152 gpd for each resident's use. The figure for Cincinnati was 162 gpd, and for Cleveland

25. Ibid.
26. On this issue, see Elkind, *Bay Cities*, 42–160, which looks at competition for water among municipalities in the San Francisco Bay region and the area around Boston.

198 gpd. Water withdrawals in that year came to 183 gpd for each person in the United States, with those in Ohio averaging 159 gpd. In Indiana withdrawals were 157 gpd, in Michigan 170 gpd, in Pennsylvania 196 gpd, in Arizona 200 gpd, in California 218 gpd, and in Colorado 245 gpd.[27]

Demand for more water came from several sources. Many of those industries remaining in Columbus were water-intensive, such as the large Anheuser-Busch brewery in the northern part of the city. (Such had long been the case, as iron and steel, starch-making, and other enterprises consumed water and then polluted it.) Then, too, after World War II water-gulping home appliances came into common use: dishwashers, clothes washers, and so forth. Increased frequency in bathing took more water. There also were many more lawns that needed to be sprinkled as Columbus sprawled outward. Between 1950 and 1970 the city of Columbus grew in size from 40 square miles to 173 square miles. One consequence of sprawl was that the need for more water was urgent.

Columbus leaders won state aid and public approval for city bond issues for the construction of two additional dams and reservoirs, each much larger than the Griggs and O'Shaughnessy dams and reservoirs. As the dams were being planned and built, Columbus officials turned to Alum Creek for a stopgap water supply. From 1949 to 1950 a small water plant was constructed on Nelson Road just south of Fifth Avenue to treat water from Alum Creek. Brownie Cornell designed the Nelson Road facility. He was the last of the engineering staff hired by John Gregory to participate in the design and construction of the Great Columbus Experiment who was still active in Columbus's water department in the 1950s. Cornell had been a field engineer in the construction of the O'Shaughnessy Dam. Placed in service in 1950, the Nelson Road Plant supplied Columbus with water for five years. It was removed from service when water from the first of the new reservoirs, Hoover Dam reservoir, began to flow.[28]

Hoover Dam and its reservoir were approved in the late 1940s and completed in 1954.[29] The dam was named after the Hoover brothers, Charles and Clarence. Impounding Big Walnut Creek, Hoover reservoir

27. Columbus Division of Water, "Water beyond 2000: Comprehensive Water Treatment and Supply Feasibility Study," Phase 1 (1990), 3, 6; and Phase 3 (1992), 10.

28. Hinds interview.

29. City of Columbus, Department of Public Service, Division of Water, "Dam and Reservoir on Big Walnut Creek," prepared by consulting engineers Burgess and Niple of Columbus, Ohio, 9 October 1952.

could supply Columbus with about 50 million gpd of water and soon provided the city with 60 percent of its water. Second was the Alum Creek Dam and reservoir, which came into service in the 1970s, adding 35 million gpd to Columbus's water supply. Linked by a conduit to each other and to a pumping station, these reservoirs were served by a new water-treatment plant on Morse Road. The plant was later named the "Hap Cremean Plant" after Warren "Hap" Cremean, a former city service director, and was built just southwest of Hoover reservoir.

Disputes sometimes accompanied Columbus's expansion of water facilities, for example, in a controversy about how to finance the construction of Hoover Dam. Residents in local communities near the projected site for the dam and its reservoir wanted federal government funds to be used, which would have given nearby residents some say in the later allocation of water. Clarence Hoover, longtime water and sewer director for Columbus, and other Columbus city officials opposed this idea, for they wanted their city to pay for the dam in its entirety and thereby control all of its water. In a session of the Columbus city council, Hoover, in a first-time-ever public display of anger, declared that the city alone would pay for the dam. Impressed by Hoover's long service to Columbus and his integrity over the decades, thirty-nine-year-old Mayor James A. Rhodes (later Governor of the State of Ohio) sustained Hoover's stance, and the citizens of Columbus financed the project.[30]

Columbus politicians used their control over their city's large, efficient water and sewer systems to ensure the outward expansion of Columbus. Mayor Maynard E. "Jack" Sensenbrenner led the city in its outward surge. He did so with the full support of members of the Columbus Chamber of Commerce, the Metropolitan Committee (a group of downtown business leaders), the Wolfe family (owners of the *Columbus Dispatch* and a very important power in the Republican Party locally), and area real-estate developers. Columbus political leaders usually agreed to make water and sewer hookups to areas around Columbus only if their residents in turn agreed to annexation to Columbus. Between 1940 and 1970 the proportion of residents in Franklin County served by Columbus's water

---

30. Conversations by the author with Conrade C. Hinds, 18 February 2014 and 26 May 2014. The stress of this controversy may have contributed to the deaths of Clarence Hoover in 1949 and Charles Hoover in 1950. It was Mayor Rhodes who named Hoover Dam after them. On Rhodes's three terms as mayor of Columbus, see Tom Diermer, Lee Leonard, and Richard G. Zimmerman, *James A. Rhodes: Ohio Colossus* (Kent, OH: Kent State University Press, 2014), 16–22.

system rose from 78 percent to 90 percent.[31] Annexation enlarged Columbus's tax base and prevented the city from being fenced in by independent municipalities. Some suburban municipalities did surround parts of Columbus—Upper Arlington to the west, Worthington to the north, and Bexley to the east—but by and large Columbus continued to move outward, usually by annexing unincorporated areas. Thus Columbus avoided "encirclement." As a consequence, Columbus's tax base remained stronger than those of Cleveland and Cincinnati, which were largely ringed by independent towns.[32] Kline Roberts, a lawyer and politician and the head of the Chamber of Commerce, recalled, "Sensenbrenner made annexation his thing. Columbus would not be surrounded like Cleveland or Cincinnati. He even threatened to annex Cleveland." Columbus officials were was not alone in their growth strategy. Officials of Lancaster also used their control over water supplies to annex outlying areas.[33]

Wil Haygood, an African American who grew up in part on Columbus's East Side, later wrote of Sensenbrenner, "He waltzed in and out of the clubs, glided onto bar stools, slapped backs. His claim to fame was grabbing land." Continuing, Haygood observed, "M. E. Sensenbrenner watched the spread of suburbia, told suburban officials if they wanted services from Columbus, they might as well annex. Then he'd twist arms and annex them. . . . The city grew."[34] Folksy "Jumping Jack" Sensenbrenner was popular with most voters and served as the very dynamic mayor of Columbus for fourteen years, 1954 to 1960 and 1964 to 1972. As a young boy, he had his photograph taken astride a jackass, hence his nickname.[35]

Columbus's new suburban customers needed to be supplied with water. Between 1953 and 1959 the city either obtained by annexation or

---

31. Mid-Ohio Regional Planning Commission, "Water Supply Plan (Revised) for Columbus, October, 1972," 4. On the details of the political steps involved in annexation, see Burgess, Planning, 26.

32. Lentz, Columbus: The Story, 137; and Hunker, A Personal Geography, 32–33. Not all areas using Columbus's water and sewer systems were annexed. Bexley used the systems from 1914, and Upper Arlington from 1919, while both remained independent. See Burgess, Planning, 38; and Waring, "Public Water," 17, 22. On how encirclement and white flight hurt Cleveland's tax base, see Stradling and Stradling, Where the River Burned, 198.

33. Contosta, Lancaster, 239. See also Jacobs, Getting around Brown, 123 (the source of the quotation).

34. Wil Haygood, The Haygoods of Columbus: A Love Story (Boston: Houghton Mifflin Company, 1998), 205–6.

35. For a biographic sketch of Sensenbrenner, see Garrett and Lentz, Crossroads, 156.

built some 247 miles of water mains. In those years Columbus supplied 16,000 new taps and water meters to areas inside the city, but another 12,000 of them went into areas beyond the city, most of which were soon annexed.[36] Sometimes expansion came at the expense of customers in well-established districts. Throughout the late 1950s petitions from the residents of Columbus's East Side, a predominantly black district, inundated the city council "to protest the lack of water pressure for the East Side of Columbus, which creates a fire hazard, makes it impossible for us to sprinkle our lawns properly, and operate dish washers or automatic laundry equipment."[37] Like the protests of Columbus's South Side residents during the Progressive era, these complaints raised environmental-justice concerns. Acrimony and conflict accompanied urban growth in Columbus.

Supplying Columbus with water while continuing to extend city boundaries outward seemed to be a never-ending spiral. A 1972 report urged city officials to look into the possibility of securing additional water from "large, buried valleys in South Franklin County" and from new dams to be built across Big Darby Creek, the Scioto River, and Mill Creek, one of the Scioto River's tributaries.[38] A far-reaching study prepared by the Columbus Division of Water in 1990 projected the city's water needs at 192 million gpd within thirty years, even taking into consideration substantial water-conservation efforts. The idea of conserving water was new in Columbus and in much of the United States. It embraced everything from using low-flow toilets and showerheads to redesigning industrial processes to consume less water. Water, Americans were coming to realize, was a finite resource. Unless actions were taken soon, the 1990 report warned, Columbus residents would face a large water deficit of 55 million gpd by 2020.[39]

The 1990 report urged that a variety of water sources be explored. By this time, the Columbus Division of Water was extracting a considerable amount of water each day from underground sources at a recently developed South Well Field, served by the new Parsons Avenue Water

---

36. Columbus Water Division, "Water Figures," State Archives Series 5052, Box 2289.

37. The many petitions may be found in State Archives Series 5052, Box 2289. The petition quoted is from 11 July 1959.

38. "Water Supply, 1972," 8–9. See also Ranney Water Systems, Inc., "Report to the City of Columbus on Preliminary Geophysical Groundwater Investigation of the Area at Junction of Alum Creek, Big Walnut Creek and Blacklick Creek, 22 November 1966," 1.

39. "Water Beyond 2000," Phase 1, pp. 14, 23, 28.

Plant. In the late 1960s and 1970s the city constructed four large wells ranging from 68 to 109 feet in depth with 6,000 feet of laterals reaching into the aquifer. City officials thought that the amount of water supplied by these wells might be readily increased. The 1990 report envisioned additional well fields tapping underground aquifers as far as 40 miles from Columbus's main pumping station. Then, too, dams might impound more reservoirs. A site on the upper Scioto River at Bellepoint seemed particularly promising. "Upground reservoirs" consisting of "circuitous or nearly circuitous embankments in which water is contained" were yet another possibility. Such reservoirs would be filled with water pumped in from streams. The "actual siting of upground reservoirs can be quite flexible," the report observed, "thereby avoiding many site-characteristic problems"—that is, difficulties encountered in building dams across streams.[40]

The report concluded that Columbus had more than enough options for water—if they were developed without delay. New underground sources might yield 110 million gpd, including an additional 77 million gpd from the South Well Field. Reservoirs impounded behind new dams on rivers and streams might yield another 166 million gpd.[41] Finally, upground reservoirs could, it was thought, deliver 187 million gpd. Over the next decade Columbus acquired 2,500 acres in Delaware County to the north for three upground reservoirs. In late 2013 the city finished the construction of an 843-acre upground reservoir capable of holding 9 billion gallons of water, more than the capacity of the Griggs and O'Shaughnessy reservoirs combined, at a cost of $123 million.[42] In mid-2015 Columbus officials also acquired land once used for a state government reformatory for boys located on the banks of the Scioto River in southwest Delaware County as the site for a new water-treatment plant. They did so over the opposition of officials of Delaware County and Concord Township, who favored having the land developed for commercial uses, thus enlarging the tax bases of their governmental entities. One of the above-ground reservoirs filled with water from the Scioto River would supply water for the plant.[43]

---

40. Ibid, 19–21, 25–26.

41. Ibid.

42. *Columbus Dispatch*, 12 November 2013, p. A13; and "Upground Reservoir Project," at www.utilities.columbus.gov, accessed on 29 November 2013.

43. *Columbus Dispatch*, 29 May 2015, p. B6; and 9 June 2015, p. B3.

# Environmental Concerns and Public Policies

Just as they did in other cities across the United States, environmental concerns increasingly influenced Columbus's search for water.[44] In the late 1960s and early 1970s clean air and water laws, along with the creation of the Environmental Protection Agency, signaled that environmentalism had reached a new, very important, stage of development in the United States. In Ohio, concerns about water quality focused upon the dumping of sewage into the Ohio River, the pollution of the Cuyahoga River in Cleveland (the river infamously caught fire in 1969), and the eutrophication (death because of lack of oxygen) of Lake Erie.[45]

The growing significance of environmental issues was clear in an amendment that members of the Columbus Division of Water made in 1991 to their report of the year before. Big Darby Creek, which had looked very promising as the site for a dammed reservoir, was eliminated from consideration because of "serious environmental concerns." Darby Creek was designated as a State Scenic River in 1984 and as a National Scenic River ten years later. The stream contained thirty-seven federally protected species of fish and mussels. It was placed off-limits to development. On the other hand, a dam on Mill Creek, which flowed into the Scioto River at Bellepoint north of Columbus, was appealing precisely because that stream was "not known to contain any threatened/or endangered species and related habitat."[46]

Environmental matters engulfed wetlands, partially protected by various federal and state laws, and pitted developers against preservationists. A developer in the southern Columbus suburb of Pickerington Ponds was forced from 2002 to 2004 to scale back his plans because they threatened water supplies for a nearby Columbus metropolitan park and wetlands. Pickerington had experienced explosive growth during the last three decades of the twentieth century, expanding from a village of several hundred people to a city of nearly 8,000 residents.[47] Even earlier, in 1999, the

---

44. Melosi, *Sanitary City,* 180–92, 225–39, looks at environmental issues about the use of water in American cities after World War II.

45. For an overview, see Kern and Wilson, *Ohio: A History,* 440–44. For more detail see Terence Kehoe, *Cleaning Up the Great Lakes: From Cooperation to Confrontation* (DeKalb: Northern Illinois University Press, 1997); and Stradling and Stradling, *Where the River Burned,* 144–72.

46. "Water Beyond 2000," Phase 2 (1991), 46.

47. *Columbus Dispatch,* 18 September 2001, p. B5; 2 December 2002, p. A1; and 2 May 2004, p. A1. On the history of Pickerington, see Contosta, *Lancaster,* 262; and *Worthington News,* 8 November 2012, p. A2.

Columbus city council, under the threat of a voter referendum (residents were opposed to new houses and additional street traffic), had revoked its support for the building of a subdivision near the Pickerington Ponds Wildlife Refuge. Residents argued that the density of the proposed housing project would harm the refuge.[48]

In mid-2013 another Columbus developer was denied permission to build on 18 acres of wetlands in northwestern Columbus near Sawmill Road, when members of neighborhood groups vehemently opposed his plans, even though the developer offered to "swap" the Sawmill wetlands for another parcel of wetlands which he would preserve not far away adjacent to the Olentangy River. An earlier developer had promised that the Sawmill wetlands would be preserved "in perpetuity," and those living in this suburban area of Columbus wanted that promise to be kept. The wetlands, they argued, improved the quality of their lives. One resident exclaimed, "Imagine being able to stop in at the Sawmill property, perhaps after a quick shopping trip to adjacent retail stores, and enjoy the beauty and serenity of this magnificent parcel."[49] Unspoiled nature and development could, she clearly thought, easily coexist. The Ohio Environmental Council awarded the Friends of Sawmill Wetlands its 2013 Conservation Achievement Award, citing the friends as "a grassroots group that worked tirelessly to block a proposed land swap that threatened this rare, high-quality wetland." The two leaders of the friends wrote in response: "We did it. We saved the wetland and can bask in the glow of the moment and then get back to work ensuring the future of our wetland."[50]

In downtown Columbus, as well as in the city's suburbs, conceptions about the proper use of water changed. In the late twentieth and early twenty-first centuries, a cleaned-up Scioto River became a magnet for residents moving back downtown and something of a tourist attraction. Enticing urban parks, walkways, and bikeways came to line the river on what was touted as the "Scioto Mile," anchored by fountains, upscale restaurants, public art, and government buildings. Some of the potential of the river for beauty and recreation, first recognized in the 1908 city plan, was realized. An effort was also made to return the Scioto River to something approaching its wild state, as two low-head dams, one just

---

48. *Columbus Dispatch*, 26 December 1999, p. 13A.

49. *Columbus Dispatch*, 12 January 2013, p. A9; 6 March 2013, p. B2; 2 April 2013, p. A15; 3 April 2013, p. B1; and 12 May 2013, p. E7 (the source of the quotation).

50. Steve McCaw and Michelle Shinew, email to the Neighbors of Stilson Highlands, 11 November 2013, in the author's possession.

north of Fifth Avenue, the other just south of Main Street, were removed from 2011 to 2014, allowing the river to run freely, or at least more freely than before. From a utilitarian transportation artery and open sewer, the Scioto River was being rehabilitated as an environmentally friendly greenbelt running through Columbus.[51]

Environmental concerns extended to sewage matters. The decision made in the 1880s to combine surface runoff and sewage had unfortunate consequences into the early 2000s for people living in Columbus. The City Planning Commission of 1908 recommended that Columbus's sewage system be "divided into two distinct schemes—one to carry storm waters and one to carry house drainage."[52] For nearly a century, however, few steps were taken in this direction. Separating sewer systems was very expensive, and overflows occurred sporadically. Only in 2002 did the city of Columbus agree with the Ohio Environmental Protection Agency to remedy this defect. The federal government entered the picture in 2010, when the U.S. Environmental Protection Agency demanded that overflows end. In 2013 Columbus possessed 2,782 miles of sanitary pipes transporting only sewage, and 2,537 miles of pipes handling just storm water; however, the city also still had 167 miles of major combined pipes.[53]

The cost of sewage remediation was estimated in 2007 at $2.5 billion. Largely to pay for the remediation, residential water and sewer rates climbed 84 percent in Columbus between 2004 and 2011. In the fall of 2013 residents approved a $445 million bond issue to continue their city's sewer upgrades. Scheduled for completion in 2023, the project revolved around boring a tunnel 20 feet in diameter, 170 feet underground, and 4.5 miles long to take sewage away from overflow points to the city's treatment plant south of Columbus.[54] Nicknamed locally as

51. *Columbus Dispatch*, 26 November 2013, p. B3; and 8 December 2013, p. F6. See also "5th Avenue Dam," at www.utilities.columbus.gov, accessed on 29 November 2013. However, five other low-head dams on rivers in Columbus were deemed to be too expensive to remove. See *Columbus Dispatch*, 23 April 2015, p. A1. For a similar change in Los Angeles, see Blake Gumprecht, *The Los Angeles River: Its Death and Possible Rebirth* (Baltimore: Johns Hopkins University Press, 1999), 235–302.

52. City Planning Commission, "City Plan," 1908, p. 16.

53. Department of Public Utilities, "Understanding Our Sewer System," 1, at http:// publicutilities.columbus.gov, accessed on 19 January 2014.

54. *Columbus Dispatch*, 12 November 2013, pp. A1, A13; and "OARS Deep Sewer Tunnel" and "A New Approach," both at www.utilities.columbus.gov, accessed on 29 November 2013. Columbus residents had company. In 2015 residents of Akron agreed to spend $1.4 billion to separate their waste-water and sewer systems, a step that included carving out a tunnel 27 feet in diameter and 6,000 feet long. See *Columbus Dispatch*, 21 June 2015, p. B7.

"the Big Dig," a takeoff on the more notorious construction in Boston with the same nickname, it was well underway in 2014.[55] Unexpected difficulties in cutting the tunnel led to further rate increases that year. In the meantime, city officials issued advisory warnings to Columbus residents whenever sewage overflows into streams and rivers were expected.[56]

The problem of sewage overflows was national in scope. In the early 2000s some 400 million gallons of sewage overflowed into urban waterways each year, and cities across the United States were trying out various "green technologies" to deal with the issue. Columbus officials adopted green technologies to reduce rain runoff at its sources, such as planting water-absorbing plants and shrubs around parking lots and vacant lots. In 2014 Columbus city officers publicly launched "Blueprint Columbus," which they described as "a thirty-year, $2.5 billion 'green' project to divert storm-water runoff from the city's sewer system to rain gardens built on vacant parcels in the city." Columbus officials planned to build 20 acres of "green infrastructure" for every 1,000 acres in thirteen specific neighborhoods, including the South Side. The program had already had a "soft start" eighteen months earlier "with some small parks and gardens in neighborhoods," especially in Clintonville on the North Side. Similarly, libraries in Worthington planted demonstration rain gardens.[57] Columbus was hardly unique. In 2014 Cleveland officials dedicated three sites as rain gardens to keep 200,000 gallons of storm water out of their city's sewer system each year, with another seven gardens planned to be open by 2019 at an estimated cost of $82 million.[58]

More generally, Columbus's Jackson Pike Plant proved unable to handle the sewage output of the burgeoning city. Upgrades boosted the capacity of the treatment facility to over 80 million gpd by the early 1960s, but that amount was still inadequate. In response to Columbus's growing needs, city engineers constructed a second sewage-treatment plant south of Columbus. Known as the "Southerly Wastewater Treatment Plant," it came online in 1967. Additions and upgrades increased the capacities and efficiencies of both sewer plants over the next four

55. *Columbus Dispatch*, 30 May 2002, p. C11; 20 July 2007, p. B5; 16 January 2011, p. B1. See also Columbus Division of Public Utilities, "Utility Update," Fall, 2007, p. 1; and *Worthington News*, 27 June 2013, p. A2.

56. *Columbus Dispatch*, 11 November 2014, p. A1; and *Worthington News*, 24 July 2014, p. A9.

57. *Columbus Dispatch*, 20 February 2014, p. A1; 10 March 2014, p. A1; and 6 June 2015, p. B5. Also see "Waste Not," *National Geographic* 224 (November 2013), unpaged; and *Worthington News*, 19 June 2014, p. A10.

58. *Columbus Dispatch*, 3 November 2014, p. B10.

decades.[59] By 2013 the Jackson Pike Plant could handle up to 102 million gpd of sewage, and the Southerly Plant had an additional daily capacity of 114 million gallons.[60] In 2015 major improvements were begun for the Southerly Plant, including efforts to reduce its smells. Sludge from both plants was handled in imaginative ways. While some was burned, buried, and sold to farmers as fertilizer, much of the broken-down waste was sold to Ohio Mulch, a private company. Ohio Mulch used the sludge as fertilizer to grow poplar trees which were, in turn, made into mulch sold to homeowners.[61]

## The Importance of Water in the Development of Columbus

This chapter, together with the previous one, has shown how important water-use developments were in shaping Columbus. Into the early twentieth century, especially during the antebellum years, waterborne diseases affected, and at times stunted, the growth of Columbus. At the same time, however, waterborne trade via rivers and canals spurred growth. Then, too, throughout the city's history, water matters encouraged the "upstream," northerly expansion of Columbus. Expansion to the south, where sewage was dumped into the Scioto River, was slow. This pattern of upstream, and specifically northerly, urban growth was common in the Midwest, where most streams—with the exception of the Ohio River, which runs mainly east to west—flow north to south. Finally, Columbus politicians often employed their power over water and sewage treatment as a club against outlying areas to force annexation to their city. Until the late twentieth century, no annexation usually meant no water or sewer connections. As a result, Columbus was not surrounded by independent municipalities and continued to grow outward, enlarging the city's tax base and helping keep city finances healthy.

In the nineteenth century Columbus often trailed larger cities in water matters. Columbus was not a metropolis like New York, Boston, or Philadelphia. Columbus was more typical of the many midsize cities across the Midwest and other sections of the United States. Private,

59. "Milestones," 5.
60. City of Columbus, Department of Public Utilities, "Water for Living" (Columbus, 2013), unpaged pamphlet.
61. *Columbus Dispatch*, 2 June 2015, p. A1. On how Cleveland officials treated their city's sludge, see Stradling and Stradling, *Where the River Burned*, 194.

local water systems lasted well into the nineteenth century in these cities. Columbus, however, moved ahead of the curve on urban water developments in the early twentieth century. The city's leadership in water matters was most pronounced during the Progressive era, when in the space of just a few years residents approved building new water-purification, sewage-treatment, and garbage-reduction plants. Their optimism about the prospects for their city, tempered by fears of waterborne diseases like typhoid fever, led to favorable votes on bond issues needed for a municipally owned and operated water and sewer system. It helped as well that Columbus did not have excessively large sunk costs in an established water system from earlier times. The city's engineers were able to learn from the experiences of others and to experiment with new processes.

Finally, chapters 2 and 3 show that politics were as important as engineering matters in determining how water systems in Columbus played out. The path dependence of engineered systems was often significant, in, for example, the century-long question of whether to separate or combine storm water with sewage. Even so, the present was not always determined by the past. Columbus residents demonstrated in the Progressive era that they could break away from past practices in crisis situations, such as outbreaks of typhoid fever, when given reasonable political leadership. Politics always mattered, as residents of Columbus's South Side repeatedly found to their dismay.[62] Columbus's water and sewer systems in use in the early 2000s were the result of changing public policies as much as changing technologies. Politics were also important in shaping patterns of land use, the topic of the next two chapters.

---

62. Environmental- and social-justice issues also arose in water-use matters in the city of Zanesville just to the east of Columbus in central Ohio. Predominantly black areas in Zanesville had difficult times obtaining city water hookups. See *Columbus Dispatch*, 16 February 2014, p. A1.

# CHAPTER 4

# Land Use in a Changing City

As in most other American cities, a mixture of public and private actions shaped land use in Columbus. Columbus's layout initially focused on the statehouse in Statehouse Square, and other public buildings helped define the burgeoning town's design in the antebellum years. Private decisions, however, were also important, as merchants, retailers, and manufacturers chose locations for their businesses and as inhabitants sought dwelling places. Privately owned, city-chartered streetcar companies encouraged urban expansion between about 1870 and 1920, as did the increasingly widespread use of automobiles after 1900. Columbus residents sought to channel spatial expansion through a 1908 city plan, an attempt that largely failed as the city sprawled outward along streetcar lines and highways. An examination of Columbus's 1908 scheme provides valuable insights into the strengths and weaknesses of planning efforts during the Progressive era of the early 1900s.

This chapter and the following one examine the development of land-use policies in Columbus. In this realm, Columbus residents usually followed, rather than led, what was being done by urbanites in larger, coastal cities. The sense of urgency that sparked massive changes in water use in Columbus during the early 1900s was generally lacking. There was no land-use equivalent of the crisis of the typhoid epidemic of 1904–6, no death of a United States senator like Mark Hanna. Even so, land-use developments in Columbus were substantial, on par with those in other midsize, midwestern metropolises.

## Land Use in the New Capital City

Columbus began its existence as the capital of the state of Ohio. As historian Charles Cole has observed, "Columbus was made the permanent state capital before it was a town."[1] The act of the General Assembly establishing Columbus as the capital specified that those seeking designation of the town as the capital would "convey to this state a square of ten acres and a lot of ten acres, and to erect a state house, such offices, and a penitentiary." In return, the legislature would appoint a "director" to survey and lay out the town. The director would determine the width of streets and alleys and would "select the square for public buildings, and the lot for the penitentiary."[2]

The 10-acre Statehouse Square, donated by the city's founders to help persuade the state legislators to designate Columbus as their state's capital, lay at the center of the new town. The politicians appointed the surveyor Joel Wright of Warren County as the director to prepare a plat for their new capital, which he did in early 1812. Franklin County Surveyor Joseph Vance did "most of the legwork." A gridiron of streets ran in the four directions outward from the square: High Street north-south to the west, Broad Street east-west to the immediate north, Third Street north-south on the square's eastern boundary, and State Street east-west just to the south. The streets were wide for the day. High Street measured 100 feet in width, and Broad Street an even wider 120 feet. Small city lots were available for purchase around the square, as were larger ones farther out to the east of Seventh Street. Separating the two types of lots between Fourth and Seventh streets was a swath of undivided land called the "Central Reservation," which the founders held back from sale for their future disposition. The original plat of Columbus also set aside 10 acres for the construction of a state penitentiary southwest of Statehouse Square on the Scioto River, south of its eastern bend into the town.[3]

---

1. Cole, *Fragile Capital*, 9.

2. State of Ohio, *Laws*, vol. 10, chapter 34, as reprinted in *Documentary Heritage*, eds. Shriver and Wunderlin, 142.

3. Cole, *Fragile Capital*, 11; Ed Lentz, "Power Evolved at State and High," *Worthington News*, 15 January 2015, p. A6; Garrett and Lentz, *Crossroads*, 27; and Lentz,

The original boundaries of Columbus were North Public Lane (later Nationwide Boulevard) to the north, South Public Lane (later Livingston Avenue, named after a pioneer family) to the south, the Scioto River to the west, and East Public Lane (later Parsons Avenue) to the east. Surveyor Wright drew his inspiration for street names partly from those in use in British and eastern United States cities—hence his designations of High Street and the Public Lanes. Philadelphia had a High Street and a Broad Street at the time. Wright was in good company. Many other midwestern cities used the same names for their streets. Lancaster, for example, had a Broad Street and a High Street.

Columbus's streets did not run along a true north-south axis. Instead, they deviated 12 degrees to the west of true north, allowing them to line up with streets laid out earlier in Franklinton to the west across the Scioto River. The streets in Franklinton in turn corresponded in their north-south orientation to magnetic north, not true north, with 12 degrees being the deviation between the two directions. "A good supposition," historian Ed Lentz has concluded, "is that Franklinton was laid out in a hurry."[4] In fact, few American cities had streets running precisely north-south. New York City, Philadelphia, Detroit, and Savannah, all of which were constructed on gridiron plans, did not. Instead, their street plans were oriented to their waterfronts. Columbus's Statehouse Square, and thus the streets around it, were similarly somewhat oriented to the flow of the Scioto River to the west.

Essential in the founding of Columbus, governmental actions remained important throughout the antebellum years. Borough and city ordinances outlawed slaughterhouses, tanneries, rendering plants, and the like inside city boundaries, leading to their establishment south of Columbus's city limits. Built for the most part by entrepreneur Peter Hayden on the edges of a deep ravine filled with a gushing stream, which came to be called "Hayden's Cut," they added decidedly unpleasant pungency to the air of Columbus's South Side.[5] Likewise, ordinances sometimes mandated building materials in the interest of preventing fires and determined when and where markets could be held. The original city market was held in the middle of High Street, south of Rich Street in 1814, an example of how

---

*Columbus: The Story,* 42–45.

4. Wright's original map of Columbus has been lost. In the 1820s Wright drew a map of his plat of Columbus from memory. See Lentz, *As It Were,* 3 (the source of the quotation), 25–27 on street names. See also Contosta, *Lancaster,* 9, 20–21.

5. Lentz, *As It Were,* 118.

streets were seen as public places, a distinction lost when streetcars and automobiles later took them over.[6]

State government actions were also significant in influencing Columbus's physical layout, as might be expected for a capital city. Buildings that housed state services developed over several decades and helped demarcate Columbus's growth pattern. Preceding even the construction of the statehouse was the construction of the state penitentiary, a three-story building erected from 1813 to 1816 on 10 acres set aside for that purpose in the original plat of Columbus, at what would become the southwest corner of West Main Street and Marconi Boulevard overlooking the Scioto River. The first public building in Columbus, the penitentiary owed its early construction to the fact that state officials intended to erect other buildings with prison labor, which they did. A larger prison was built just down the hill in 1818. Soon overcrowded, the penitentiary was moved in 1834 to a new location along Spring Street in what was countryside to the north. It had some seven hundred cells, along with "schools, shops, hospitals, and recreational facilities." A fire killed 320 inmates in 1930, but the penitentiary continued in use for five more decades. Closed as recently as 1984 and demolished four years later, the penitentiary had been located such that it encouraged Columbus's northward migration. The first statehouse, a two-story brick structure on the southwest corner of Statehouse Square at the intersection of State and High streets, was replaced by a grand "Greek revival temple" of a statehouse at the center of Statehouse Square. Built over several decades as state revenues permitted, it opened in early 1857. Both statehouses reinforced the square as the center of activities in Columbus. When street numbering for individual addresses began in the late 1850s, the system took the intersection of High and Broad streets on the northwest corner of Statehouse Square as its starting point.[7]

Additional state buildings included schools for the blind and deaf. In 1827 legislation established "an asylum for the education of the deaf and dumb," and a school for them was built several years later on a 10-acre lot near the intersection of Town Street and Washington Avenue, several blocks east of Statehouse Square, "near the town but removed

---

6. Cole, *Fragile Capital*, 29, 162; Lentz, *Columbus: The Story*, 58; and Winter, *A Concise History of Columbus*, 44.

7. Arter, *Columbus Vignettes*, vol. 2, p. 20; Cole, *Fragile Capital*, 16, 117–34; Lentz, *As It Were*, 10; Ed Lentz, "First Prison Sat on Donated Land," *Worthington News*, 6 November 2014, p. A6; and Ed Lentz, "City Wasn't Born with Address System," *Worthington News*, 16 January 2014, p. A6.

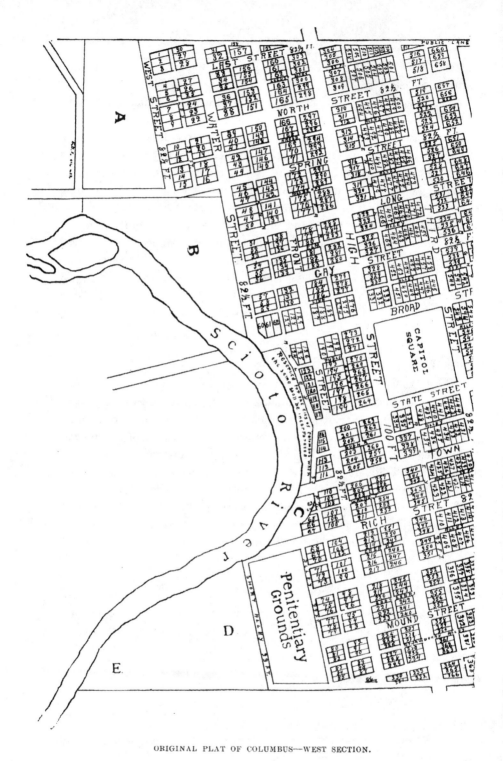

ORIGINAL PLAT OF COLUMBUS—WEST SECTION.

**Figure 4.1.** Joel Wright's Map (Drawn in the 1820s) of Columbus in 1812. This map reveals plans for a city oriented toward the state capital and the Scioto River. (Reprinted from Lee, *History of the City*, vol. 1, pp. 202–3)

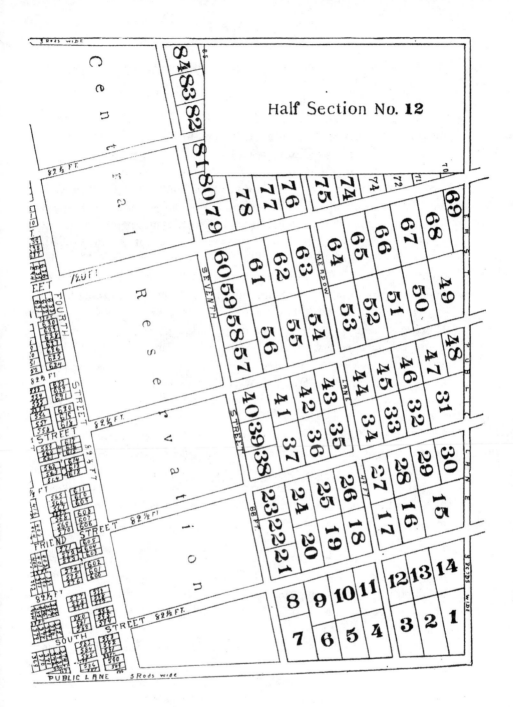

ORIGINAL PLAT OF COLUMBUS—EAST SECTION.

from the bustle." A school for the blind was established in 1839 on 9 acres at Main Street and Parsons Avenue to the southeast. After moving to new sites earlier, the schools relocated to locations in northern Columbus in 1953. State legislation authorized building a place for the treatment of the mentally ill in 1835, and a state lunatic asylum, constructed with prison labor, opened three years later on 30 acres on the north side of Broad Street about half a mile east of Columbus's center. By the 1860s a common Sunday activity for the residents of Columbus was to "prepare a picnic lunch and take one's leisure amid handsome grounds and gardens of The Lunatic Asylum."[8] A fire destroyed the asylum's main building in 1868, with the loss of six lives. That structure was not rebuilt. Instead, the institution moved to the Hilltop area in West Columbus. The new building there, the Columbus State Hospital, was the largest structure under one roof in the United States until the building of the Pentagon.[9]

As impressive as the state buildings was the Columbus City Hall. However, for most of the antebellum years there was no city hall, and borough, and later city, officials met in various inns and taverns. After 1850 they convened in a room on the second floor of the new city market just south of Town Street between Third and Fourth streets. Only in early 1872 was a city hall opened on the south side of State Street across from Statehouse Square. The City Hall building contained a post office, a library room, and offices for the city's newly formed Board of Trade. Council chambers on the second floor were "frescoed with watercolors, and the bar is covered with a handsome carpet of brilliant colors." A public hall on the third floor measured 140 feet in length and 70 feet in width and could accommodate 3,000 seated residents. Here, council members met until the City Hall was destroyed by fire in the early 1920s. The site later became home to the Ohio Theatre.[10]

Private actions complemented governmental ones in shaping Columbus. Land sales started in June 1812, with lots selling mainly near the intersection of Broad and High streets. The terms for the sales of lots in Columbus were standard for the time. As a newspaper advertisement explained, "One-third [was] to be paid at the time of purchasing; and the remaining two-thirds in two annual installments, with interest." Due

8. Cole, *Fragile Capital*, 108–16; Lentz, *As It Were*, 32–35, 42–47, esp. 34, 44; Winter, *A Concise History*, 69–71; and Wooley and Van Brimmer, *Second Blessing*, 65–78.

9. Ed Lentz, "1868 Fire Destroyed Lunatic Asylum," *Worthington News*, 20 November 2014, p. A6.

10. Ed Lentz, "First City Hall a Sight to Behold," *Worthington News*, 26 June 2014, p. A6.

to slow sales, terms were soon liberalized to 20 percent down, with the remainder due in four equal annual payments. Prices fell during the War of 1812, remained low well into the 1820s, but picked up from the 1830s onward.[11] Front Street, which ran north-south one block west of High Street, developed into an early-day residential street, as did Broad Street eastward from High Street. Most homes were not elaborate, as numerous log cabins nestled next to more refined dwellings. One account observed, "The cabin of the Ohio pioneer was usually laid up with round logs, notched into one another at the ends and chinked between with wooden blocks and stones." Continuing, the report noted, "The chimney was built outside of the walls of crossed wooden strips, daubed with clay. At its base it extended into a large open fireplace, with a firm lining of stones." "The roof," the account concluded, "was made of clapboards, five or six feet long, riven from oak or ash logs, and held down by being weighted with stones or poles."[12]

Different land uses existed cheek-to-jowl in the developing town. A two-story brick tavern was built in late 1812 at the corner of High and State streets, and the Worthington Manufacturing Company put up a store to sell dry goods, hardware, and groceries near Broad and High streets not long afterward. No public zoning ordinances or private-deed covenants specified permissible land uses; nor would they until the twentieth century.

The private building probably having the greatest impact on early Columbus was what became the Union Railroad Station, a "giant, rambling, barn of a structure" built in 1850 at the terminus of the first railroad to enter the city, the Columbus and Xenia line. It served the station needs of all of the railroads entering Columbus for twenty-five years. Situated just north of North Public Lane, Union Station helped pull Columbus's growth northward. Two additional union stations were built on that site in later years, 1875 and 1894. The third one boasted "elaborate toilet rooms, a private smoking room, barber shop, bathrooms, dining room, lunch counter and buffet . . . all comforts and conveniences of the first-class hotel."[13] Designed by nationally known architect Daniel Burnham, it was torn down in the name of urban redevelopment during the mid-1970s.[14]

11. Garrett and Lentz, *Crossroads*, 26, reprints the land advertisement.

12. As quoted in Ed Lentz, "1800s Settlers Faced Difficult Times," *Worthington News*, 23 January 2014, p. A6. See also Cole, *Fragile Capital*, 11; and Ed Lentz, "Settlers Built Simple Log Cabins," *Worthington News*, 26 March, 2015, p. A6.

13. Arter, *Columbus Vignettes*, vol. 1, p. 59.

14. Lentz, *Columbus: The Story*, 61; and Lentz, *As It Were*, 101 (the source of the quotation).

The movement into Columbus of new groups of people seeking economic and social advantages helped shape the city's growth. Most of the earliest settlers in the city came from Kentucky and Virginia. (West Virginia did not become a state until 1863, when she broke away from Virginia during the Civil War.) Especially in its early decades, Columbus had a "border-state" quality about it, especially when compared to Cleveland. Lancaster, just south of Columbus, had a similar makeup in its early population; Worthington, just to the north, was by contrast composed initially of migrants from New England.[15] William Neil was one such southern migrant to Columbus. The city's wealthiest residents initially lived away from the clamor of High Street, along Front and Third streets. Poorer inhabitants lived closer to where they worked or owned their business. Neil lived on the top floor of the inn he built on High Street across from the statehouse, and David Deshler at first resided with his wife Betsy in home quarters in his carpentry shop at Broad and High streets.[16]

Historians Kevin Kern and Gregory Wilson have recently argued that Ohio initially grew up "not so much as a society as a community of communities."[17] Historians Andrew Cayton and Peter Onuf have concluded much the same about the Midwest as a whole, writing, "The Midwest was more like an ethnic and cultural checkerboard than the proverbial melting pot."[18] From its earliest days, Columbus possessed elements of social diversity. Franklin County had 43 "free people of color" in 1810, 132 in 1820, 288 in 1830, and 573 in 1840. African Americans lived along Hayden's Cut. They also resided along West Long and West Spring streets. Some 216 African Americans lived in Columbus by 1832, about 10 percent of the town's population, a proportion that remained about the same in 1840 but that dropped to 7 percent ten years later. Some 650 African Americans made Columbus their home in 1870. All were free blacks, as Ohio's constitution had outlawed slavery.[19] While most African Americans were unskilled workers, some were skilled laborers, artisans, and business owners—barbers, carpenters, tailors, and draymen, for example. They lived in clusters throughout the city, not in any

---

15. Contosta, *Lancaster*, 14–15; and Berquist and Bowers, *The New Eden*.

16. Garrett and Lentz, *Crossroads*, 27; and Lentz, *Columbus: The Story*, 61–65.

17. Kern and Wilson, *Ohio: A History*, 126. Cayton, *Ohio: The History of a People*, 43, makes the same point.

18. Cayton and Onuf, *Midwest and the Nation*, 27.

19. Mark, *Negroes in Columbus*, 7; and *African-American Settlements and Communities in Columbus, Ohio*, ed. Toni Smith (Columbus: Columbus Landmarks Foundation, 2014), 13, published online at http://columbuslandmarks.org, accessed on 4 April 2015.

single district.[20] Still, about one-half of the African Americans residing in Columbus lived in the Long Street district by 1860, and about one-third still lived there ten years later.[21]

German and Irish immigrants entered Columbus in significant numbers from the 1830s and 1840s. Many Irish had built Ohio's canals, suffering from malaria as they did so, and some stayed on in Columbus. They lived along North Public Lane and nearby streets. In 1850 about 6 percent of Columbus residents were from Ireland. Germans congregated south of Peter's Run, which was south of Rich Street near Hayden's Cut. They resided on South Public Lane and streets to the south in what became known as the Old South End and later as German Village. Here they had kindergartens, German-language schools and newspapers, singing societies, athletic societies and clubs, churches, and the Lutheran Theological Society. Some opened breweries, as did the Hoster family in the 1830s, the origin of the Columbus Brewery District. Germans called the Columbus residents living west of the Scioto River, mainly Virginians, "pinchguts," because of their alleged stinginess. Residents from New England were known as "cold dumplings." By 1870 German-born immigrants composed about 13 percent of Columbus residents. Like other midwestern cities, Columbus thus possessed a major population of Germans. By 1890, in all of the most populous cities of the Midwest the largest number of foreign-born residents came from Germany. Columbus also was a young city, with children and youth making up 43 percent of its population in 1840.[22]

Immigrant neighborhoods began developing, with Columbus's riverfront left to business establishments and the homes of various, less prosperous residents.[23] Relations among groups in the various neighborhoods were not always friendly. Conflict between some of Columbus native white and immigrant German residents developed in the 1850s. Native groups coalesced into the aptly named Know-Nothing Party, which was opposed to Catholics and immigrants, as part of a national movement.

20. Smith, *African-American Settlements*, 13–16.

21. Weisenburger, *Columbus during the Civil War*, 4.

22. Cole, *Fragile Capital*, 78, 83–84, 214; Teaford, *Cities of the Heartland*, 59; and Winter, *A Concise History*, 59–62. For more detail on Germans in Columbus, see La Vern J. Rippley, *The Columbus Germans* (Baltimore: J. H. Furst Company, 1968). Population figures are on p. 3. On the migration of Irish and Germans to Ohio, see Kern and Wilson, *Ohio: A History*, 136–37. See also Meyers, Meyers, and Walker, *Look to Lazarus*, 21.

23. Cole, *Fragile Capital*, 213; and Garrett and Lentz, *Crossroads*, 77. On midwestern developments, see Cayton and Onuf, *Midwest and Nation*, 87.

The party was particularly strong in the Midwest. Violence broke out in 1855; armed conflict between Germans marching in a Fourth of July parade and onlookers resulted in the death of one of the spectators. That violence led in turn to the construction of an arsenal by the state in 1860 to look over Germans in South Columbus. Built on the site of the original state penitentiary, the arsenal functioned as an armory through World War I. It was later used by the Ohio National Guard and still later became home to the Columbus Cultural Arts Center.[24]

With economic and population growth came spatial expansion, as Columbus moved outward in all directions, but especially to the north and east. By the 1860s and 1870s, factories and warehouses were beginning to migrate outward from the downtown core to the margins of the city. That of Buckeye Steel was one of them. Likewise, only a handful of private residences remained on High Street near the statehouse. Most downtown inhabitants moved east or north. Like most other American cities, Columbus was a walking city in its preindustrial decades, with its inhabitants able to get around the expanding, but still small, town on foot. In the antebellum years residents could easily traipse from their homes to their places of businesses and to the stores they patronized.[25]

## The First Parks in Columbus

Columbus acquired its first public parks in the antebellum years and shortly thereafter. Lincoln Goodale donated 40 acres that he had acquired just north of the city to Columbus as the first public park in 1851. Goodale had prospered as a doctor, pharmacist, and storekeeper in Franklinton and Columbus. He set up a general store and pharmacy in a two-story building on High Street between State and Town streets shortly after Columbus was created. Goodale lived upstairs in the building's second story. There, he did well financially, perhaps becoming the first millionaire in Columbus. Unmarried, Goodale wanted to give something back to Columbus—hence his gift of undeveloped land to create what was only the third urban park in the United States. City officials had underbrush cleared out in 1852, but little else was done until the

24. Lentz, *As It Were*, 60–63. For the details of the 1855 conflict, see Rippley, *Columbus Germans*, 18.

25. There is an extensive literature on America's walking cities and how they changed with the coming of streetcars. For a lucid summary, see Christopher W. Wells, *Car Country: An Environmental History* (Seattle: University of Washington Press, 2013), 9–10.

COLUMBUS O. 2-12-07. &c. 4399

Goodale Park Lake

Figure 4.2. Goodale Park in 1907. Located just north of Columbus's downtown, Goodale Park was intended to be an island of peace and quiet in a growing commercial and industrial city. (Courtesy of the Columbus Metropolitan Library)

park served as a training camp during the Civil War, only to be returned to its parklike appearance after the conflict. By the time Goodale died in 1868, the park featured a large pond with a fountain, a circular drive, and stately trees. It served "as a quiet place to give people refuge from the day-to-day confusion of urban life." By 1885, according to a publication for the Columbus Board of Trade, the park possessed "a growing collection of wild animals," which was expected to "become quite a menagerie."[26] In 1888 sculptor J. Q. A. Ward, who had been born in Urbana, Ohio, was commissioned to prepare a bust of Goodale to grace the park's entrance. Photographs of the park from 1889 to 1890 reveal bucolic scenes, with, however, a telephone pole in the background.[27]

With its restful, peaceful setting, Goodale Park was established in the park tradition of Frederick Law Olmsted, the leading designer of parks in the United States in the nineteenth century, including Central Park in New York City. To planners such as Olmsted, the purpose of

26. Columbus Board of Trade, "Columbus," 74.

27. Arter, *Columbus Vignettes*, vol. 2, p. 14; *Columbus Dispatch*, 25 April 2010, p. G1; Condon, *Yesterday's Columbus*, 53; Lentz, *As It Were*, 15 (the source of the quotation); and Wooley and Van Brimmer, *Second Blessing*, 55–57.

parks was to uplift the human spirit by exposing urbanites to carefully manicured nature, for example, through sinuous drives around meadows and ponds.[28] That Goodale Park did, but over time it also became home to more vigorous activities, including a Fourth of July celebration in 1913. In whatever form, Goodale Park helped pull residents north to build fashionable homes near Capital University, which was then located at Goodale Avenue and High Street, north of railroad yards at Union Station.[29]

Schiller Park in German Village began its life in 1867, when Columbus purchased land in an area called Stewart's Grove for the creation of what was then called City Park. It was soon renamed Schiller Park after the German poet Friedrich von Schiller, and since 1891 it has featured a bronze statue of the poet. Like Goodale Park, Schiller Park possessed beautiful trees, stately drives, and a pond with a fountain, encompassing romantic park ideals. Members of the Columbus Board of Trade touted the park's "rustic bridges and diminutive islands, and well-laid-out drives and walks, with hedges, shrubbery and flowers," which made it "a delightful resort for men, women, and children." Schiller Park was renamed Washington Park during World War I as part of the revulsion many Americans felt for all things German (the Cincinnati city council even banned the serving of pretzels in saloons during the conflict). Anti-German hysteria was short-lived, and after the war the park's name reverted to Schiller Park. The park never totally lost its "uplifting" mission, as Shakespeare's plays were performed there each summer in the late twentieth and early twenty-first centuries.[30]

Franklin Park, just south of East Broad Street and west of Alum Creek, rounded out the major parks created in Columbus by the end of World War I. Franklin Park began as the site for the Ohio State Fair in 1874. The fair remained there until 1886, when it moved to its present location off Seventeenth Avenue. The area was used by local agricultural societies when the fair was not in session and became a city park in 1890. The state fair's horse-racing track could still be discerned in the early 2000s as the 1-mile-long path rimming the park's perimeter. In 1895 a large glass conservatory was put up in the park, inspired by the recently

28. Laura Wood Roper, *FLO: A Biography of Frederick Law Olmsted* (Baltimore: Johns Hopkins University Press, 1973).

29. Ed Lentz, "City's 4th a Quieter Affair in 1913," *Worthington News*, 4 July 2013, p. A6; and Lentz, *Columbus: The Story*, 77. Capital University later moved to Bexley, an independent town just east of Columbus.

30. Arter, *Columbus Vignettes*, vol. 2, p. 12; and Rippley, *Columbus Germans*, 45.

completed Chicago Columbian Exposition. It remained the focus of the park in the early twenty-first century.[31]

In line with Progressive era thinking, in the early 1900s some Columbus residents began pushing for parks and playgrounds that featured active pursuits. Members of the Young Ladies Playground Association and the Federated Women's Clubs began urging the creation of a city recreation department in 1908. Two years later, Columbus officials established just such a recreation department, with an annual budget of $6,000, to oversee ten playgrounds, playing fields, bathing beaches, and an outdoor sports program. By 1912 five recreation centers, offering crafts, sports, and dramatics, had also been opened, one being in the auditorium of city hall. The first city-owned golf course opened in 1920 next to the Dublin Road Water Works.[32]

Columbus residents also used land not officially set aside as parkland for picnics and other outdoor activities. Land around the Dublin Road Water Works quickly became "a Mecca on pleasant Sundays."[33] So did lands around Griggs Reservoir and the waters of the lake. Ice boating developed on the frozen expanse of the reservoir in winter months. A reporter for the *Ohio State Journal* wrote in 1907 that "George C. Urlin, prominent in Columbus business and social circles," had become "the city's pioneer at ice boating." He ran his craft, named *Ice Prince*, on Griggs reservoir at "a clip of 90 miles per hour." A photograph of Urlin and his boat showed a craft with a jib and a very large mainsail.[34]

## Streetcars, Urban Expansion, and Amusement Parks

Columbus underwent tremendous spatial expansion as it grew in population with burgeoning industrialization in the late nineteenth and early twentieth centuries. As late as 1860 most Columbus residents lived in the compressed area between South Public Lane (Livingston Avenue) and North Public Lane (Naughten Street).[35] However, historian Ed Lentz has explained that by the 1890s, "the boundaries of the city were stretching

31. *Columbus Dispatch*, 25 April 2010, p. G1; Lentz, *As It Were*, 64–67; and Rippley, *Columbus Germans*, 9.

32. *Columbus Dispatch*, 25 April 2010, p. G1.

33. City Plan Commission, "Report," 1908, p. 35. On similar developments nationally, see Smith, *City Water*, 145.

34. *Ohio State Journal*, 7 February 1908, p. 4.

35. Weisenburger, *Columbus during the Civil War*, 3–4.

out to well beyond the 2-mile ring one might draw on a map." That ring was the effective walking distance of earlier times. By Columbus's centennial in 1912, the city's boundaries were much farther out from the downtown. By 1920 the city limits were about where they would remain into the 1960s.[36]

Columbus's growth continued to the north. In that direction, city boundaries encompassed the Ohio State University, which had been founded in the 1870s on William Neil's land, and then extended considerably beyond that institution. To the west, Columbus's limits embraced Franklinton, annexed in 1864, and then moved out of the lowlands onto a ridge to which many state institutions, such as the insane asylum, had moved. This area became known as the Hilltop. Eastward, Columbus came to include fashionable neighborhoods along Broad Street toward the town of Bexley across Alum Creek. City boundaries also extended into the industrial district of what became known as the South Side, south of Peter's Run. This district is where Buckeye Steel, like many other industrial enterprises, moved in the early 1900s.

The coming of streetcars allowed Columbus to spread out. The first streetcar venture began operations in Columbus in 1863, a horse-drawn line operating for about a mile and a half along a single track on downtown High Street. Other lines soon followed, until by 1875 they radiated outward from the statehouse in all four directions.[37] The lines shared certain drawbacks: they were slow, only as fast as a horse or a mule could plod, about 3 miles per hour; cars were cold in winter and hot in summer; and the smell of horse manure permeated the air.[38]

The electrification of streetcar lines revolutionized cities. From 1887 to 1888 Richmond, Virginia, opened the first electrical streetcar system in the United States. Faster and more comfortable than horse-drawn cars, electric streetcars quickly replaced animal-powered vehicles. By the close of 1893 streetcar companies had electrified about 7,000 miles of their lines in the United States, 60 percent of the total. Within another decade 98 percent of the lines were electrified, some 30,000 miles. Electric streetcars could carry passengers at 5 miles per hour (or even faster in some cases), allowing people to live farther from their places of work than in

36. Garrett and Lentz, *Crossroads*, 85; Lentz, *Columbus: The Story*, 97; Lentz, *As It Were*, 141–43; and Larry Saylor, "Street Railroads in Columbus, Ohio, 1862–1920," *Old Northwest* 1 (September 1975), 291–315, map after p. 292.
37. Saylor, "Street Railroads," 294.
38. Lentz, *Columbus: The Story*, 98; and Lentz, *As It Were*, 98.

earlier times, encouraging the development of new neighborhoods and suburbs. Walking cities gave way to mechanized ones.[39]

Columbus boasted its first electric streetcar line in 1887, one extending from downtown east along Broad Street to the state fairgrounds in Franklin Park. The city was served by 88 miles of streetcar lines in 1900, nearly all of which had been electrified. By 1910 three major lines extended north, including one that ran up High Street 10 miles to Worthington, well beyond Columbus's northern boundary. Several others went to the northeast. Five lines went east from downtown, including one that reached across Alum Creek into Bexley. Six lines extended west, including two that went to suburbs or villages beyond Columbus's city limits. By contrast, just three short lines served the South Side.[40] Altogether, Columbus possessed 71 miles of streetcar routes, nearly all of which were double-tracked, by 1917.[41]

At about the same time, electric interurban cars, traveling longer distances at higher speeds than streetcars, linked Columbus to nearby towns and cities such as Urbana, Newark, London, Springfield, and Zanesville. By 1916 Ohio was home to 2,869 miles of interurban lines, and Columbus was the hub for eight lines. (Ohio boasted the first interurban line in the United States, one just east of Columbus connecting Newark to Granville. At the time of World War I Ohio possessed the most interurban mileage of any state.) One interurban line extended northwest from Columbus to the town of Magnetic Springs, several miles west of the Scioto River. Attracted by the supposed healing qualities of the spring's waters, about 10,000 people, mainly from Columbus, flocked to the town's bathing establishments and hotels as late as the 1930s. Advances in science and changes in recreational habits led to the town's demise after World War II. Just a handful of houses remained there in the early 2000s.[42]

---

39. Wells, *Car Country*, 14. The classic work on streetcars and urban development is Sam Bass Warner, Jr., *Streetcar Suburbs: The Process of Urban Growth in Boston, 1870–1900* (Cambridge, MA: Harvard University Press, 1962).

40. Andrea D. Lentz, "The Question of Community: The 1910 Street Car Strike of Columbus, Ohio," Master's thesis, Ohio State University, 1970, p. 6. A map of Columbus's streetcar lines and ward boundaries may be found on p. 76.

41. Saylor, "Street Railroads," 291, 304.

42. Arter, *Columbus Vignettes*, vol. 1, p. 55; *Columbus Dispatch*, 18 May 2014, p. B2; Kern and Wilson, *Ohio: A History*, 284; and the author's observations during a trip to Magnetic Springs, 8 March 2014.

Streetcars offered a good example of the combination of public and private planning. Private companies located, designed, built, and operated the lines. However, Columbus's city council regulated how those lines were run by granting them franchises, for which the lines paid the city, which spelled out terms of operation. Individual city ordinances were passed by the council for each franchise. Terms of operation stiffened as time passed. The first franchise, granted in 1862, stipulated little about how the Columbus Street Railroad would serve the public. It set no rates or schedule, nor did it require that the company contribute to the maintenance of the street upon which its tracks ran. Within a year, however, the city required that all franchise street-railroad construction plans be approved by the city's civil engineer and specified that the lines could not impede the free flow of traffic on the streets or the drainage of water from the streets. Later regulations specified distances to be maintained between the cars and set fares. Additional regulations required that the lines help maintain the streets upon which their tracks were built and set schedules by which cars had to run. Speed was limited to 5 miles per hour, and cars were required to be kept in good repair, "so as not to imperil the lives, limbs, or health of passengers."[43]

Electrically powered street railroads brought tighter city regulation. City ordinances stipulated that only straight wooden poles or painted iron ones could carry electric lines for the railroads. The speed limit was raised to 14 miles per hour, but that speed was usually not achieved in Columbus's increasingly crowded downtown. Service intervals were set at 15 minutes between cars on some lines. From 1901 streetcars had to be heated whenever the temperature fell below 35 degrees Fahrenheit. However, motormen's cabs remained in the open and were cold in the winter. One Columbus streetcar operator had his toes frostbitten and as a result left Columbus for the sunny climes of southern California. Columbus city council members became involved in streetcars in other ways. The city built a tunnel under steam-railroad tracks near Union Station in 1875, preventing what might have been massive traffic snarls, since steam lines ran along High Street there. Similarly, in 1891 the city built a bridge for an electric-streetcar line over steam-railroad tracks on Fourth Street. Columbus city councilmen considered having their city own and build street railroads on several occasions, but they never did. Instead, city councilmen kept rates low and terms of service high. The cars were comfortable and cheap. For a nickel, one could ride just about anywhere

---

43. Saylor, "Railroads," 292–301, esp. 296.

in Columbus (or for even less, as a packet of tickets costing a quarter gave seven rides).[44]

With the construction of streetcars, new neighborhoods developed and old ones expanded. "For the most part," historian and archivist Andrea Lentz has explained, "residential construction expanded away from the central business and industrial districts and was furthered by ambitious tract developments as well as individual building." These neighborhoods included Indianola Highlands around the Ohio State University; the Hilltop west of Franklinton; another neighborhood near Franklin Park off Broad Street; and yet another one south of German Village, the previously mentioned South Side. The expansion of electric-streetcar lines and real-estate development went hand in hand.[45] Municipalities served by electric streetcars from Columbus incorporated in the early 1900s: to the west, Marble Cliff in 1901, Grandview Heights in 1906, and Upper Arlington in 1918; to the east, Bexley in 1908; and to the north, Linden Heights in 1908.[46]

Such suburban development was especially typical of midwestern cities. Compared to other regions, the Midwest was a land of homeowners, not renters, with more and more people living in suburbs. In 1890, of the fifty-eight American cities having over 50,000 residents, Toledo ranked first in the percentage of home ownership, at 46 percent. Grand Rapids was number two, with nearly 45 percent, and Milwaukee, Detroit, and Dayton were close behind. In New York City, by contrast, the home-owing proportion of residents was just 6 percent.[47] There was room in the Midwest for cities to spread out, allowing the building of individual homes, a characteristic less typical of eastern areas.

Streetcar and interurban franchisees constructed privately owned amusement parks in Columbus to boost travel and revenues on their lines, as was occurring in many cities across the United States, but especially in the Midwest.[48] The Columbus Railway, Power & Light Company owned Olentangy Park at the end of one of its lines in northern Columbus in 1896. The park's theater was advertised as "the finest summer

44. Ibid, 296, 306.

45. Ibid, 307–8; Andrea Lentz, "Question of Community," 6; and Ed Lentz, *As It Were*, 97–100.

46. Burgess, *Planning*, 38.

47. Teaford, *Cities of the Heartland*, 77.

48. On the development of amusement parks by electric-streetcar companies across the United States, see Lauren Rabinovitz, *Electric Dreamland: Amusement Parks, Movies, and American Modernity* (New York: Columbia University Press, 2012).

amusement palace in this country." It seated 2,248 people and hosted shows twice a day, including "all the leading vaudeville artists, as well as comic operas and minstrel stars." The park boasted a "boat house, dance pavilion[, and] a score of modern park amusements." The street railway company also came to own Minerva Park to the northeast, near a connection with an interurban line running to northern Ohio, on 150 acres, including a lake. This establishment featured bowling alleys, a merry-go-round, a scenic railroad, and a shoot-the-chutes water ride. It also had baseball fields and tennis courts. Its casino could accommodate 2,500 people and offered "shows ranging from light opera to vaudeville and all legitimate theatrical entertainments." Indianola Park in northern Columbus was a third amusement grounds, served by the Fourth Street car line. It boasted the largest swimming pool in Ohio, 140 feet by 238 feet. The city of Columbus provided water and sewer services to those parks within its boundaries. Parks such as these prospered as long as street railroads did, with the last park closing in Columbus in 1937, unable to compete with the radio and movies, and ravaged by the Great Depression of the 1930s.[49]

Streetcar lines had decidedly significant impacts on Columbus and other cities across the United States. With their tracks usually running down the middle of streets, streetcars tended to take over the avenues upon which their tracks ran, especially when their rails were double-tracked, ending most other functions of the streets, for instance, as sites for markets. Markets moved out of streets into buildings next to thoroughfares. Photographs of Columbus make this shift clear. A photograph of the City Market House at Town and High streets in the 1870s shows the substantial structure in the street, but a photograph of the new Central Market at Rich and High streets just before World War I pictures the building at the side of the streets.[50]

Then, too, the northerly and westerly directions of the streets upon which most streetcars ran reinforced the tendency of Columbus to develop along a north-south axis. Water and land developments went hand in hand in shaping Columbus's growth to the north and away from the south. In particular, the downtown began spreading out in a linear fashion north-south along High Street. Into the early twenty-first century

---

49. "Columbus, Ohio, 1900: Illustrated Guide to the City and Pleasure Resorts with Map and Street Railway Directions. Compliments of the Columbus Railway Company" (Columbus: Columbus Railway Company, 1900), unpaged pamphlet. See also Arter, *Columbus Vignettes*, vol. 2, pp. 59, 70; and Condon, *Yesterday's Columbus*, 65–67.

50. Condon, *Yesterday's Columbus*, 36, 72.

Columbus's downtown had an elongated, linear shape, stretching for several miles along High Street. In the early 2000s a proposal, one not yet realized, was posited to reintroduce streetcars or construct a light-rail system in Columbus that would run lines north-south on High Street. A successful downtown circulator bus route established in early 2014 was long and linear. It operated city buses north along High Street from German Village, through the downtown, to the Short North—a boutique area of restaurants, art galleries, shops, and residences—just north of the downtown. Buses returned south on Front Street one block to the west.[51]

A 1922 investigation of street railroads in Columbus specified their impacts on the commerce of the city's thoroughfares, especially High Street. Eight lines, the report observed, converged on High Street in the downtown between Broad and Long streets. More streetcars passed by that point than in any other part of Columbus. Consequently, that area was "the heart of the retail section, from which a string of stores extend in every direction." As car lines turned off High Street, east onto Long Street and west and onto other streets, "the stores decrease a little." North along High Street between Spring Street to Chestnut Street, "a little more pronounced decrease is noticed in the grade of store." Farther north of Chestnut, "a still more pronounced decline takes place." Even so, "thus far High Street has become congested with retail stores." Still farther north, where fewer lines extended, stores were located only at main intersections with High Street: at Fifth Avenue; at Tenth and Eleventh avenues and Woodruff Avenue on the campus of the Ohio State University; and around Arcadia Avenue even farther north.[52]

Columbus's downtown was anchored at its south end by the Lazarus Department Store. A Jewish immigrant from Germany, Simon Lazarus opened a small men's clothing store south of Statehouse Square, three doors from the southwest corner of High and Town streets, in 1851. Benefiting from a demand for clothing during the Civil War, he expanded his shop in 1864 by purchasing an adjacent store. Twelve years later he added a store on a nearby vacant lot. He passed his growing store on to his sons Fred and Ralph in 1877. Fred had come to Columbus from Germany with his parents when he was one year old. He began working in his father's store at age sixteen. Ralph followed in his older brother's footsteps. The brothers bought most of the block around the store

---

51. *Columbus Dispatch*, 23 January 2014, p. B6; and 27 February 2014, p. B4.

52. Forest Ira Blanchard, "An Introduction to the Economic and Social Geography of Columbus, Ohio," Master's thesis, Ohio State University, 1922, pp. 36–38.

to form "one large retail emporium." In 1909 Fred opened a new six-story F. & R. Lazarus & Co. building at the northwest corner of High and Town streets, where it long remained Columbus's leading department store. (Ralph had died in 1903.)

At its height in the mid-twentieth century, the Lazarus Department Store controlled one-third of the retail activity in Columbus, a feat, several historians have noted, "no other store in the country ever matched." Run by four generations of Lazarus men, the store conducted activities that dominated social life for many Columbus residents as well as dominating economic matters. Sales at Lazarus rose from $65,000 in 1880; to $695,000 in 1907; to $13 million in 1929; and to $45 million in 1961 (for clothing alone). Being in the right place at the right time—in a rapidly expanding city whose people needed clothing and home wares—and paying close attention to the precise needs and desires of Columbus residents proved the keys to success. It helped, too, that Simon Lazarus brought $3,000, a substantial sum, with him from Germany to enter business in the United States and that he could depend on family, friends, and religious associates for help. Social capital was always important. The store's seasonal alterations brought people downtown, and its eleven restaurants and many lounges acted as gathering places. Many retailers such as Lazarus clustered along High Street. All of Columbus's retail clothing establishments could be found within a three-block area on that street in downtown Columbus as late as the 1870s.[53]

While streetcars helped downtown merchants such as Simon Lazarus and his sons prosper, they also contributed to downtown congestion, for most had one of their termini there. Numerous lines dropped off and picked up their passengers within just a few blocks of each other. The upward movement of downtown buildings added still more people to downtown crowds.

Columbus acquired its first "cloud scrapers," not yet quite skyscrapers, around the turn of the twentieth century. Designed by Chicago architect Daniel Burnham, the Wyandotte Building opened in 1897 just southwest of Broad and High streets. It stretched eleven stories into the sky. Such buildings were going up in downtowns across the United States, made possible by the use of both steel structures, which replaced older,

---

53. Huntington, "Fred Lazarus," in *Men behind the Guns*, 141-42; Lentz, *As It Were*, 53–55; and Marc Lee Raphael, *Jews and Judaism in a Midwestern Community: Columbus, Ohio, 1840–1975* (Columbus: Ohio State University Press, 1979), 38–41. For more detail, see Meyers, Meyers, and Walker, *Look to Lazarus*, 15 (the source of the quotation), 33, 42, 70, 100.

masonry-bearing walls, and steam-powered (later electric-powered) elevators. Business leaders added even taller, veritable skyscrapers to Columbus's skyline in the 1920s.[54] Tallest was the AIU Citadel (now the LeVeque Tower), which was named after a Columbus-based insurance company, the American Insurance Union, whose workers and executives inhabited it. Completed in 1929, the structure stood 555.5 feet high, half a foot taller than the Washington Monument. One writer has described the building in the following words: "Never merely a monument to the moneychangers, 'the Citadel' was to be the emblem of a new age of fraternal freedom and civic greatness." After the American Insurance Union collapsed during the Great Depression, the building was purchased by Leslie LeVeque, a Columbus developer, and John Lincoln, Chairman of the Cleveland Electric Company, in 1945. The building then became known as the LeVeque Lincoln Tower. In the 1970s the LeVeque family took sole control of the building, which was thereafter called the LeVeque Tower, before selling it to the investment group Tower 10 in 2011. The skyscraper remained a Columbus landmark in the early twenty-first century.[55] Buildings like these made sense downtown, where land was expensive, but by concentrating people in small areas, they added further to congestion.

Automobiles also contributed to that congestion. Henry Ford's Detroit factory began making Model Ts in 1908 and started mass producing them from 1913 to 1914. Historian Christopher Wells has aptly labeled resulting automobile congestion nationwide then as "a deluge of traffic." That traffic led urbanites to try to improve city streets. Smoother street pavements, the elimination of at-grade steam-railroad crossings, and widened streets (which often eliminated public space on sidewalks) helped. So did the use of stop signs, stoplights, and painted street lines, all of which came into use right before World War I. Columbus police employed a large umbrella with "stop" and "go" painted on different sides to regulate the flow of traffic on High Street in 1914, the same year in which Cleveland authorities began using traffic lights. By turning the umbrella,

---

54. On skyscrapers as a midwestern phenomenon, see Teaford, *Cities of the Heartland*, 73.

55. Arter, *Columbus Vignettes*, vol. 1, p. 23; *Columbus Dispatch*, 11 April 2014, p. D2; and Lentz, *As It Were*, 133–36, 169–71. For more detail, see Michael A. Perkins, *Leveque: The First Complete Story of Columbus' Greatest Skyscraper* (Bloomington: Author House, 2004), ix (the source of the quotation). After her husband's death in 1975, Katherine S. LeVeque lived in an apartment high in the tower. She became best known for financing the renovation of the Palace Theatre on the ground level of the building.

**High Street North from Gay Street, Columbus, Ohio.**

Figure 4.3. Regulation of Downtown Traffic with a Street Umbrella in 1914. Columbus's police employed a large umbrella with "stop" and "go" painted on different sides to regulate the flow of traffic on High Street in 1914. (Courtesy of the Columbus Metropolitan Library)

Columbus police changed the direction of traffic. Police traffic squads—designated to untangle traffic jams—and educational programs to inform pedestrians against dangerous behaviors such as jaywalking in cities like New York were also parts of the answer. In 1915 street accidents, many involving pedestrians, killed over two and a half times as many people in New York City as murders: 659 versus 260.[56]

Street improvements in Columbus began after the Civil War, but progress was not easy, as a look at efforts to rebuild the city's major commercial thoroughfare, High Street, shows. Deeply rutted by wartime traffic, High Street was regraveled in 1865, but the gravel did not stand up to the demands of traffic. Next, city officials tried a wood-block pavement, which proved "clean, quiet, and comfortable to ride on." However, a failure to keep up with repairs allowed the wooden pavement to decay. By 1873 the wood blocks were judged to be "a failure." The city council had downtown High Street paved with asphalt in 1875, but again

---

56. Kern and Wilson, *Ohio: A History,* 294; and Wells, *Car Country,* 24, 86–104, esp. 91.

problems developed when repairs were not made in a timely fashion. The basic difficulty was that business owners whose firms fronted High Street had to pay for most repairs. Many were reluctant to do so and dragged their heels, with the result that little was accomplished until 1886. In that year members of the Columbus Board of Trade persuaded state legislators to pass an act allowing Columbus—and only Columbus, among all of Ohio's cities—to sell bonds to finance street improvements. Politicians were tired of getting stuck in mud around their statehouse. High Street promptly received a pavement of first-class asphalt, upon which repairs were kept up.[57]

More generally, Columbus officials increased expenditures on street improvements from $7,032 in 1876 to $1.5 million a decade later. Street construction continued into the early 1890s, with 85 miles of paved roads laid down between 1886 and 1893. However, street building stuttered and then stopped after 1893. City funds were needed for other purposes, such as new water and sewer lines, and Columbus's debt had risen from less than $2 million in 1886 to more than $7 million in 1893. Above all, the onset of a major depression, which lasted for about three years, cut city revenues dramatically.[58]

Private improvements to streets in Columbus occurred from time to time. Occasionally, individual business owners on High Street, discouraged by delays in actions by the city council, made their own street improvements, which resulted in a patchwork of smooth pavements alternating with deep ruts and potholes along the avenue. Then, too, business leaders sometimes beautified streets. William Deshler, a son of Betsy Deshler, paid to have trees planted to line both sides of Broad Street east of the downtown in 1857, making it, by one account, "one of the most beautiful avenues in America." The trees lasted until 1922, by which time automobile exhaust, traffic accidents, and diseases had killed them.[59]

For the most part, however, Columbus streets, like those in other American cities, were in a sad state of disrepair in the early 1900s, barely able to handle the increasing volume of traffic. Columbus residents faced other urban problems. Parts of Columbus—despite growth and, after the depression of the mid-1890s, renewed prosperity—seemed run-down and in need of a facelift to many—in particular, Flytown, located northwest of downtown, and the Bottoms, situated inland from the west bank of the

57. Speer, "Urbanization and Reform," 188–200, esp. 189–90.
58. Ibid.
59. Ibid; and Lentz, As It Were, 39.

Scioto River. These districts were home to poorer blacks and whites and had turned into something like slums. Columbus's downtown waterfront was littered with smoking factories and dilapidated warehouses.[60] Gone were stately homes in the downtown area, shifted east toward Bexley along Broad Street. Columbus's city hall was also glaringly inadequate for the needs of a modern city. In the optimistic Progressive era some Columbus residents sought to remedy these situations through city planning.[61]

They were hardly alone. City dwellers across the United States tried to remake their metropolises through America's first urban-planning movement in the opening decades of the twentieth century. As cities grew tremendously in size and population, turning the United States into an urban nation by 1920, old ways of doing things proved inadequate. Streets were congested to the point of slowing traffic to a standstill and retarding the growth of urban economies; water and sewer systems did not work, leading to epidemics of waterborne diseases; open spaces had nearly disappeared in cities, for few parks existed; and, more generally, the forces of industrialization seemed to be running amok, threatening the established social order. Comprehensive urban planning in what became known as the "City Beautiful movement" (1890s and 1900s) promised solutions. Plans drafted by the nation's first generation of professional city planners encompassed new street systems; civic centers, parks, and boulevards; and, for coastal metropolises, revamped harbor facilities. Planners envisioned all of the separate parts of their plans as operating harmoniously to advance cities economically and socially.[62]

---

60. For one person's look at some of the problems Columbus residents faced, see Charles B. Kolb, "Helping Up the Man Who Is Down; Or, Seven Years in the Slums" (Columbus: no publisher listed, 1910), a thirty-two-page pamphlet available in the library and archives of the Ohio Historical Society (Ohio History Connection). Born in eastern Ohio, Kolb moved to Columbus, found religion, and worked in a Protestant mission house on Seventh Street in downtown Columbus.

61. On urban reform in Columbus during the early 1900s, see Michael Pierce, "Washington Gladden's Columbus: The Politics of Municipal Reform in Columbus, Ohio, 1885–1915," Master's thesis, Ohio State University, 1993.

62. William Wilson, *The City Beautiful Movement* (Baltimore: Johns Hopkins University Press, 1989). Much has been written about Progressive era city planning. For a discussion of the scholarly literature on the City Beautiful movement, see Blackford, *Lost Dream*, 3–11. Much of the City Beautiful movement took its inspiration from efforts to remake Paris in the 1800s. See Stephane Kirkland, *Paris Reborn: Napoleon III, Baron Haussmann, and the Quest to Build a Modern City* (New York: St. Martin's Press, 2013). On the history of city planning in the United States more generally, see John W. Reps, *The Making of Urban America: A History of City Planning in the United States* (Princeton: Princeton University Press, 1965); and Mellior Scott, *American City Planning Since 1890* (Berkeley: University of California Press, 1969). For more-critical accounts of

Planning could be, proponents argued, a way to get cities ahead of urban rivals and a means to dampen conflict among different groups in cities. Business leaders were often in the forefront. They were optimistic about the futures of their metropolises, *if* proper actions—as they defined them—were taken. They were, however, pessimistic in believing that if such actions were not taken, and not taken quickly, their cities would fall behind urban rivals and degenerate into social chaos. Often associated with progressivism, the City Beautiful campaign shared the complexity of that larger movement in trying to look forward to an increasingly urban and industrial nation and at the same time glimpsing backward at an imagined simpler, small-town America. Like those espousing progressivism, proponents of City Beautiful hoped to include many disparate groups and ideas within their ranks.[63]

## The 1908 City Beautiful Plan

In Columbus the City Beautiful planning movement began in 1900 with agitation from members of the Columbus Board of Trade for a "Better and Greater Columbus." Among other matters, this effort resulted in the construction of the water, sewer, and garbage plants as discussed in chapter 2. There was also consideration for "parks, parkways, and playgrounds," beginning with an address to those belonging to the board in the spring of 1902, followed by a similar presentation a year later "through cooperation of the City Federation of Women's Clubs and the Board of Trade."[64]

Mayor Robert Jeffrey was of prime importance in furthering planning. He was the son of Joseph A. Jeffrey, who had been born in Clarksville, Ohio, in 1836. The senior Jeffery had a varied career in finance in Cincinnati and Columbus before entering manufacturing through the purchase of the Lechner Mining Machine Company in the capital city in 1878. By 1906 this firm—with Joseph Jeffrey as its president, and known as the Jeffrey Manufacturing Company—had more than 1,000 employees

city planning, see Christine Boyer, *Dreaming the Rational City: The Myth of American City Planning* (Cambridge, MA: MIT Press, 1983); and Richard Fogelsong, *Planning the Capitalistic City: The Colonial Era to the 1920s* (Princeton: Princeton University Press, 1986).

63. On city planning and reform in the Midwest in the Progressive era, see Teaford, *Cities of the Heartland,* 137–46.

64. City Plan Commission, "Plan," 1908, pp. 5–6.

turning out electrical machinery, elevators, and mining machinery in a large plant on 13 acres of land. Robert Jeffrey was born in 1873. After graduating from Williams College, he attended law school at the Ohio State University but completed his education at a Columbus business college. He worked his way up in Jeffrey Manufacturing, and he was the assistant manager of the works when nominated to become mayor of Columbus by the Republican Party in 1903. Jeffrey was strongly endorsed by the nonpartisan Municipal Union, an organization that had developed over several years to back progressive candidates for office, and he won election handily. He was well known in Columbus by then, having been the President of the Columbus Board of Trade in 1902. As mayor, Jeffrey pushed the city council to pass an ordinance requiring him to establish a commission to prepare plans for a general park system for Columbus late in 1904. The council did so. Jeffrey also won the council's approval for water and sewer plants at about this time. He was, an admiring publication exclaimed, "a young man of wonderful capacity and energy."[65] His administration was generally recognized to be "progressive and honest."[66]

An eighteen-member planning commission appointed by Jeffrey met for the first time on 22 December 1904 and chose George W. Lattimer, a Columbus business leader, as its chairman. Bolstered by a $500 appropriation from the Board of Trade, commission members performed preliminary work on park planning but then turned to three professional planners and architects from New York for advice. The experts were unanimous in recommending further study of "the park and improvement needs of Columbus, not from the esthetic point of view only, but for the comfort of the citizens and the betterment of living conditions." The report of the three outsiders called for the preparation of a plan for "a comprehensive park, playground, and parkway system."[67]

Widespread business and professional support followed. The Board of Trade, the City Federation of Women's Clubs, and the Playground Association were joined by all Columbus newspapers in endorsing the idea of planning. After sponsoring several public meetings on the topic of planning, the city council appropriated $5,000 to employ outside experts to draft a plan for "the streets, alleys, parks, boulevards and public grounds of the City of Columbus" in the fall of 1906. A five-member commission composed of Austin Lord, a New York City architect; Charles Lowrie,

65. Huntington, "Joseph A. Jeffery"; and "Robert H. Jeffrey," both in *Men behind the Guns*, 113-14. See also Arter, *Columbus Vignettes*, vol. 2, p. 71.
66. *Columbus Citizen-Journal*, "Robert H. Jeffrey," in *Columbus Mayors*, unpaged.
67. City Plan Commission, "Plan," 1908, pp. 5-6.

a New York City landscape architect; Albert Kelsey, a Philadelphia architect; H. A. MacNeil, a New York City sculptor; and Charles Mulford Robinson, a nationally known city planner from Rochester, began meeting in early 1907. Three of the five—Robinson, Lowrie, and Lord—had composed the earlier three-member commission, and the other two, Kelsey and MacNeil, had been involved in designing a monument to William McKinley, which had been placed on the statehouse grounds. (Robert Jeffrey served as a member of the commission that oversaw the siting of the sculpture, which was dedicated in the fall of 1906.) The five commissioners knew Columbus well. After meeting throughout 1907, sometimes in Columbus, at other times in New York City, they presented their plan as a report to the mayor and city council of Columbus in early 1908.[68]

The commissioners thought big. They took as their scope the city of Columbus and its surrounding areas. They sought especially to "harmonize" the city's different functions as a political, industrial, and educational center. To do so, they called for substantial alterations and additions to the physical layout of Columbus, operating, in a manner typical of progressives, on the assumption that environmental changes would alter the character and behavior of the city's inhabitants for the better. Above all, the commissioners sought orderliness and system. Their plan, they averred, would assure Columbus residents of "beauty, harmony, economy, and convenience."[69]

They began their report by suggesting ways to make streets more efficient and beautiful. They recognized a hierarchy of streets: parkways linking parks to avenues, avenues rapidly carrying heavy city traffic, streets conveying less traffic at slower speeds, and alleys and rural footpaths. The commissioners recommended improvements for each type in such matters as paving and widening. They wanted sidewalk obstructions to be removed, and they desired that limits be placed on street-sign advertising. Below-ground public toilets would grace streets near the statehouse, as would above-ground public art in the form of "civic sculpture" and attractive benches. A large open-air pool should, they thought, be built near the statehouse. Like reformers in other cities, planners in Columbus believed that clean working-class citizens would be less susceptible to disease and would be less disorderly. Steam-railroad, interurban, and electric-streetcar street crossings needed to be eliminated or made safer.

---

68. Ibid, 6–7.
69. Ibid, 9–10, 26.

Similarly, bridges, viaducts, and stations should be upgraded and beautified. The commissioners urged making the "coordination and systematiz-
ing" of railroads and street railroads operating in Columbus the subject
of a future report. For the time being, they recommended that all unnec-
essary trolley-wire and electric-wire poles be taken down.[70]

Next the commissioners turned from streets to parks, for they saw the
two as intricately related. Employing standard arguments of their day, the
commissioners stressed that parks needed to be made available for everyone, including "the working population." Everyone in Columbus would
benefit from parks, because parks would boost private property values,
"immensely increase the efficiency of labor," and "attract to the city a
better class of labor." Social control was implicit throughout the 1908
planning scheme. The business and professional men and women pushing the plan were certain that they knew what was best for other groups
in Columbus. Moreover, parks and parkways, planners claimed, would
help Columbus in its competition with other cities by making Columbus
a more enjoyable place in which to live. As with streets, the commissioners recognized a hierarchy of parks. There should be, they thought,
small parks and playgrounds within about half a mile of the homes of all
Columbus residents. Schoolyards might be used as playgrounds, if up-to-
date play equipment such as swings and teeter-totters were provided.[71]

The commissioners called for the creation of four large "interior"
parks, linked by a circular boulevard and parkway 100 to 300 feet wide
around Columbus. Heading the list was a park complex for the South
Side, which, for once, received its due. This proposed park's features
included "a recreation park, a long river promenade and speedway, free
from street crossings, and two driveways." The recreation park would be
sited "on the tract next west of the Scioto and on both sides of Greenlawn
Avenue" to the south. Second would be a Westside Park across the Scioto
River from downtown, to be reached by proposed parkways from the
south and northeast and via a beautified Broad Street bridge. The park
grounds would consist of two parts: "The highland, or westward section, breezy, well shaded, and with fine outlooks, is admirably fitted for
general park purposes. The lowland, or eastward section, which is about
a third of the total area, is well-suited for athletic fields, playgrounds,
and water features." The commissioners were always trying to balance
older park ideas, which favored relaxed, serene, scenic vistas, with newer

70. Ibid, 13–24.
71. Ibid, 27–29.

park concepts stressing orderly, but vigorous, exercise. Third, a Northern Park might be constructed inland along the Olentangy River to the north of Goodale Street. It would be "naturally of a quiet and restful character" but would also include playgrounds. Finally, Franklin Park could be upgraded to become an eastern interior park along Alum Creek featuring "open lawns, offering pleasant far views." The park would also contain playgrounds and a lake, which might be used for swimming in the summer and ice skating during the winter.[72]

Beyond the circular boulevard linking the four interior parks would be "large, outlying reservations or country parks." They would serve as destinations for "all-day outings, as objective points for drives and rides" and would "preserve forever to the public the most beautiful of the surrounding scenery." Radial streets emanating from downtown Columbus would give city residents easy access, the commissioners thought, to the countryside parks. The boundary between city and country could thus be blurred. The commissioners urged consideration of the creation of several specific country parks. They wanted one to be created 5 or 6 miles to the southwest of Columbus, another along the "romantic" Olentangy River south of Worthington, and yet a third around Griggs Reservoir.[73]

A proposed civic center focusing on the statehouse provided the keystone to the 1908 plan for Columbus. This center would be "the heart of the city, that center of life blood, in a civic and traffic sense, of the community." The commissioners recommended sprucing up the statehouse to restore it to its 1850 design. An open mall or parkway flanked by monumental governmental and office buildings would extend westward across the Scioto River, opening a pleasing vista for Columbus residents. Just east of the statehouse would be "a City Hall, a future Government Building, possibly other State Buildings, an Art Gallery and a Music Hall." The governor's mansion would be nearby.[74]

The commissioners closed their plan with the statement that they fully realized that an undertaking of this kind is "not to be entirely achieved in one generation, or, perhaps, in several."[75] They were correct. The plan and models of it were put on public display at the office of the Board of Trade in early 1908. Columbus's city newspapers reported favorably on the plan, especially the section devoted to the capital mall on the Scioto River. However, like the commissioners, newspaper reporters

72. Ibid, 29, 33, 42, 44.
73. Ibid, 45–46.
74. Ibid, 47–56.
75. Ibid, 57.

THE PROPOSED CIVIC CENTER

Figure 4.4. The Proposed Civic Center Looking West in 1908. A proposed civic center focusing on the statehouse provided the keystone to the 1908 plan for Columbus. (From the 1908 plan, p. 51)

questioned whether the plans would ever be adopted "on account of their enormous cost."[76]

The consideration of a city plan in Columbus was part of a more general "civic revival" taking place in urban centers across Ohio and the Midwest. Writing about midwestern progressivism in the early 1950s, historian Russell Nye observed, "The Midwest's spirit of protest is simply its own, compounded out of its geography, its culture, its economic and social history." He thought it was an attempt "to reaffirm eighteenth-century democratic faith and to preserve it against the rising tide of skepticism, and, as they called it, 'plutocracy.'"[77] Several decades later, historian Jon Teaford added, "The Midwest led the nation not only in industrial advances but in the effort to right the wrongs of city government." He further noted, "The region's self-designation as the promised land of democracy combined with its boundless confidence and its Germanic homeowning electorate thus made it ripe for reform messages."[78] Reforming politics, particularly in Toledo and Cleveland, and adopting segments of city plans were part and parcel of the reawakening of civic spirit in the Progressive era. This civic revival in Ohio represented "the reawakening of the faith in cities as positive agents of civilization."[79]

That was true to some degree in Columbus, certainly much more so than in Cincinnati, where old-style city bosses ruled. Columbus was an exciting and innovative place to be in the Progressive era. Some business leaders, such as S. P. Bush of Buckeye Steel, ran state-of-the-art factories based on principles of efficiency and welfare capitalism.[80] Mayors such as Robert Jeffrey worked with nationally known engineers such as John Gregory and the Hoover brothers to remake their city's water system and

76. *Columbus Evening Dispatch,* 4 February 1908, pp. 1, 4 (the source of the quotation). See also *Ohio State Journal,* 4 February 1908, pp. 1, 8.

77. Russell B. Nye, *Midwestern Progressive Politics: A Historical Study of Its Origins and Development, 1870–1950* (East Lansing: Michigan State University Press, 1951), 3, 27.

78. Teaford, *Cities of the Heartland,* 111–13.

79. Robert H. Bremner, "The Civic Revival in Ohio: The Fight against Privilege in Cleveland and Toledo, 1899–1912," PhD diss., Ohio State University, 1943, p. 4. On Toledo, see Shirley Leckie, "Brand Whitlock and the City Beautiful Movement in Toledo, Ohio," *Ohio History* 91 (1982), 5–36. On Cleveland, see Stradling and Stradling, *Where the River Burned,* 102. For an overview of urban reform in Ohio, see Kern and Wilson, *Ohio: A History,* 324–31. For a summary of developments in Ohio's northern cities, see Cayton, *Ohio: The History of a People,* 220–26.

80. Mansel G. Blackford, "Scientific Management and Welfare Work in Early Twentieth Century American Business: The Buckeye Steel Castings Company," *Ohio History* 90 (Summer 1981), 238–58.

end waterborne diseases. Some Protestant ministers preached the "social gospel," which emphasized changing society for the better, especially for working-class urbanites. Nationally recognized Washington Gladden, speaking from the pulpit of the First Congregational Church at Broad and High streets, a post he assumed in 1882 at the age of forty-six, was best known. He served a term as a reforming member of the Columbus city council from 1901 to 1902.[81]

Over a century of time, many of the parks postulated in Columbus's 1908 plan were constructed, as were some of the civic-center buildings and streets. However, no mall with a vista west across the Scioto River appeared, except for about a year during the mid-1980s, when the demolition of a downtown building to make way for new construction briefly opened that view, which was indeed magnificent. The 1908 plan was never realized in anything approaching its entirety, and little was immediately accomplished in the Progressive era.

Several reasons accounted for the failure of Columbus residents to adopt the 1908 plan. Other issues, most notably the need for the new water and sewer plants, were more pressing and consumed available city funds. The coming of World War I also made Columbus's City Beautiful plan seem much less urgent. Then, too, the plan had limitations that detracted from its appeal. It said little about major concerns of many Columbus residents, such as improved housing. Housing simply was not a concern of most urban planners then. In fact, the Columbus plan called for the destruction of decayed housing without putting forward any ideas about where displaced inhabitants would live. One person's slum was, of course, another's home. Nor did the plan consider the impacts of automobiles very much, which is perhaps understandable since they were in their infancy. The Columbus Auto Club had only ninety members in 1906. The advent of mass automobility would soon make large portions of the Progressive era's City Beautiful plans obsolete. Americans' embrace of cars made urban planning much more difficult in the United States than in European nations, where public transportation systems long ruled the day. The Columbus plan was also silent about Columbus's employment base and population structure.[82]

---

81. Pierce, "Gladden's Columbus," 3. On Gladden's ideas see Jacob H. Dorn, *Washington Gladden: Prophet of the Social Gospel* (Columbus: Ohio State University Press, 1966).

82. For brief discussions of Columbus's 1908 plan, see Burgess, *Planning*, 22; and Lentz, *Columbus: The Story*, 111–13.

The Columbus plan was typical of other City Beautiful schemes across the United States. Streets, parks, and civic centers received much more attention than did the lived experiences of people. Asked about her city's 1908 plan in 1991, one of Columbus's leading urban planners— Beth Clark, the supervisor of the city's master plan—characterized it as "romantic" and "not tied in with the decision-making process." Continuing, she observed, "Ours is more practical. What we're after here is a decision-making tool with a lot of community participation." Critics rejoined, however, that the planning process of the early 1990s failed to produce the kinds of "stirring ideas" found in the 1908 plan. Planning, they thought, had become too tied up in technicalities and did not consider human experiences broadly enough.[83]

## The City Beautiful Plan and the Neighborhoods

Most basically, Columbus's city plan failed to win wholesale adoption because planners and their backers wanted to force middle-class values on others, who resisted that effort. Conflict accompanied planning. Class, ethnic, and racial differences separated Columbus residents. Columbus hosted immigrants from southeast Europe in the late nineteenth and early twentieth centuries, part of a massive migration to the United States. By 1910 about 9 percent of Columbus residents had been born outside of the United States. Then, too, African American communities further developed in Columbus, as blacks moved from the South to northern cities as part of the Great Migration before, during, and after World War I.[84] Columbus's African American population doubled during the war. In 1910 about 7 percent of Columbus residents were African American, compared to 2 percent of Cleveland's and 5 percent of Cincinnati's. By 1930 some 81 percent of people living in Columbus were native whites, but another 8.4 percent were foreign-born whites, and 10.6 percent were African Americans.[85]

Groups of African Americans were scattered over much of the city by the start of World War I. A sizable group lived just north of the Ohio

---

83. As quoted in "1908 Columbus Planners," *Columbus Dispatch,* 22 April 1991.

84. Blanchard, "Geography"; and Lentz, *Columbus: The Story,* 109–11. On African Americans in Ohio between 1880 and 1930, see Kern and Wilson, *Ohio: A History,* 302–7. African Americans composed about 5 percent of the state's population in 1930.

85. William Kaufman, "The Neighbors of the South Side Settlement, 1940," Master's thesis, Ohio State University, 1943.

State University, and another resided farther south around Fifth Avenue close to railroad lines and many industries. A third black group lived a mile west of the Olentangy River, between King Avenue and North Star Avenue, where they owned "small patches of cultivated ground." "In the heart of the city," African American groups resided in Flytown, on the eastern bank of the Olentangy River, and in an area south of Broad Street along the Scioto River. Some blacks also lived in Steelton, a district of the South Side. Others lived in the Hilltop, west of Franklinton. This group was "the most prosperous" and was reported as possessing "neat, attractive homes."[86]

While African Americans lived throughout many sections of Columbus, their segregation in the East Side was increasing. An investigator for the Ohio State University, Mary Louise Mark, found that by the time of World War I, "While negro real estate men denied the statement that negroes depreciate land values around them, they told the writer of numerous cases of white people selling at a sacrifice in order to leave negro sections and of the refusal of whites to buy property in communities where negroes lived." The same report observed the development by World War I of a particularly large black area "known as the East Long Street district located two blocks north of Broad Street," forming "a long, narrow strip running parallel to Broad Street for a distance of two miles."[87] J. S. Himes Jr., a historian studying the racial situation in Columbus in 1942, concluded that by World War I, "one after another the privileges enjoyed by old [African American] residents were denied— theaters, hotels, cafes, restaurants, public places."[88] Jim Crow had come to Columbus, as "black access to white hospitals, movie houses, schools, hotels, and restaurants was uniformly restricted by the 1920s."[89]

Segregated schools served Columbus students from the 1850s. By 1855 four all-black schools "dotted the east Side, serving virtually all of the city's black schoolchildren." African American students were consolidated in one larger school in 1871, until that dilapidated establishment was torn down a decade later. A period of school integration followed, after the Ohio Supreme Court declared in 1888 that local school boards could not maintain separate schools for blacks and whites.

---

86. Blanchard, "Geography," 79–82.

87. For more details on African American population changes in Columbus between 1890 and 1920, see Himes, "Forty Years," 141–43; and Mark, *Negroes in Columbus,* 5–29, esp. 5–6, 77 (the sources of the quotations).

88. Himes, "Forty Years," 150.

89. Jacobs, *Getting around Brown,* 7.

Nonetheless, all-black schools returned to Columbus with the opening of the Champion Avenue Elementary School in 1909. Members of the Columbus School Board manipulated attendance boundaries to create four additional all-black schools by the early 1940s. Segregated schools remained the norm for decades. By 1964 Columbus had fifty schools that were either all-white or all-black. Only federal-court-ordered desegregation altered this situation in the late 1970s, a topic dealt with in chapter 5.[90]

Two communities absorbed many of the immigrants from southeast Europe. One was Flytown, an approximately twenty-five-block area roughly square in shape with about half a mile on each side. Situated west of Neil Avenue north of downtown, it took the Olentangy River as its western boundary and railroad yards and industrial plants—Columbus Forge & Iron, Columbus Coop Foundry, the Simplex Foundry, and the like—as it southern limits. Early residents included Irish, German, and Welsh immigrants. However, in the late nineteenth and early twentieth centuries, Italian immigrants, among others from southern and Eastern Europe, came to live there in increasing numbers, forming "Italian Village." St. Francis of Assisi Church, built in 1895 on Buttles Avenue, became a religious and social center. Not far away was a Greek Orthodox church, signaling the contribution of Greek immigrants to life in Columbus. An investigator in 1922 observed of Flytown that it had "long been a foreign section." Continuing, his report noted that in its early days Flytown was dominated by "north European nationalities" but that it was "changing to south European nationalities." A smaller Italian community existed for a time in the unincorporated village of San Margherita on the west side of the Scioto River, near where Italians quarried stone.[91]

The South Side attracted even more immigrants from southeast Europe, along with African Americans and white Appalachians. Part of the South Side had been well established by German immigrants in the nineteenth century. They settled in the northern and western portion in a district soon known as "German Village," some 233 acres bounded by Livingston Avenue on the north and Nursery Lane to the south.[92] Farther east and south in the South Side lived Greeks, Italians, Poles, Hungarians, and members of other immigrant groups, intermingled with African

90. Ibid, 12–15.

91. Blanchard, "Geography," 87–88, 92; Burgess, *Planning*, 16; and Hunker, *A Personal Geography*, 113–16, esp. 113.

92. Jody H. Graichen, *Remembering German Village* (Charleston, SC: History Press, 2010).

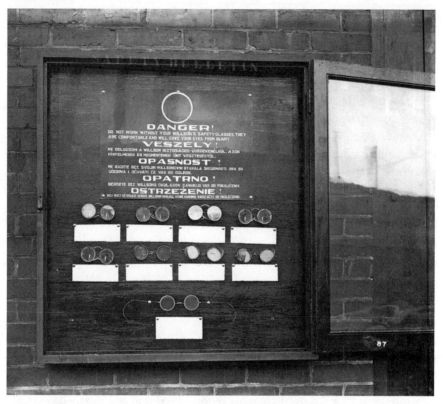

**Figure 4.5.** Safety Poster at Buckeye Steel Castings in 1915. Printed in many languages, this safety poster suggested the southern and Eastern European origins of workers in heavy industry in factories in Columbus's South Side. (From the author's collection)

Americans and whites increasingly from Appalachia.[93] By 1922 the area was home to "about a dozen nationalities."[94]

Part of the South Side became known as "Steelton," where Buckeye Steel Castings, Carnegie Steel, American Rolling Mills, Federal Glass, Keever Starch, and other industrial ventures had factories. Executives at Buckeye Steel Castings printed safety notices in a wide range of southern and Eastern European languages and sponsored English-language and "Americanization" classes for their workers. The many factories contributed to the "south end smell." In the early 1900s the letterhead of the

---

93. Hunker, *A Personal Geography,* 109–13; and Lentz, *Columbus: The Story,* 127–29.

94. Blanchard, "Geography," 91.

stationery of Buckeye Steel proudly showed the company's plant belching thick, black smoke into the air from numerous smokestacks, a symbol of economic progress. The odor also owed a lot to Columbus's sewer plant, just to the west. The stench persisted into the early 2000s, retarding regional growth.[95]

Conflict occurred in Columbus's multicultural society, with ethnic, racial, and class friction boiling over. Most violent was a strike by street-car men in 1910, just two years after the park commissioners had sub-mitted their city plan to Columbus's mayor and city council. Striking for better working conditions and higher wages, the men were opposed by strikebreakers, city police, and, at times, members of the Ohio National Guard. "Carmen and strikebreakers clashed repeatedly, exchanging bar-rages of rocks, bricks, rotten eggs, and gunfire," historian Andrea Lentz has observed. The strike dragged on for months and tore apart the social fabric of Columbus.[96] In the immediate wake of the strike, offi-cers of Columbus's leading manufacturing firms—including former mayor Robert Jeffrey of Jeffrey Manufacturing and S. P. Bush of Buckeye Steel Castings—formed the Ohio Manufacturers' Association. The organiza-tion was established, according to the secretary of its executive commit-tee, "to offset the organization of labor and socialistic interests." Bush served as the body's second president in 1912.[97] Racial violence was less common in Columbus than in other Midwest cities, but it did occur. A 1913 report observed of Columbus, "It is not so much a rabid feeling of prejudice against the Negroes because their skin is black as it is a bit-ter hatred of them because they are what they are in character and hab-it."[98] Columbus was one of the midwestern cities in which the Ku Klux Klan was reborn and thrived during and immediately after World War I. In 1924 hundreds of members of the Klan marched through downtown

---

95. On the continuing South Side smell, see *Columbus Dispatch,* 18 September 2003, p. C1; 12 June 2005, p. A1; 15 September 2011, p. B3; and 11 November 2013, p. B1. Mike Harden, a well-known journalist for the *Columbus Dispatch,* wrote in 2005 of Steelton, "The neighborhood was a stew of Hungarians, Italians, Slovenians, and Croa-tians. Appalachians arrived daily." As quoted in Meyers, Meyers, and Walker, *Look to Lazarus,* 142.

96. Andrea Lentz, "Question of Community," 9. On the violence, see also Moore, *Franklin County,* vol. 1, pp. 239–40. Columbus was a center for labor organization, with the American Federation of Labor formed at a meeting in the city in 1886 and the United Mine Workers of America organized at another meeting there four years later.

97. Ohio Manufacturers' Association, "Executive Committee's Report," 28 April 1914, Ohio Manufacturers' Papers, the Ohio Historical Society (Ohio History Connec-tion) library and archives.

98. As quoted in Himes, "Forty Years," 136.

**Figure 4.6.** The Industrialized South Side in 1915. Industrial work dominated life in Columbus's South Side. (From the author's collection)

Columbus in full regalia on their way to burn a cross in a public park.[99] Columbus society was thus fragmented along several lines, and comprehensive urban planning faded in the contentious atmosphere.

Even had Columbus residents wanted to immediately implement the entire 1908 plan for their city—and most did not—political considerations would have made that proceeding difficult. In the state of Ohio, municipalities were creatures of the state. That is, throughout the nineteenth century and into the twentieth century, the state government retained large powers over what cities could and could not do. Only with statewide approval of a new state constitution by public vote in 1912 did Ohio's cities attain "home rule"—that is, freedom from many state-imposed restrictions on municipal actions. Home rule meant that city officials had more power to run city affairs without having to obtain the approval of state legislators. Columbus adopted a new city charter under

---

99. Lentz, *Columbus: The Story*, 110. On racial violence and the revival of the Ku Klux Klan in Ohio, see Kern and Wilson, *Ohio: A History*, 306, 368–70.

the terms of that state constitution in 1914, setting the stage for future planning activities.

There were downsides to the new municipal arrangement, however. Under the new city charter, Columbus had seven councilmen elected at-large, replacing an eighteen-member city council elected from nine wards. More efficient, the new council was not necessarily more democratic than the old one. In fact, it tended to be dominated by businessmen and professional men who had name recognition and who could afford to run citywide campaigns. The charter effectively disenfranchised African Americans. Since voting was citywide, not by ward, African Americans, who had earlier sent black representatives to city council, no longer did so. They lacked the citywide presence needed to vote members of their communities into office.[100]

## Land Use and Planning during the Progressive Era

The conflicts taking place in Columbus before World War I were harbingers of later discussions and disagreements about how best to develop the city's downtown and neighborhoods, conversations extending into the early 2000s. Over at least a century of time, tensions have existed between different groups on these issues. While most Columbus residents probably backed the general idea of city planning in the Progressive era, they disagreed on many of the details, and, as has often been the case, "the devil is in the details." Friction continued into the early 2000s on land-use matters, as we shall see in the next chapter. In that chapter we shall also observe how Columbus residents continued to try to shape their city through a mixture of public and private actions. We shall see as well additional tensions between business developments and environmental changes, with shifts in the balance between the two. Less was accomplished in Columbus in land-use planning than in water-use matters. Urgency was lacking. Nothing similar to the cholera and typhoid epidemics, which catalyzed planning for clean water, energized planning for land use. To the contrary, Columbus residents, who were unified on water matters, proved to be divided along many lines on land issues and remained so into the twenty-first century.

---

100. Pierce, "Gladden's Columbus," 1; and Himes, "Forty Years," 136–37, 177.

CHAPTER 5

# Land Use and
# Urban Development

Closely intertwined public and private efforts continued to shape land use in Columbus after World War I. Like other people in many cities across the United States, large and small, Columbus residents adopted a public zoning code. City officials drafted their original code in 1923, revised it in 1948 and 1949, and largely rewrote it in 1954 and later years. Even more important in determining land use, however, were covenants to private deeds. Beginning in the early 1900s and spreading to common use during the 1920s and later decades, restrictive covenants specified who could live where in what types of dwellings, again as was typical of developments in cities throughout the United States. The continuing expansion of their city led Columbus citizens to engage in some forms of regional planning after World War II, even as they refined zoning and covenants. The decisions of city officials affecting the downtown, suburbs, and shopping centers also became increasingly important in shaping the contours of growth. The development of a metropolitan park system and a regional zoo and aquarium were part of this evolution.

This chapter examines the exigencies of modern land-use planning in a typical midwestern city, especially how interactions between public and private efforts shaped that metropolis. Reflecting the changing nature of Columbus, this chapter sprawls a bit to cover the widening variety of issues important to land use in the city.

## Public Zoning and Private Covenants

Turning away from City Beautiful schemes, which increasingly seemed overly romantic, American urban planners and reformist-minded lawyers working with them embraced zoning, which seemed to be a more hardheaded, more practical way to try to channel the development of cities. For planners and reformers, zoning promised to end housing and street congestion by specifying exactly what types of buildings could be constructed in each section of a city and designating how many people could live in them. Population densities, reformers thought, could be controlled and slums eliminated. Cities would become more livable places, as commercial and industrial establishments were excluded from residential neighborhoods. Planners were often joined by real-estate agents eager to have city officials zone land uses in ways that allowed them to develop exclusive subdivisions featuring high-priced homes. Private and public efforts to control land use went hand in hand, as developers wrote restrictive covenants into deeds of the house plots they sold. Covenants spelled out what types of houses might be constructed on what sizes of lots and who might live in the houses. Those private covenants often preceded public zoning, with zoning ordinances frequently simply adopting provisions from covenants.[1]

Planning seemed urgent, as American cities spread outward during the 1920s and later. Electric streetcars began urban decentralization, but it was furthered by Americans' embrace of automobiles. Automobile registrations soared from 77,400 in 1905 to more than 8 million in 1920 in the United States, providing vehicles for the expansion and dispersal of cities and their suburbs. And dispersal there was. During the 1920s in the eighty-five American cities having populations of 100,000 people or more, the populations of suburban areas grew an average of 39 percent, while those of urban areas rose just 19 percent. People moved out from cities' cores. The Great Depression slowed, but did not halt, this type of growth. In 1940, 13 million Americans lived in urban or suburban districts not served by public transportation but reached only by automobiles. Most of the suburbanites of the 1920s were relatively wealthy, people in the top one-fifth of America's income distribution. This

---

1. For discussions of zoning in general, see Burgess, *Planning*, 1–5, 59–79; and Marc Weiss, *The Rise of the Community Builders: The American Real Estate Industry and Urban Land Planning* (New York: Columbia University Press, 1987).

phenomenon contrasts with that which occurred during mass suburban-ization after World War II. Then, the middle three-fifths of Americans as measured in terms of income began moving outward.[2]

Expansion in Columbus followed national trends, as the city annexed 7,600 acres, about 12 square miles, during the 1920s. Additions con-tinued in later decades, with Columbus growing in size from 24 square miles in 1920 to 135 square miles in 1970. At the latter date, 549,000 of the 833,249 people living in Franklin County resided in Columbus proper, with the rest living in independent municipalities.[3] Historian Ed Lentz has observed of Columbus during the 1920s, "A whole new gener-ation of automobile suburbs sprung up around the city beyond the 3- and 4-mile ring of streetcar suburbs." Many of the suburbs, such as Bexley and Upper Arlington, were populated by residents in the top one-fifth of Americans in terms of income distribution. However, others, like Clin-tonville and Hilltop, then considered suburbs, were more solidly middle class, foreshadowing developments after World War II. All of them owed their expansion to the automobile.[4]

City officials began zoning land use within Columbus's boundaries in the early 1920s. As allowed by their new city charter of 1914, city coun-cilmen set up a six-member planning commission chaired by the mayor in 1921 and charged that body with drafting a zoning ordinance "in the interest of the public health, safety, convenience, comfort, prosperity of general welfare." After consulting with Robert Whitten, a nationally known urban planner, the commissioners presented the councilmen with a zoning proposal covering all of the land within Columbus's boundaries, which the councilmen in turn adopted as a city ordinance on 6 August 1923. The city had no other comprehensive urban plan at the time. As in most other American cities, zoning preceded other forms of planning.[5]

The 1923 zoning code designated five ways that land might be used. In dwelling-house districts "tenement houses, apartment houses, stores, and industries" were prohibited. Only family homes were allowed. Moreover, dwelling-house districts were subdivided. Those zoned for

2. Wells, *Car Country*, 87, 161.

3. Burgess, *Planning*, 7, 43, 116.

4. Lentz, *Columbus: The Story*, 113. On the expansion of Clintonville and the northern march of Columbus's boundary to Morse Road by 1927, see Lentz, *As It Were*, 178.

5. As quoted in Burgess, *Planning*, 80–81. On the composition of the commission, see City of Columbus, City Planning Commission, "The Columbus Zone Plan, 1923" (Columbus: City Government, 1923), 2.

single-family houses required at least 4,800 square feet per lot. However, only 2,400 square feet per family were needed in areas where two-family homes were permitted. Apartment-house districts were subdivided into three types of areas according to how large lots were per family: 1,200 square feet (thus allowing four families on a standard lot of 4,800 square feet), 600 square feet (eight families), and lots having no density restrictions, intended for hotels. Front and back yards were required of all dwellings. "Grass and trees," the commissioners observed, "make an attractive home environment and are almost essential to the normal and healthful development of children." Sentiments of the 1908 City Beautiful plan, stressing the impact of the environment on character development, were echoed in that statement.[6]

The plan defined commercial districts and two types of industrial districts. The scheme recognized a central business district downtown, where commercial establishments might intermingle with light industries such as newspaper printing. The zoning plan called for "a large expansion" of this area. During the mid-1920s and into the 1930s, Columbus business and political leaders secured passage for important bond issues to rebuild the downtown, which had not fully recovered from the ravages of the 1913 flood, actions that helped pave the way for growth after World War II. The 1923 zoning plan also recognized the need for "local business centers" at "approximately half mile intervals throughout the residence sections," where no industry was allowed. Two types of industrial districts won recognition. In the first type "certain semi-nuisance industrial processes" were not permitted, but in a second type they were. These industries included "chemical plants, gas plants, boiler-making, structural iron works." Some sorts of industrial businesses were excluded from within Columbus's city limits altogether, harking back to ordinances of the 1820s and 1830s: tanneries, slaughterhouses, cement making, and fertilizer manufacturing.[7]

The 1923 zoning plan set four height restrictions for different types of buildings: 50 feet, 75 feet, 100 feet, and 150 feet. Taller buildings could be constructed within specified height districts only if the taller portions of the buildings were set back in staircase fashion from lot lines: 1 foot back for every 2 feet of additional height in the 50-foot and 75-foot districts, and 1 foot for every 3 feet in the other two. To make zoning palatable to property owners, the commissioners specified that the zoning ordinance would apply only to future construction; it would "not affect existing

---

6. Planning Commission, "Zone Plan," 3–9, esp. 9.
7. Ibid, 9–10; and Garrett and Lentz, *Crossroads,* 128.

uses of property." Housing was allowed in commercial and industrial districts, but not vice versa. Nor were apartments allowed in dwelling-house districts. A building inspector would enforce the zoning ordinance, and the plan specified that "no building permit will be issued unless the building and its proposed use conform to the zoning regulations."[8]

The commissioners closed their plan with a long section justifying zoning. "Zoning," they stated, was "a conscious, intelligent effort to direct the building of the city in accord with a well-considered plan." Like "good industrial management," they asserted, the plan would bring about "orderly growth and expansion of plans." More specifically, zoning would, they concluded, prevent "the development of great blighted areas" and "congestion of population." Zoning, they claimed, would spur economic growth in Columbus and help their city move ahead of urban competitors. Above all, zoning would "conserve property values" and "attract money . . . for investment in real estate."[9] City councilmen adopted all of the specifics in the commissioners' plan as Columbus's first city zoning ordinance.

By this time, the 1923 zoning report pointed out, twenty-two American cities had adopted zoning codes, placing 27 percent of the nation's urban population in zoned municipalities.[10] People in Los Angeles had adopted a comprehensive zoning code in 1908, followed by residents in New York eight years later. Zoning received a significant boost in 1924, when the U.S. Department of Commerce, led by Herbert Hoover, drafted and disseminated the Standard Zoning Enabling Act nationwide. A further impetus came two years later, when the Supreme Court of the United States upheld the constitutionality of zoning by municipalities, even though zoning infringed on private property rights, in a case in involving the small northern Ohio town of Euclid, *Euclid v. Ambler*. By 1928 residents in 525 American cities had adopted municipal zoning plans, and by 1930 some nine hundred had, encompassing 80 percent of American urbanites in zoned communities.[11]

Nor was zoning limited to the United States. Frankfurt, Germany, is usually recognized as the first city to engage in comprehensive zoning,

8. Planning Commission, "Zone Plan," 11–12.
9. Ibid, 18–19, 22.
10. Ibid, 24.
11. Burgess, *Planning*, 72. For more detail, see Theodora Kimball Hubbard and Henry Vincent Hubbard, *Our Cities To-Day and To-Morrow: A Survey of Planning and Zoning Progress* (Cambridge, MA: Harvard University Press, 1929); and Seymour I. Toll, *Zoned American* (New York: Grossman Publishers, 1969).

doing so in 1891. In Great Britain paternalistic employers set up strictly zoned company towns, such as William Lever's Port Sunlight near Liverpool, just a short time later; and in 1932 and 1947 the parliament passed legislation allowing towns and cities to engage in zoning.[12] Zoning spread to Japanese cities during the 1920s and later decades. An act passed in 1919 by the Japanese Diet (the national legislature of Japan) divided all urban lands in Japan into four types or zones: residential, commercial, industrial, and unrestricted. The law established permissible materials, heights, and lot coverage and uses for buildings in the different zones; it remained the basic zoning law for the nation's cities into the late 1960s.[13]

Columbus officials found their city's 1923 zoning code adequate for their needs for several decades, especially as new construction ground to a halt during the 1930s. The value of building permits issued in Columbus in 1933 was only 3 percent of what it had been in 1928. However, Columbus politicians revisited zoning as building picked up after World War II. In early 1948 they divided the single commercial zone into four different types of categories—Business Districts A, B, C, and D—in descending order of what was allowed in each. In Business District A, for example, only banks, office buildings, private schools, radio and television stations, and telephone exchanges were permitted. In Business District D, the broadest category, even bottling works, dance halls, garages, second-hand car lots, and premises where poultry were killed for retail sales were allowed.[14] A year later the city councilmen split the dwelling-house class into three categories, including one for single-family homes covering no less than 1,500 square feet on lots of 4,800 square feet. Further zoning changes took place in 1954, when the councilmen adopted a new code, which was more complex than its predecessors, designating three classes of single-family homes: one for one-to-four-family homes and

12. Mansel G. Blackford, *The Rise of Modern Business: Great Britain, the United States, Germany, Japan & China* (Chapel Hill: University of North Carolina Press, 2008), 162. For more detail, see Daniel Rodgers, *Atlantic Crossings: Social Politics in a Progressive Era* (Cambridge, MA: Harvard University Press, 1998), 177; and John Sheail, *An Environmental History of Twentieth-Century Britain* (Houndmills, Basingstoke, UK: Palgrave, 2002), 17–23.

13. Blackford, *Pathways to the Present*, 132–33. For more detail, see Andre Sorensen, *The Making of Urban Japan: Cities and Planning from Edo to the Twenty-First Century* (London: Routledge, 2002), 85–114.

14. City of Columbus, "Ordinance No. 194-48," passed 1 March 1948, State Archives Series 5039, Box 18,414, vol. 35, archive and library of the Ohio Historical Society (Ohio History Connection).

three classes of apartments. The new code also specified in more detail than before four commercial categories and two manufacturing zones. Recognizing the growing importance of automobiles, the plan included a new land-use class in "parking." The 1954 zoning ordinance had a wider variety of building-height and lot-size requirements than earlier ones.[15]

The 1954 zoning code regulated land uses within Columbus's boundaries into the late 1970s. A new code adopted in 1979 recognized eight major types of residential districts, six sorts of commercial-land uses, four types of manufacturing districts, and two types of land uses for parking. Planning had become less top-down than before, as nine area commissions advised city officials on zoning matters in their districts, although final decision-making power rested with members of the city council. The area commissions in existence in 1979 were the Capitol Square Commission, the Clintonville Area Commission, the Driving Park Area Commission, the Franklinton Area Commission, the German Village Commission, the Italian Village Commission, the Near East Area Commission, the University Area Commission, and the Victorian Village Commission.[16]

In a nod to regional planning, which was becoming increasingly common in the United States at this time, Franklin County officials established a zoning commission in 1943, which implemented a zoning code for all of the unincorporated land in the county in late 1948. Following the lead of Columbus's councilmen, the county commissioners established four classes of single-family homes based on the size of their lots and the square footage of homes per family: three classes of multiple or apartment houses based on the square footage required per family; two types of commercial districts; and two types of manufacturing districts, each with its own building-height and building-line restrictions. Unlike the Columbus zoning code, that for Franklin County also recognized farmhouse, tourist-camp, and trailer-coach-park zones.[17]

The Franklin County Planning Commission became the Franklin County Regional Planning Commission in 1950. With regional planning established, at least on paper, both Columbus and Franklin County officials could, and did, apply for and receive federal government funds to

---

15. Burgess, *Planning*, 84–85, 136–39. See also Patricia Burgess Stach, "Real Estate Development and Urban Form: Roadblocks in the Path to Residential Exclusivity," *Business History Review* 63 (Summer 1989), 356–83, esp. 380.

16. Columbus City Council, "Zoning Codes, 1979 and 1983" (Columbus: City Government, 1979, 1983), pamphlets.

17. Franklin County Planning Commission, "Franklin County, Ohio, Zoning Resolution, Adopted November 12, 1948," pamphlet.

support regional planning and redevelopment efforts for housing, water, and sewer improvements. The existence of regional planning was, in fact, a prerequisite for federal funding of projects. Members of the regional commission included representatives from the governments of Franklin County, townships, the city of Columbus, and smaller municipalities and villages.[18]

In 1969 the Franklin County Regional Planning Commission was substantially expanded, leading to the organization's transformation into the Mid-Ohio Regional Planning Commission (MORPC) that year. MORPC experienced controversies. In the early 2000s the recurring question resurfaced of how much power representatives from the city of Columbus should have. Within a few years the matter was partially ironed out, and there was "a perception, if not reality, that township trustees have more of a say in developments that impact them, although Columbus still maintains the whip hand as a result of its control over the extension of water and sewer lines."[19] By 2014 MORPC was a voluntary association of forty-four local governments in twelve counties in central Ohio—unincorporated townships, but also villages, towns, and cities. According to one of its officers, MORPC existed to serve "the region through planning, direct service, public policy information, and innovative programming and intergovernmental coordinating services in areas of transportation, land use, energy, the environment, and housing." The body's website claimed that "MORPC is committed to collaboration and developing bold new strategies that continue to make the region stand out both nationally and regionally."[20]

Late in 2014 MORPC, in collaboration with several private planning bodies, issued a report titled "Insight2050," which addressed demographic changes expected to occur in central Ohio over the next thirty-five years as the region gained a projected 500,000 new residents. The report called for "denser, mixed-use developments to replace outward urban sprawl."[21]

Columbus-area residents thus took important steps to implement zoning. But what did zoning actually accomplish? Probably not much. Urban

18. Burgess, *Planning*, 131–35.

19. *Columbus Dispatch*, 5 June 2003, p. A7.

20. "Perry, Prairie Townships now in MORPC Fold," *Worthington News*, 4 February, 2014, p. A4. See also MORPC, "Overview," at www.morpc.org, accessed on 12 February 2014.

21. *Columbus Dispatch*, 11 November 2014, p. A1; 26 November 2014, p. A12; and "Insight2050," at www.morpc.org/Insight2050, accessed on 30 November 2014.

historian Patricia Burgess, who examined the history of zoning in Columbus between 1923 and 1970 in great detail, concluded that it achieved
little in guiding the growth of the city. Much land was grandfathered in
its uses as of 1923; numerous, substantial zoning variances were granted
over the decades; and, when new land acquired by Columbus was zoned,
the categories and restrictions usually just repeated what had already
been put in place by real-estate developers. Power lay more with the private developers than the council members. The Columbus city council
created a permanent city planning commission only in 1953, and the city
possessed an overall plan to guide its expansion only in 1957.

Harland Bartholomew, a nationally known private urban planner, was
hired as a consultant to prepare Columbus's first comprehensive city plan
since 1908. Between 1954 and 1957 members of his firm prepared reports
on many aspects of the Columbus metropolitan area, including land use,
demographics, schools, parks, housing, streets and transportation, public buildings, and the downtown. All of these topics were subsumed into
a master plan put forward in 1957, a plan that was intended to guide
Columbus's growth for a generation. The plan recognized that "as the
Capital of Ohio, the seat of the Ohio State University and a growing center of trade and industry, Columbus is already a good city." However,
it went on to observe, "we believe it can be made into an even better community. It is to this better, more efficient, more pleasing, and more livable
metropolis that this plan is dedicated." The scheme made detailed recommendations for each of the separate issues first dealt with in the individual 1954–57 reports. In its conclusion, the 1957 master plan called upon
Columbus residents to use the plan "as a guide for all public improvements and for the general direction of growth," thus ensuring "economy,
efficiency, and orderliness throughout the Columbus area." Those goals
could be met, the planners thought, through "subdivision control, zoning,
the capital improvement program, and urban redevelopment."[22]

The objectives were not met. Columbus officials, Burgess has correctly
declared, "did not use zoning to plan and direct growth and development for the benefit of the city as a whole." Instead, "they reacted to the
requests of individual property owners on a one-by-one basis to protect
property value." "Columbus adopted only the form," she observed, "not

---

22. Harland Bartholomew and Associates, *A Summary Report: The Master Plan
Columbus Urban Area Prepared for the City Planning Commission and the Franklin County Regional Planning Commission* (St. Louis: Harland Bartholomew, 1957),
unpaged preface, and p. 90.

the substance, of planning."[23] That outcome was common. Looking at impacts of zoning nationwide, historian Christopher Wells has concluded that "zoning laws had virtually no effect, primarily because interwar ordinances quite reasonably reflected existing land-use patterns." "To do otherwise," he has observed, "would [have] require[d] the complete reconstruction of big cities."[24]

More specifically, too much land in Columbus was zoned for commercial use, much more than was actually employed for trade. Moreover, frequent rezoning allowed commercial uses to invade poorer, often black, residential districts, raising environmental-justice and social-equity issues. Burgess's study revealed "little indication that either the council or zoning board intended to use zoning in a racially discriminatory manner." However, that was the consequence, if unintended. African Americans were affected "when city officials acceded to property owners' requests" for zoning variances, allowing the intrusion of commercial and industrial businesses into their districts, such as the growing one on the East Side. "Zoning actions affecting land near the central city," Burgess concluded, "lessened residential quality."[25]

Restrictive deed covenants attached to land sales by private developers did more to guide land usage in Columbus than did zoning. Modern deed restrictions date to efforts by real-estate operators to create subdivisions in Riverside, California, in 1871; in Short Hills, New Jersey, in 1877; in Wissahickon Heights, Philadelphia, a few years later; and in Kenilworth, Illinois, in 1891. Developers of Shaker Heights near Cleveland pioneered the use of deed restrictions in Ohio.[26] Typically, developers used deed restrictions to exclude nuisances, such as slaughterhouses, from their subdivisions; indeed, they often prohibited most forms of businesses. They usually specified building setback distances and building-lot-coverage maximums

---

23. Burgess, *Planning*, 97. Elsewhere, Burgess has concluded of Columbus, "Zoning actions followed the economic value of land. They protected the neighborhoods of middle-income or upper-income residents, but lower-income neighborhoods were subject to changes that offered the potential of greater profits." See Patricia Burgess, "Of Swimming Pools and 'Slums': Zoning and Residential Development in Post-World War II Columbus, Ohio," in *Planning the Twentieth-Century American City*, eds. Mary Corbin Sies and Christopher Silver (Baltimore: Johns Hopkins University Press, 1996), 215–39, esp. 215.

24. Wells, *Car Country*, 138.

25. Burgess, *Planning*, 152.

26. Burgess, "Real Estate Development," 357–62; and Patricia Burgess Stach, "Deed Restrictions and Subdivision Development in Columbus, Ohio, 1900–1970," *Journal of Urban History* 15 (November 1988), 42–68.

to ensure the provision of open spaces, and they often set requirements for the types of houses to be constructed. Single-family homes made of specific materials worth certain minimum amounts of money were the norm. Deed restrictions also often forbade selling homes to racial or ethnic groups such as African Americans, Jews, and Asians, until the Supreme Court of the United States held such restrictions as legally unenforceable in *Shelley v. Kraemer* in 1948.[27] The goal of most developers was to create attractive, parklike subdivisions whose building lots could be sold at high prices. Most deed restrictions were set to last an initial thirty years, with their renewal automatic unless homeowners voted to amend or eliminate them.

Before 1900 Columbus developers made little use of restrictions, but after that date they increasingly included setback and building-price minimums in deed restrictions. In the early 1900s building-size minimums and racial restrictions also began appearing in covenants to deeds. Between 1900 and 1920 one-quarter of the deeds in new subdivisions forbade selling homes to African Americans, Jews, or Asians. Some added Italians to the prohibited list. Restrictive covenants became more common during the 1920s, with even more of them forbidding sales to "undesirables," "foreigners," and "foreigners of the Dago class." Few new subdivisions were platted during the 1930s, but building boomed after 1945. Most subdivisions laid out between 1945 and 1970 continued to have setback and use restrictions. More covenants than in the past specified a maximum density of building per acre, and many boasted housing-price and housing-size minimums.[28]

Some deeds continued to have indirect racial restrictions. Developers evaded the Supreme Court's 1948 decision for a few years by including deed restrictions which required that home buyers join the subdivision's country club or community association. The membership required a positive vote, often a unanimous one, of its members as a prerequisite to buying land or houses. Then, too, the high minimum house prices and the large-size requirements for houses kept most African Americans out of "exclusive" subdivisions. At any rate, the federal government agency that insured many house mortgages, the Federal Housing Authority (FHA), refused to insure mortgages in racially mixed or minority neighborhoods on the assumption that property values in such districts would decline. That decision froze African Americans out of many urban areas.[29] The

27. Burgess, *Planning*, 30–32.
28. Ibid, 40–45, 106–12.
29. Ibid, 113.

actions of real estate subdividers and agents of the FHA did more than those of city zoning authorities to segregate Columbus. Members of the Columbus Department of Building and Zoning Services usually accepted whatever restrictions subdividers had first put in place.

Columbus developed in the twentieth century through the combined decisions of public zoning authorities and private developers of subdivisions, but the actions of land developers were more important. The restrictive deed covenants they established covered much of the land eventually annexed by the city of Columbus and were rarely altered by zoning authorities. In her richly detailed account, Burgess concluded, "During the twentieth century's first half, Columbus real estate developers large and small collectively shaped the urban area." Continuing, she observed, "Through the choice of site and the nature of the restrictions they imposed, land developers established the city's social and spatial structure."[30]

True enough, and very important. However, developers chose their sites in accordance with parameters laid down in large part by circumstances beyond their control. For instance, relatively few built in the South Side. Odors from the sewer plant and industries made that district unappealing to the creators of subdivisions. Between 1900 and 1970 a scant 6.6 percent of Columbus's real-estate development took place there. For the most part, real-estate operators in Columbus expanded on established patterns of urban development. They rarely struck out in completely new directions. Columbus continued to grow mainly to the north and the west.

## The Development of Upper Arlington

Two brothers, Benjamin and King Thompson, showed that deed covenants could be powerful tools in the creation of subdivisions in their development of the suburban municipality of Upper Arlington. Zoning, while significant, was less important. Situated west of the Olentangy River about 4 miles northwest of downtown Columbus, Upper Arlington was from its inception before World War I a carefully planned community for upper-middle-class residents. It remained largely a bedroom suburb of Columbus in the early 2000s, possessing relatively few commercial establishments and almost no industrial ones. From a group of just six houses

30. Ibid, 29 (the source of the quotation), 121.

on ten roads at its founding, Upper Arlington grew to a bustling community of 5,370 people in 1940, a home for 28,486 residents in 1960, and a small city of about 35,000 inhabitants in 2012.[31]

The Thompsons met on Christmas Eve, 1913, with James Miller, a prominent farmer and landowner, to purchase almost 1,000 of his acres, soon to become the nucleus of Upper Arlington. They chose Miller's farm for their new subdivision for its high ground (they were starting Upper Arlington just months after the 1913 flood), its closeness to Columbus, and the absence of any industrial pollution. They noted in an early advertising brochure that winds blew from west to east, away from their community toward Columbus. No sewer or garbage odors polluted the air. A photograph taken around 1900 shows the "vast expanse of the Miller farm," with a mansion on top of a hill surrounded by "manicured fields and squared hedges."[32]

Born in Georgetown, Ohio, in 1876 and 1879, respectively, King and Ben Thompson attended the Ohio State University, Ben in engineering, King in law. They decided to go into land development soon after their graduations, forming a real-estate partnership in 1907. After initially working with Charles Johnson, another Columbus developer, they struck out on their own, specializing in sites northwest of Columbus's downtown. Between 1916 and 1922 they platted 1,335 lots in five subdivisions, many of which featured winding streets and shade trees. However, they had to share developments in these regions with others and wanted to create a planned community of their own—hence their purchase of land for Upper Arlington. They formed the King Thompson Company to develop the Miller farm in 1917. Ben generally handled the business details, with King acting as the more thoughtful driving force.[33]

Four hundred inhabitants successfully petitioned the state government to incorporate their settlement as the Village of Upper Arlington in 1918. King was conversant with efforts by J. C. Nichols to create a "Country Club District" of homes in a suburb of Kansas City and desired to do the same in Upper Arlington. The first advertising pamphlet for Upper

---

31. Thompson Buck, "Company and Community: The King Thompson Company and Upper Arlington, Ohio, 1913–1929," Senior Honors Thesis, Ohio State University, 2011, p. 17. King and Ben Thompson were great-great uncles to Thompson Buck. I directed this thesis. See also *History of Upper Arlington: A Suburb of Columbus, Ohio,* ed. Marjorie Gavin Sayers (Columbus: Upper Arlington Historical Society, 1977), 32.

32. Buck, "Company and Community," 17.

33. Ibid, 18–22; and Burgess, "Deed Restrictions," 55–58.

Arlington was titled "The Country Club District; 1000 Acres Restricted; Upper Arlington." The village had gently winding streets, plenty of trees, and a golf club. It was intended to be a residential community for professional and business people working in Columbus. The first lots were platted in 1914, and the village grew rapidly after World War I, with 4,100 lots laid out by 1950, about half of them in the 1920s. As president of the Upper Arlington Company, the Arlington Ridge Company, and the Ashbury Company, King Thompson controlled these developments closely during this time period, with input from Ben.[34]

Nearly all of the land was set aside for single-family homes. In only two small areas were commercial uses allowed. Deed covenants specified generous setbacks (40 feet in most areas, but 150 feet for lots fronting on the golf club) and lot sizes. Minimum building costs were high: $5,000 to $6,000 per dwelling during the 1920s, $8,000 to $10,000 for houses near the golf club in the 1930s, and $15,000 for houses built near the club during the 1940s. Deed covenants were not racially restrictive at first, but covenants in the 1920s and later were. No lots or houses could be sold to African Americans. Residents in Upper Arlington were among those who got around the 1948 Supreme Court decision by requiring membership in a community association as a prerequisite for land purchases. So intent were the Thompsons on the sale of residential lots that they long forbade even church construction in most areas. When members of Upper Arlington's city council passed their first zoning ordinance in 1927, it encompassed most elements of the Thompsons' deed covenants, including the ban on churches. Nearly all of the land was zoned exclusively for single-family residences. No apartments were permitted. The two small commercial areas were allowed, but no land was zoned for industrial usage. Setback and yard requirements preserved those established in deed covenants.[35]

Upper Arlington's officials annexed hundreds of acres of farmland after World War II, along with some contiguous areas that had been platted in the 1910s and that contained modest homes. Some residents unsuccessfully opposed those actions, because they thought the acquisitions would degrade their property values and alter their bucolic lifestyle. In the 1950s and later decades some churches, a few apartments, and more commercial buildings were permitted, but the city council enforced the code to keep the upper-income residential suburb in that state from the time

---

34. Buck, "Company and Community," 25–42; and Burgess, "Deed Restrictions," 58–59.

35. Buck, "Company and Community," 22–23; and Burgess, *Planning*, 59–60, 168–69.

STREET VIEW OF ANDOVER ROAD, UPPER ARLINGTON,
SHOWING HOMES BUILT BY E. RAY EVANS

Figure 5.1. Upper Arlington in 1926. Upper Arlington had gently winding streets, plenty of trees, and a golf club. It was intended to be a residential community for professional and business people working in Columbus. (Courtesy of the Columbus Metropolitan Library)

the first zoning code was adopted.[36] Zoning went hand in hand with deed restrictions to retain Upper Arlington the way most residents wanted it.

The growth of suburbs occurred across the United States but was an especially strong movement in the Midwest, home of the automobile. Between 1920 and 1940 the percentage of metropolitan residents living outside of central-city limits rose from 17 percent to 25 percent in Chicago, from 14 percent to 28 percent in Cleveland, from 28 percent to 40 percent in St. Louis, and from 36 percent to 42 percent in Cincinnati.[37]

## The Downtown, Neighborhoods, and Shopping Centers

A reporter observed in a front-page article for the *Wall Street Journal* in 1990 that Columbus was "an anomaly in the middle of the Rust Belt, a booming center of banking, insurance and other service industries."

36. Burgess, *Planning*, 106, 172.
37. Teaford, *Cities of the Heartland*, 205.

Columbus was an exciting city. The reporter asked, "Where can you find a large bowling league for homosexuals, the first Henri Bendel's store outside of Manhattan and the kind of avant-garde art that would pique Jesse Helms' interest?" The answer, of course, was not San Francisco or Key West, but Columbus, "no kidding."[38] Similar articles multiplied over the next two decades. Another front-page essay in the *Journal* noted with approval in 2001, "During the country's near-delirious economic expansion, Columbus buzzed along—but without much buzz." There was "little irrational exuberance," but lots of "plain vanilla" economic expansion.[39]

Substance lay behind such statements. Columbus seemed to be much more like Sun Belt than Rust Belt cities. By 2000 Columbus had become the nation's fifteenth-largest metropolis in terms of city population, and the population of Columbus's standard metropolitan area was expected to soon surpass those of Cleveland and Cincinnati. (Columbus's standard metropolitan area was, however, only the thirty-seventh-largest in the United States.) Greater Columbus's population was increasingly diverse. About 18.5 percent of Franklin County's residents were nonwhite in 1990, but 21 percent were eight years later. In 2000 about 5 percent of the people living in Columbus's standard metropolitan area were foreign-born, with two-thirds of them having arrived in the region within the previous decade. Particularly noticeable was an influx of refugees from Somalia. By the early 2000s Columbus possessed the second-largest population of Somalis in any American city, only after Minneapolis.[40] Columbus was also home to 10,000 Bhutanese/Nepali refugees.[41]

In spatial reach, Columbus was larger than any other city in Ohio. "We're a bright light in the state of Ohio," crowed Columbus Mayor Michael B. Coleman in 2004.[42] Like the Sun Belt cities, Columbus was decentralized. Historian Steve Conn observed in 2014, "Columbus's population density, at about 3,400 people per square mile, is half that of Cleveland's and about the same as the density of Dallas."[43] Even

38. *Wall Street Journal*, 23 August 1990, p. 1.

39. Ibid, 22 February 2001, p. 1.

40. *Columbus Dispatch*, 19 September 1999, p. B6; 26 January 2001, p. C4; 18 March 2001, p. A1; 11 July 2004, p. A1; 27 March 2015, p. A1.

41. "Asianam Volunteer Information with Local Refugee Community," email received by the author on 24 February 2014.

42. *Columbus Dispatch*, 13 January 2004, p. A8. See also ibid, 1 August 1999, p. B1; and 28 May 2003, p. C1.

43. On Columbus as a Sun Belt–like city, see Steve Conn, *Americans against the City: Anti-Urbanism in the Twentieth Century* (New York: Oxford University Press, 2014), 217–26, esp. 218.

tourism seemed to be thriving, as Columbus emerged as a major center for regional and national conventions. In 2002 the president of the Greater Columbus Convention and Visitors Bureau claimed that 178,000 Columbus residents owed their jobs directly or indirectly to tourism, probably an exaggerated figure.[44] Columbus seemed to combine some of the most appealing aspects of Sun Belt cities, such as economic growth—which created jobs—with midwestern affordability, especially in the prices of houses.

Columbus's emergence as a major American metropolis took people, including many of the city's residents, by surprise. A reporter for the *Columbus Dispatch* observed in 2003 that "Columbus often doesn't behave like the nation's 15th largest city."[45] Columbus residents frequently made that point during the opening years of the twentieth-first century. In 2006 *Money* magazine ranked Columbus as the eighth-best large American city in which to live, prompting humorist Joe Blundo, a columnist for the *Columbus Dispatch,* to ask, "If a city crashes *Money* magazine's best-of-place-to-live list and no one has heard of the place, does it make a sound?"[46] "Obscurity," Blundo opined, tongue-in-cheek, suited Columbus just fine. Others lamented, however, that Columbus lacked any meaningful sense of identity, and business leaders often talked about the need to develop a nationally recognized "brand" for their city. Columbus was clearly no longer "the good old Columbus town" of the early 1900s. However, just what the city was and was becoming was unclear to many. Wil Haygood, an African American who grew up on Columbus's East Side and went on to become a nationally syndicated newspaper writer, observed in 1997, "Essayists and poets haven't written much about my Columbus by way of explaining its texture and mood. Perhaps it's a little too elusive. . . . Maybe it's because sometimes it can seem otherworldly."[47] In part, confusion stemmed from Columbus's never-ending expansion.

People continued to move outward from Columbus's core, a shift that had begun in the late nineteenth and early twentieth centuries with their adoption of electric streetcars. Authorized by an act of Congress in 1956 and financed mainly by the federal government, the construction of interstate highways spurred additional sprawl. Ohio secured its share of federal funds for the construction of interstate highways. A report by the

---

44. *Columbus Dispatch,* 12 October 2002, p. B10; and 5 March 2014, p. D1.
45. Ibid, 20 July 2003, p. F1.
46. Ibid, 23, July 2006, p. H1.
47. Haygood, *The Haygoods,* 216.

head of the Ohio Department of Highways observed with pride in 1962, "Latest reports of the U.S. Bureau of Public Roads place Ohio once again out in front of all other states in the utilization of Interstate Highway funds." Between 1959 and 1963, the report noted, "the Ohio Department of Highways placed 349.6 miles of Interstate Highways under contract at a total cost of $676,118,822." Those funds were very important for Ohio's cities. "More than half of this investment," the report concluded, "was for Urban Interstate Highways, serving the long neglected traffic needs of Ohio's cities."[48] Interstate Highway 71, which sliced through Columbus north to south, connecting the city with Cleveland and Cincinnati, and Interstate 70, which ran east-west, opened new areas around Columbus to development. So did Interstate 270, which ringed Columbus and was completed in 1975.[49] Many of the freeways were designed to move people quickly in and out of Columbus's downtown. Perhaps not surprisingly, Lazarus officials served as unpaid consultants to those designing where the interstates would run.[50] Even more important initially, however, was the straightening and widening of State Route (SR) 315, which ran north-south along the western banks of the Scioto and Olentangy rivers, encouraging the continued movement of Columbus-area residents to the west and north.

Columbus's inner suburbs initially benefited most from highway construction. Upper Arlington, just west of SR 315, experienced a population boom from 5,000 residents in 1940 to 35,000 thirty years later. Grandview Heights, just south of Upper Arlington, saw its population rise at a slower rate, increasing from about 7,000 to 8,500 in the same decades. To the north, Worthington experienced a population explosion from 1,600 to 16,000 residents. To the east, Bexley underwent a population expansion from 8,700 to 15,000 inhabitants. Whitehall, a suburb east of Bexley, had fewer than 5,000 residents in 1940 but more than 25,000 by 1970.[51]

More was involved in the outward growth of Columbus and other American cities than highway building. The work of the Federal Housing

---

48. Ohio Department of Highways, *4-year Report to the Governor, 1959–1962* (Columbus: F. J. Heer, 1962), 38, as reprinted in *Documentary Heritage,* eds. Shriver and Wunderlin, 197; and Kern and Wilson, *Ohio: A History,* 400–402.

49. On the history of the interstate highway system, see Mark H. Rose, *Interstate: Express Highway Politics, 1941–1956* (Lawrence: University Press of Kansas 1979); and Wells, *Car County,* 270–77.

50. Meyers, Meyers, and Walker, *Look to Lazarus,* 96.

51. Burgess, *Planning,* 169.

Authority (FHA) and the Veterans Administration (VA; now called the U.S. Department of Veteran Affairs) in guaranteeing long-term mortgages at low rates of interest, along with other forms of aid to veterans under the G.I. Bill, spurred movements to single-family homes in new subdivisions. People wanted houses in what they imagined would be almost parklike settings. Few Americans initially gave much thought to possible downsides, such as highway congestion and environmental damage, as bulldozers moved into the countryside to build roads and prepare home sites. Real-estate developers were happy to make these wishes come true—to encourage them, in fact. "Fueled by federal incentives, postwar growth machines churned out subdivisions outside nearly every American city, the residents of which experienced near-complete segregation by race, income, and, to a lesser extent, age," historian Wells has concluded.[52]

Columbus residents differed from inhabitants in some cities in their expansionary experiences. By their control over water and sewer connections, city officials forced the annexation of contiguous, unincorporated areas, allowing urban sprawl into countryside for decades. In a bit of boosterism, writers for the *Columbus Dispatch* commented on this circumstance in 2007. "The aggressive growth policy Sensenbrenner spun in motion during a record 14 years as mayor, beginning in 1954," they thought, "catapulted Columbus from a cowtown with a good football team to a dynamic urban gem that sparkled as its Ohio sister cities rusted." Columbus expanded, they pointed out, from 39 square miles in 1950 to 210 square miles in 2000, "adding more than 80 square miles more than Ohio's other six biggest cities combined."[53] In fact, only Columbus and Madison, Wisconsin, of all of the Frost Belt cities in the United States, annexed much in the way of outlying land after World War II. They were outliers in the Midwest.

Retail stores followed people. In the 1920s and 1930s individual shops along busy thoroughfares and at their intersections, which had

---

52. Wells, *Car Country*, 260. Not all suburbs were inhabited by middle-class whites. Elaine Lewinneck, *The Working Men's Reward: Chicago's Early Suburbs and the Roots of American Sprawl* (New York: Oxford University Press, 2014), shows the importance of immigrants and working-class whites in the formation of early suburbs.

53. *Columbus Dispatch*, 9 December 2007, p. A1. Much has recently been written about urban and suburban expansion in the United States after World War II and the implications of that expansion for the natural environment. See esp. Adam Rome, *The Bulldozer in the Countryside: Suburban Sprawl and the Rise of American Environmentalism* (New York: Cambridge University, 2001); Jon C. Teaford, *The Metropolitan Revolution: The Rise of Post-Urban America* (New York: Columbia University Press, 2006); and Wells, *Car Country*, 251–88.

existed in streetcar days, were replaced by neighborhood shopping centers serving people with automobiles. Regional shopping malls came
after World War II, featuring extensive parking lots and other amenities.
Between 1949 and 1953 one to three regional malls opened each year in
the United States, with the pace rising to seven openings in 1954 and to
five in 1955. Located on the outskirts of cities, shopping centers and malls
were built where relatively inexpensive land was available, a necessity for
large parking lots, and where middle-class people with money to spend
lived. They were sited where arterial roads or freeways allowed easy
access for large numbers of shoppers. By 1961 fifty-eight regional malls
boasted at least half a million square feet of floor area in cities across
the United States. Zoning codes spurred the growth of shopping centers,
for the codes usually required new stores to provide ample parking for
customers. So did policies of the FHA, which as early as the mid-1930s
encouraged shopping-center developments. The goals were to create con-
venient shopping experiences, to untangle urban congestion, and to earn
profits for developers.[54]

Developer Don M. Casto built the first modern shopping center in
central Ohio in 1948, the Town and Country in Whitehall on Columbus's eastern edge. Born in Cleveland in 1898, Casto came to Columbus
in 1912. After graduating from North High School in 1917, he served in
the American Army in France during World War I. Gassed and severely
wounded, he received citations for bravery in action. Upon returning to
Columbus, Casto attended the Ohio State University and then went into
real-estate work, associating at first with King Thompson. He established
his own firm in 1923, with offices downtown. An inveterate traveler,
Casto was one of the passengers onboard the dirigible *Graf Zeppelin* on
the airship's first commercial flight from the United States to Germany
in 1928.[55] By 1948, Casto had been experimenting for twenty years
with shopping configurations designed for people driving automobiles.
Initially, he was thwarted in his desire to build by the exigencies of the
Great Depression and World War II. He was, however, able to put up
a thirty-store grouping called the Grandview Avenue Shopping Center
in 1931, with off-street parking for four hundred automobiles. In 1948

54. Wells, *Car Country*, 262–69. See also Lizabeth Cohen, "From Town Center to
Shopping Center: The Reconfiguration of Community Marketplaces in Postwar America," *American Historical Review* 101 (October 1996), 1050–81; and Thomas C. Hatch-
ett, "U.S. Tax Policy and the Shopping Center Boom of the 1950s and 1960s," *American
Historical Review* 71 (October 1966), 1082–110.

55. Moore, *Franklin County*, vol. 3, pp. 1316–17.

Casto developed the above-mentioned Town and Country Shopping Center on 48 acres in Whitehall, the first regional parking-lot shopping center in the world. A risky venture, derided at first as "Casto's Folly," it soon became known as "Casto's Coup," as it attracted major tenants such as J.C. Penney.[56]

In short order after World War II, Casto and others developed shopping centers on the outskirts of Columbus: the Great Southern, Great Western, Great Eastern, and Northern Lights. A second generation of shopping centers even farther out from downtown followed in the late 1950s and 1960s: Eastland, Westland, and Northland.[57] These shopping centers dominated retailing in Columbus into the 1990s, when a third generation of mammoth regional malls was built around Columbus's outer belt, Interstate 270: the Mall at Tuttle Crossing opened in 1997 to the northwest; the Polaris Fashion Place opened in 2001 to the north, just off Interstate 71; and the Easton Town Center opened in 1999 off Interstate 270 to the northeast. In 2015 ground was broken for a large outlet mall just off Interstate 71 about 10 miles north of Polaris. As before, shopping centers moved in the directions people were going to live, sometimes in advance of those migrations. No large malls were established to the south. The South Side smell, a result of the operations of factories, the sewage-treatment plant, and garbage-disposal facilities, held developers at bay.

What freeways gave, they could also take away. There were losers as well as winners in the postwar migration of people and stores. As in many other American cities, Columbus's downtown lost customers and stores to outlying shopping centers.[58] Large downtown department stores, including Lazarus, the Union, and Fashion, were severely hurt by shopping-center competition. Some fought back by building branches in shopping centers and in suburban shopping areas. The Union established the first suburban branch, opening one in Upper Arlington in 1947.[59] With some reluctance, Lazarus's officers opened branches of their department store in the Westland Mall (1962), the Northland Mall (1964), and

---

56. Garrett and Lentz, *Crossroads*, 138, 141; and Meyers, Meyers, and Walker, *Look to Lazarus*, 61, 88–89.

57. On initial shopping-center developments in Columbus, see Lentz, *Columbus: The Story*, 122–23; and Lentz, *As It Were*, 180–83.

58. Robert Fogelson, *Downtown: Its Rise and Fall, 1880–1950* (New Haven: Yale University Press, 2001). On the decline of city centers in Ohio, see Kern and Wilson, *Ohio: A History*, 406–7.

59. Meyers, Meyers, and Walker, *Look to Lazarus*, 139–40.

**Figure 5.2.** The Town and Country Shopping Center around 1948. Don Casto developed the Town and Country Shopping Center on Columbus's East Side right after World War II. (Courtesy of the Columbus Metropolitan Library)

the Eastland Mall (1966). Lazarus also opened a branch in Upper Arlington's Kingsdale Shopping Center (1971). By 1981 the Lazarus group was composed of sixteen stores in and beyond Columbus. Under new ownership via merger, Lazarus later opened stores at the Mall at Tuttle Crossing (1997), the Polaris Fashion Place (2001), and the Eastland Town Center (2001). As retail establishments left Columbus's downtown, the district became something of a ghost town by the late 1970s. A local humorist joked that one might shoot a cannon down High Street without hitting anyone, if one could find someone to fire the cannon.[60] The number of residents living downtown collapsed from nearly 30,000 in 1950 to about 3,500 fifty years later.[61]

---

60. Lentz, *As It Were*, 183. On Lazarus, see *Columbus Dispatch*, 8 August 2004, p. F1; and Meyers, Meyers, and Walker, *Look to Lazarus*, 104–11, 134–36.

61. Meyers, Meyers, and Walker, *Look to Lazarus*, 13. For a nostalgic look at Columbus's downtown, illustrated with many photographs, see I. David Cohen, *Sorry, Downtown Columbus Is Closed: The Golden Era of Columbus—A Salute to a Bygone Time* (no publisher or place of publication listed, 2009).

The impact of freeways was not limited to shopping. Controversy attended the construction of Interstate 270, the outer belt ringing Columbus. As planned during the 1950s and 1960s, the northern segment of this freeway would have passed south of Worthington, cutting through the Ohio School for the Deaf and Dumb just north of the Graceland Shopping Center. "Vigorous lobbying" led to its relocation north of Worthington. A second conflict arose about the exact route for the eastern section of the outer belt. Columbus airport authorities wanted it pushed east to allow room for the future extension of runways, which were located inside the proposed outer belt. Residents in Gahanna to the east objected to this eastward siting of the freeway and pushed back. The result was a compromise, giving Interstate 270 an eastward bulge.[62] Interstate 70, which ran east-west, was located in a deep trench near where Hayden's Cut had once been and cut off the South Side from downtown and the rest of the city.

In the South Side a multicultural district had developed between the two world wars. An investigation by the head of the South Side Settlement House in 1940 provides a valuable snapshot of the area as it existed right before World War II. About two-thirds of the households were headed by native-born whites, about a quarter by immigrants or their children, and about one-twelfth by African Americans. Of those born abroad, the largest proportions came from Hungary, Italy, Yugoslavia, and Romania. West Virginia and Kentucky provided the greatest numbers of native-white migrants.[63] The survey revealed employment disparities. Over half of the white residents had skilled or semiskilled jobs, especially in manufacturing enterprises; about one-eighth was white-collar workers; and another one-eighth was unemployed. It was different for African Americans. One-half worked as unskilled laborers, and 17 percent were unemployed. Most homes had electric lighting, indoor toilets (98 percent did, as sewers were extended into the South Side), and running water in kitchens. Most homes also possessed radios, but less than a quarter had telephones. Just over half of the households had automobiles. In each category, ownership rates were lower for African Americans; less than a quarter had automobiles. Five theaters served the area, and nearly everyone went to the movies at least once every week or two. African Americans faced social segregation and had to sit upstairs in balconies or go to

62. "Interstate 270 (Ohio)," at http://en.wikipedia.org/wiki/Interstate_270_(Ohio), accessed on 9 June 2015.

63. Kaufman, "Neighbors," 6, 7, 16–19, 23–32.

the one theater that catered exclusively to blacks. Commercial dance halls were also popular places of entertainment, attended by young men and women alike.[64]

The South Side, including German Village, fell into disrepair in the mid-twentieth century. German Village was rehabilitated as an upscale living area in the 1960s and later. The gentrification of German Village forced out some long-time residents who were no longer able to afford living there. The future of the rest of the South Side seemed less promising. Children's Hospital, which moved in 1924 from its original 1894 location near Franklin Park to Seventeenth Avenue and Stone Street, provided a focal point for the South Side, as did churches, restaurants, and taverns, some of which came to feature Appalachian music. Dwight Yoakum, a Kentucky native, became a country-music star after growing up in Columbus during the 1960s and 1970s. His song "Readin', Rightin', and Rt. 23" referred to the main north-south highway from central Kentucky to central Ohio.[65] However, the deindustrialization of Ohio and Columbus hit the South Side hard. To the extent that Columbus still had factories after World War II, most were in the South Side, and many shuttered their gates in the 1970s and later decades. Some renovation took place in the area, though not nearly as much as in German Village.[66]

Another formerly immigrant and African American district no longer exists. Most of Flytown disappeared after World War II, erased by freeway construction (the building of an interchange for Interstate 670) and urban redevelopment, called the "Goodale Redevelopment Project." Some 118 acres were cleared, displacing 547 families, 71 individuals, and 73 businesses. Most recently, Westminster-Thurber, an upscale retirement community, has been constructed there, near Neil and Buttles avenues.[67] In 2014 those preparing a report on African Americans in Columbus for the nonprofit Columbus Landmarks Foundation concluded that the elimination of Flytown was "an example of the 'planned' destruction of an African American community in Columbus."[68]

---

64. Ibid, 36–40, 51, 55, 60, 62.

65. On the migration of Appalachians to Ohio, see Cayton, *Ohio: The History*, 291–301, esp. 296–98.

66. To view the South Side, see "South Side," WOSU TV Public Media's "Columbus Neighborhoods," produced in 2013. On some renovation in Merion Village, south of German Village, see *Columbus Dispatch*, 7 April 2014, p. B1.

67. Blanchard, "Geography," 87–88, 92; Garrett and Lentz, *Crossroads*, 144; and Hunker, *A Personal Geography*, 113–16.

68. Smith, *African-American Settlements*, 46.

The construction of Interstates 70 and 71 tore through Columbus's largest African American district, that on the East Side—dividing it and isolating black neighborhoods from the downtown.[69] A 2014 report on African American communities in Columbus concluded about the impact of Interstate 70 on one such predominantly black community, Hanford Village: "In the mid-1960s the State of Ohio chose this location for the path of Interstate 70 and the Alum Creek Interchange. This created a physical barrier between the new and old parts of the community . . . destroyed numerous homes, and a sense of history—a historic marker in the neighborhood references 'the highway divided them.'"[70] Such was not unusual in Ohio or across the nation.[71] Interstate 75 ran through the West End of Cincinnati, destroying that area's black neighborhood.[72] Various interstate freeways cut up several communities in Cleveland as well. One of the few to avoid that fate was Shaker Heights, whose wealthy and well-connected residents successfully resisted the threatened incursion of an expressway.[73] Historian Conn has written eloquently about the impact of interstate highways on Columbus's neighborhoods and downtown: "The beltway that ringed downtown was a marvel of automotive efficiency—at least initially—but it cut off the center of the city from the neighborhoods that once bordered it." He concluded that the highways "created a circular chasm of dead space in the heart of the city, a vehicular moat which turned downtown into something like an office-tower island."[74]

Most controversial was the construction of Interstate 670, a freeway connecting Columbus's downtown to the airport to the east and to SR 315 on the west side of the Olentangy River. This "Connector," as the freeway was called, provided a west-east route across much of the city, with a northeastern extension to the airport. It was built at considerable environmental and social costs. In particular, building the Connector

---

69. Lentz, *Columbus: The Story,* 30–31; and Edward Lentz, "Rationalization and Reform: The Columbus Urban League, 1942–1962," Master's thesis, Ohio State University, 1969, pp. 98–102.

70. Smith, *African-American Settlements,* 49–50.

71. Freeways often cut through African American and other minority districts in cities. See Raymond Moll, "Stop the Road: Freeway Revolts in American Cities," *Journal of American History* 30 (July 2004), 674–706; and Zachary M. Schrag, "The Freeway Fight in Washington, DC: The Three Sisters Bridge in Three Administrations," *Journal of Urban History* 30 (July 2004), 648–73.

72. Cayton, *Ohio: The History,* 344.

73. Stradling and Stradling, *Where the River Burned,* 181–85.

74. Conn, *Americans against the City,* 223.

added greatly to the destruction already done to African American communities by Interstates 70 and 71. It also encouraged urban sprawl to the northeast.

Columbus's business and political leaders had begun thinking of a connector in the early 1950s. A six-lane freeway from the downtown to the airport along Leonard Avenue was proposed in 1957, as was an expressway along Seventeenth Avenue between Interstate 71 and the airport. Further study of routes came in the 1960s and early 1970s. In the mid-1970s the Mid-Ohio Regional Planning Commission (MORPC) recommended that the Connector (labeled I-670 for the first time) be constructed in the Leonard Avenue corridor and that Seventeenth Avenue become an arterial street, recommendations approved by the city of Columbus, the Ohio Department of Transportation (ODOT), and the Ohio Division Office of the Federal Highway Administration. The die seemed to be cast: the Connector would be built.[75] In fact, much of it had already been constructed. The initial stretch of Interstate 670 actually built, that section between SR 315 and U.S. Highway 23 (High Street), was opened to traffic in 1961—designated as part of Interstate 71. This expressway was extended east to the Interstate 71 freeway heading north in 1966, and it was called Interstate 670 from then on. It was not, however, complete, for backers wanted a major extension to the airport.[76]

Environmental and budgetary issues intruded. Construction of a western segment of Interstate 670 would have required the relocation of a stretch of the Scioto River, to which members of the newly created U.S. Environmental Protection Agency objected. Plans had to be redesigned. Then, too, a major nationwide recession hit Ohio hard in the early and mid-1970s, limiting new highway construction by federal and state governments. Budgetary issues continued into the 1980s. During a major budget crunch in the early 1980s, Walter Smith, the head of ODOT, declared in a notorious statement that he wanted Interstate 670 taken off his books, because it was a "local route" not needing federal or state funding.[77]

75. U.S. Department of Transportation, Federal Highway Administration, "Interstate 670 Extension: Final Joint Environmental Impact Statement," typescript report, 16 July 1981, pp. I-3 through I-6.

76. Anonymous, "Interstate 670 Ohio," pp. 1–2, at http://www.interstate-guide.com /i-670_oh.html, accessed on 7 June 2015; and Sandor Gulyas, "I-670 East Plans," p. 1, at http://www.roadfan.com/670east.html, accessed on 7 June 2015.

77. Gulyas, "I-670 East Plans," p. l.

Even more than budgetary and environmental matters, social issues delayed the completion of Interstate 670 from the downtown to the airport. Many in Columbus favored constructing the Connector. Members of the Columbus Chamber of Commerce saw it as essential for the continued economic growth of their city; members of the AFL-CIO favored it as creating jobs; members of the Columbus Board of Realtors supported it as a tool to help "substantially diversify and expand" their city's economic base; and doctors and administrators of the Franklin County Health Planning Council supported it as improving access to their hospitals. Leslie Wexner, the head of The Limited, was just beginning the development of New Albany to the northeast of Columbus and favored the extension of Interstate 670 eastward as a way of reducing the commuting time to Columbus's downtown for residents in his upscale, planned community. Some residents living in the areas to be paved over also favored highway construction, for the mitigation payments they would receive would allow them to move into housing in newer, more upscale districts. Those preparing the 1981 environmental impact statement for the building of the Connector estimated that the project would "displace some 109 households, including an estimated 355 persons." It would also "displace 18 businesses, 4 institutions and require about 592 acres of land for right of way." They admitted that "it will adversely affect some cohesive, black neighborhoods" but thought that "no neighborhood will suffer more than a minor impact." Positive impacts were weighed against these negative ones: the freeway extension would "result in substantial benefits related to accessibility, reduced congestion and enhanced development potential."[78]

However, many Columbus residents objected to the planned freeway extension. About three-quarters of those living in the affected communities opposed it. From 1982 to 1983 investigator Olivia Flakes interviewed 100 residents, 96 of whom were African American, and reported, "Most residents realistically fear that relocation would mean deterioration of both physical condition of housing and social aspects of the present community(ies). Many of the residents believe that the highway would not be to the advantage of the current residents. They feel it is to the advantage of the suburbanites (largely white society) and the business community of

--------

78. Olivia Flakes, "Citizen Participation in Public Policy: A Case Study of Interstate 670 in Columbus," Masters thesis, Ohio State University, 1983, p. 53 (the source of the quotation); Jacobs, *Getting around Brown,* 183; and U.S. Department of Transportation, "Interstate 670 Extension," iii, vii, B-14 through B-19.

the central business district."[79] African American political leaders joined them. Jerry Hammond and Ben Espy, African American city councilmen, opposed building Interstate 670 through black neighborhoods. Hammond acknowledged the need for a connector but was against the chosen route, which he thought would destroy the stability of many of Columbus's predominantly black neighborhoods. He believed a mass-transit rail system was a better alternative. Members of ODOT and MORPC rejected a rail system as too expensive. Espy opposed Interstate 670 because he thought that the desires of black residents in affected areas were not given proper consideration. He initially served on an advisory board for the planning of the Interstate 670 extension but soon resigned.[80]

Giving organization to opposition was the Coalition of Concerned Citizens Against 270. An umbrella organization, the coalition was composed of civic associations representing numerous communities: Shepard, Brentnell, Trevitt Heights, St. Mary's, East Columbus, Eastgate, Cumberland Ridge, Italian Village, and the city of Bexley. Most of these communities were made up mainly of African American residents.[81] Members of the coalition were against building the Interstate 670 extension, claiming, "It is time that the Federal government cease the allocation of funds to state and local governments for projects that adversely affect only minorities and poor people." Coalition members feared "the displacement of people and the depreciation of property in presently stable communities." Improved bus transportation, redesigned streets, carpooling, and a redistribution of traffic by staggering work hours by businesses could, coalition members thought, solve traffic problems.[82]

Nonetheless, the Interstate 670 extension was built, with the approval of most members of the Columbus City Council, ODOT, and the U.S. Department of Transportation. Opposition came to naught, and the proposed route was altered little. The final route was chosen in 1984, but additional funding shortfalls delayed construction. In 1993 the first of fifteen construction projects composing the extension of Interstate 670, the section connecting downtown to the airport, was opened to traffic. In addition to greatly speeding up transportation from Columbus's downtown to its airport, the Connector also greatly reduced the time needed to reach the airport for largely white middle-class suburbanites in

79. Flakes, "Citizen Participation," 53.

80. Ibid, 36–37.

81. Ibid, 40.

82. U.S. Department of Transportation, "Interstate 670 Extension," B-21 through B-28.

Upper Arlington, Marble Cliff, and Grandview Heights west of Colum-bus. By 2003 the entire extension was completed. Final sections opened included a "cap" of shops and restaurants along High Street on a bridge connecting the Short North to the downtown.[83]

The freeways damaged an African American community (or actually a group of communities) that had grown up on Columbus's East Side. Altogether, about a quarter of the residents of the Near East Side were displaced. The eastward extension of Interstate 70 alone led to razing half of the homes in Hanford Village, where "dozens of black servicemen and their families had settled after the war." The residential population of downtown areas, largely African American, fell by half between 1950 and 1964.[84]

From the 1920s most African Americans in Columbus had come to live on Columbus's East Side, as their numbers increased and social seg-regation in Columbus became more pronounced. A major reason the East Side emerged as the main African American district may have been that the city's wealthiest residents, who lived nearby on East Broad Street, wanted to have "negro 'help' nearby." A 1928 report observed, "The Long Street region [in the East Side] was near enough for convenience and also far enough away to keep Broad Street exclusive." In addition to Long Street, Mt. Vernon Avenue served as the East Side community's main commercial venue. In 1940 one of the nation's first public housing projects, Poindexter Village, replaced the dilapidated Blackberry Patch community, "rows of shacks devoid of sanitation and amenities," on the East Side.[85] Increasingly concentrated in the East Side, African Americans composed 12 percent of Columbus's population in 1950, but 22 percent thirty years later. By way of comparison, African Americans made up 16 percent of Cincinnati's residents in 1950 and 34 percent in 1980. The corresponding figures for Cleveland were 16 percent and 44 percent.[86]

A lively, if segregated, black community developed on the East Side. As early as 1922 an investigator reported that there were "10 Negro phy-sicians, 6 dentists, 10 churches, 2 drug stores, 2 undertakers, and over

83. Anonymous, "Interstate 670 Ohio," 1; and Sandor, "I-670," 1.

84. Jacobs, *Getting around Brown,* 11.

85. Mark, *Negroes in Columbus,* 18. See also Smith, *African-American Settlements,* 20–21, 35–36. The East Side became known as "Bronzeville," a term that originated in Chicago. For brief descriptions of fourteen clusters of African Americans in Columbus before many moved to the East Side, see Smith, *African-American Settlements,* 32–59.

86. On the Great Migration of African Americans out of the South into Ohio and the impacts of that migration on Ohio cities see Cayton, *Ohio: The History of a People,* 281–91.

100 Negro-owned homes" in just the Jefferson-Garfield blocks on East Long Street.[87] A bit later, artist Aminah Robinson, who lived in Poindexter Village, expressed the energy of the people of the district in paintings and collages, as in her depictions *Vegetable Man* (1979; sculpture), *The Umbrella Man* (1996; sculpture), *Unwritten Love Letter #003: The Chickenfoot Man* (1988; pen and ink, thread, and found objects on hand-dyed envelope), and many others. So did Elijah Pierce, a barber, in wooden carvings of people and street scenes.[88] Wil Haygood, living as a teenager in a housing development on the East Side during the late 1960s and early 1970s, later recalled Mt. Vernon Avenue as being "busy as fire," with numerous stores, nightclubs, and theaters. Freeway construction severely altered the district after World War II, as did the movement of middle-class African Americans to other sections of Columbus when social and residential segregation eased. Haygood left Columbus to become a journalist for the *Boston Globe* in the 1980s. He returned as a scholar-in-residence at the Thurber House on Jefferson Avenue on the western edge of the East Side in 1994. He found a Mt. Vernon Avenue very different from that of his youth, with "so much [that] seemed to be vanishing, getting away." It seemed to him that "Mt. Vernon Avenue was all echoes now, memories." Some renovation occurred in the 1990s and early 2000s, as, for example, in the refurbishing of the Lincoln Theatre.[89]

For Columbus's mayors from the 1940s into the1980s, the downtown always had a high priority as the beating heart of their city—certainly a higher priority than did most neighborhoods, in particular East Side ones. Mayors used their imagination and creativity to lead downtown business and political leaders in resisting the rise of suburbia. In 1945, just as the shift in shopping to suburban malls was beginning, Mayor James Rhodes met with one hundred "prominent community social, political, and economic leaders" in a Metropolitan Committee to develop "worthwhile projects requiring public funding." Over the next twenty-two years, Columbus voters approved bond issues totaling $82 million for civic improvements, many of which were put forward by that committee, and most of which aimed at improving downtown. Through leveraging with state and federal government funds, the bond issues brought in hundreds of millions of dollars to Columbus for slum-clearance projects, school

---

87. As quoted in Himes, "Forty Years," 143.

88. Viewed by the author at the Columbus Museum of Art in the early 2000s. On Aminah Robinson, who died in 2015, see *Columbus Dispatch*, 24 May 2015, p. B3.

89. Haygood, *The Haygoods*, 129, 334. See also Cayton, *Ohio: The History of a People*, 346–47.

construction, hospital expansion, and airport modernization.[90] Even as they rather reluctantly established suburban branches, Lazarus's leaders remained committed to the downtown, spending $12 million on the renovation and expansion of their flagship store between 1946 and 1961. This work included the building of four downtown Lazarus parking garages.[91]

The commitment of Columbus's downtown business and political leaders to continued growth for their businesses and development for their city helped ensure that the integration of the city's schools went smoothly. As we have seen, Columbus developed a segregated school system from the 1920s onward. In part, school segregation simply reflected the de facto segregation of housing and neighborhoods in Columbus. However, it also resulted from long-term efforts made by the city's largely white school board to keep schools segregated. Columbus, in effect, operated a dual school system, one for whites and a separate one for African Americans. In 1977, more than two decades after members of the U.S. Supreme Court declared such arrangements unconstitutional in their landmark *Brown v. Board of Education in Topeka, Kansas* in 1954, Judge Robert M. Duncan, writing for the Federal Court of Appeals for the Sixth Circuit, declared that the way the Columbus Public Schools (now called Columbus City Schools) operated was unconstitutional. In his decision in *Penick v. Columbus Board of Education,* which was upheld by the U.S. Supreme Court two years later, Duncan ordered the school board to desegregate Columbus's schools. That school board had been divided for several years between four white members largely opposed to desegregation, especially to the use of busing to achieve desegregation, and three black members who favored desegregation.[92]

Members of Columbus's business and political leadership, including especially members of the powerful Columbus Chamber of Commerce, supported desegregation, including busing, and worked hard to make it a success—a stance unusual among business leaders in American cities then. They wanted, above all, to avoid any violence during school desegregation, for they had seen an example of such violence in the desegregation of Boston's schools several years earlier. They greatly feared that violence would stain Columbus in the national media, retarding business and urban growth in central Ohio. They established the Metropolitan Columbus Schools Committee, headed by Rowland Brown, the CEO of

90. Garrett and Lentz, *Crossroads,* 180; and Lentz, *Columbus: The Story,* 124–25. See also Conn, *Americans against the City,* 219.

91. Meyers, Meyers, and Walker, *Look to Lazarus,* 82, 89, 99.

92. Jacobs, *Getting around Brown,* 64–119.

Buckeye Steel, to work with Columbus residents to make school desegregation occur without incident. It did, as the busing of 35,636 students on 6 September 1979 proceeded smoothly.[93] Thus the same business leaders who supported the construction of freeways, which damaged and sometimes destroyed black communities, supported school desegregation. And they did so for the same reason: both actions were seen as aiding Columbus's economic ascent.

However, the aftermath of school desegregation in Columbus revealed limits to the visions of the city's business and political leaders. Rowland Brown wanted the Metropolitan Columbus Schools Committee to stay in existence to further the integration of blacks and whites in Columbus, but the body dissolved in 1980. With initial school desegregation working, most members of Columbus's business and political leadership thought that they had done enough. Members of the Chamber of Commerce, in particular, wanted to return to what they viewed as strictly economic matters to push their firms and their city ahead on the national scene.

Movement by whites to suburbs that were not part of the Columbus Public Schools, and thus not covered by Judge Duncan's desegregation order, increased. Then, too, the boundaries of the city of Columbus and the Columbus Public Schools, which had been the same into the early 1960s, diverged to the detriment of the school district. As Columbus expanded by requiring the use of city water and sewer connections as a means to force annexation, the areas covered by the school district lagged far behind the annexed land. By 1979 the Columbus Public Schools served just 109 of the city of Columbus's 180 square miles and just 80 percent of its students. The remaining city of Columbus students were taught in the schools of independent municipalities such as Dublin, Westerville, and Worthington. When Columbus annexed land, the students did not automatically join the city of Columbus school system: that move required the permission of the Ohio State Board of Education. Faced with growing opposition from parents in the newly annexed areas, who did not want their children to attend Columbus schools, board members increasingly withheld that permission. Columbus Public Schools lost valuable tax bases as a result. Acrimonious conflict broke out between members of the Columbus school board and their counterparts in the suburbs, leading to mitigation and a compromise in 1986, but that compromise greatly favored the suburban school districts.[94]

---

93. Ibid.
94. Ibid, 120–78.

Making matters even worse, real-estate agents, land developers, bankers, and insurance-company officers basically redlined the entire Columbus school district, almost halting the construction of new houses there. Instead, they steered clients to the suburbs. Between 1980 and 1990 the number of housing units in the city of Columbus increased by 18 percent, but the number in the Columbus school district fell by 2 percent. Gregory S. Jacobs, the scholar who has most carefully studied school desegregation in Columbus, has concluded, "In essence, the health of the city school district was sacrificed to preserve the expansion of the city itself." Writing in 1998, he found that "the gradual abandonment of urban education in Columbus has resulted in both the concentration of poor and African American students within the central city school district and the emergence of a politically powerful form of defensive activism within the overwhelmingly white suburban systems."[95]

Problems with Columbus's public education system continued into the 2010s. Some were beyond the power of people in the Columbus school district to change. As long as Ohioans relied largely on local property taxes to fund the operations of their schools, poor school districts would remain poor. Although the judges on the Ohio Supreme Court ruled on several occasions in the 1990s and early 2000s that relying on such funding violated their state's constitution, it continued. Other problems were of their own making. In the early 2010s some Columbus school administrators and teachers falsified school records to increase state funding for their district—not all funding was local—moves that led to criminal investigations and convictions.

Columbus's business and political leaders refocused their attention on the downtown, if, in fact, that attention had ever wandered from that district. Columbus leaders established a downtown convention center in the 1980s and 1990s. Located on the site of the former Union Railroad Station—torn down in 1976 much to the dismay of preservationists—the convention center traced its existence to a $36.5 million contribution from Columbus's Battelle Memorial Institute, a nonprofit organization that uses technology and science to conduct research in various areas, in 1974. Construction began in 1987, and the Greater Columbus Convention Center opened its doors on North High Street two years later, connected to a 631-room high-rise Hyatt Regency Hotel. Architectural competition for expansion of the center, funded by Leslie Wexner, began

---

95. Ibid, xiii (the source of the quotation).

in 1988, and an augmented center started operations in 1993. Further expansion and rejuvenation, paid for by the Franklin County Convention Facilities Authority, took place over the next two decades. Battelle Hall was refurbished at a cost of $40 million in 2010 to become the Battelle Grand, Ohio's largest multipurpose ballroom. New private hotels went up at nearby sites, most recently the Hilton Columbus Downtown Hotel, which is connected to the convention center by an enclosed above-street walkway. In 2014 the convention center and the Hyatt claimed 1.7 million square feet of space. The center's four main exhibition halls offered a total of 335,000 square feet of space, in which were held predominantly local and regional conventions, along with an occasional national one, such as the International Gem & Jewelry Show.[96]

Complementing the convention center was Nationwide Arena, which was built on the site of the old penitentiary. The penitentiary had been razed, against the wishes of preservationists, like the Union Station, in 1996 at the urging of Mayor Greg Lashutka and with the approval of the city council. The city had purchased the site from the state for $1, preparatory to making it available for arena development. Located just north of One Nationwide Plaza and within half a mile of the convention center, Nationwide Arena was designed to bring professional sports to Columbus. The presence of professional football and basketball teams in Cleveland and Cincinnati and the existence of strong college teams in those sports at the Ohio State University—which constructed its own indoor arena, the Schottenstein Center, in the mid-1990s—seemed to rule out professional teams in football and basketball. Baseball had possibilities, but city leaders found no way to upgrade their city's Triple-A Major League team, the Columbus Clippers. The very popular Clippers played in the 15,000-seat Cooper Stadium several miles west of downtown, just off Highway 40, the Old National Road. Hopes came to focus on professional soccer and hockey. In the end, Columbus citizens got both, but the road to acquiring the teams and their playing venues was rocky.[97]

---

96. "The Greater Columbus Convention Center," at wwwcolumbusconventions.com /theconventioncenter.php, accessed on 24 October 2014. On the history of convention centers in the United States, see Heywood T. Sanders, *Convention Center Follies: Politics, Power, and Public Investment in American Cities* (Philadelphia: University of Pennsylvania Press, 2014). Sanders is very critical of convention centers as engines of urban economic growth. His detailed account shows that they rarely meet expectations. Despite problems, the Columbus center has fared better than those in many other cities.

97. For a timeline on the development of Nationwide Arena, see *Columbus Dispatch*, 26 December 1999, p. 13A. For more detail, see ibid, 7 October 2000, p. A1.

In 1978, 1981, and twice in 1997, voters in Columbus and Franklin County rejected proposed increases in sales, property, and income taxes to fund the building of an indoor arena capable of hosting professional sports teams. The campaign for a downtown arena began with the work of Jack Gibbs, a professional educator and civic activist, in the 1970s. He led an unsuccessful drive for a property-tax increase to construct a civic coliseum in 1978. With the death of Gibbs in 1981, and the continuing rejection of tax increases as funding mechanisms, the mantle for constructing an arena and bringing professional sports to Columbus passed to private businessmen. In 1993 Mayor Lashutka, a former football player at the Ohio State University, appointed Ron Pizzuti, the city's leading real-estate developer, and John H. McConnell, founder, chairman, and CEO of Worthington Industries, a major steel fabricator located in Worthington, to lead a committee whose goal was to secure professional sports franchises for Columbus. They succeeded in landing one of the founding teams of Major League Soccer in 1994, with Dallas-based sports entrepreneur Lamar Hunt as the major investor. After voters rejected a sales-tax hike to build a soccer stadium and hockey arena in 1997, the Controlling Board of the state of Ohio approved a lease of property adjacent to the state fairgrounds for a soccer stadium several miles northeast of Columbus's downtown. This action opened the way for privately financed construction of a soccer-stadium complex. Play began there on 15 May 1998, when Columbus defeated the New England Revolution team 2–0 before a sellout crowd.[98] Touted as "America's hardest-working team," the Columbus Crew has often led its league in attendance.

The acquisition of a hockey team proved more difficult. Columbus had a very popular minor-league hockey team, the Columbus Chill, which set league records for attendance while playing games in the cramped confines of the Coliseum at the state fairgrounds. From 1996 to 1997 a Columbus investment group consisting of McConnell, Pizzuti, Hunt, and Wolfe Enterprises (whose president, John F. Wolfe, was publisher of the *Columbus Dispatch*) made a successful bid for an expansion team of the National Hockey League. McConnell provided the bulk of the $120 million winning bid, putting forward 80 percent of the offer. Wolfe Enterprises provided 10 percent, and Pizzuti and other investors came up with the remaining 10 percent. Professional hockey thus seemed to be assured for Columbus, but, again, voters refused to support tax increases to finance the necessary indoor arena. On short notice, officers

---

98. *Columbus Dispatch*, 26 December 1999, p. 13A.

of Nationwide Insurance, led by Dimon McFerson, the firm's CEO, agreed to pick up 90 percent of the cost of constructing a $150 million arena on the site of the old penitentiary, with Wolfe leading the *Columbus Dispatch* into financing the other 10 percent. As in the case of the soccer stadium, private financing, rather than public expenditures, paid for the hockey arena. Ground was broken on the 20,000-seat Nationwide Arena in mid-1998, and play began there in late 2000, with the Columbus Blue Jackets taking on the Chicago Blackhawks.[99]

Columbus business leaders were genuine in wanting to revitalize their city's downtown. They put up large sums for the Columbus Blue Jackets and Nationwide Arena. Speaking for many of the investors in the team and arena in 2000, Wolfe stated, "I told him [McFerson] two generations of my family have supported the concept of a Downtown arena; we've editorialized for 30 years in support of it. If the opportunity is there, we need to step to the plate and help." There was more to the situation, however. Over time, fees for seat licenses and corporate suites helped pay for the arena. Parking fees charged in nearby Nationwide Insurance garages also offset some expenses. In addition, in 1997 the city council approved a scheme that gave the arena developers control over 13.5 acres of land around the arena. The land was sold to Nationwide at its fair market value.[100] By early 2004 Nationwide Insurance owned fifteen buildings in what had become known as the Arena District, covering about 75 acres.[101] Rents charged to businesses in those buildings were substantial. The Arena District, somewhat ironically, also became home to a small pocket park containing remnants of the Union Station, razed about two and half decades earlier, mainly several columns from the building's façade.

Then, too, the city government provided the necessary infrastructure of street alterations, electrical and water hookups, and the like. Just how important infrastructure changes were became apparent about a decade later when casino owners wanted to locate their business operations near the arena. When businesses in the Arena District—upscale pubs, restaurants, and movie theaters—opposed the entrance of a casino into their "family friendly" area, city officials refused to make needed street changes, forcing the casino owners to site their operations west of the downtown, where street changes and other infrastructural improvements were made readily available.

99. Ibid.
100. Ibid.
101. Ibid, 11 April 2004, p. F1.

Still, the moves to develop and then protect Nationwide Arena did not ensure the arena's profitability. The arena attracted events beyond Blue Jacket games; it was a major venue, for example, for rock concerts—but not for enough of them. In 2012 the Franklin County Convention Facilities Authority (FCCFA) agreed to buy the facility. In a complicated agreement, Nationwide Insurance lent the FCCFA about $43 million to pay for the purchase (a sum much less than the original construction cost). The FCCFA, in turn, would receive income with which to make payments (to be completed in 2039) from casino tax revenues collected by both the city of Columbus and Franklin County. In addition, the Ohio Department of Development pledged a decade-long $10 million loan to the FCCFA to assist in the facilities' purchase. When the arena owners proved reluctant to meet the team's request for lower rental rates, these arrangements were seen as necessary to keep the Blue Jackets in Columbus.

Columbus's revenues were essential to this plan. In early 2011 council members authorized the mayor to pledge a growing share of the city's revenues from taxes on the casino to help the FCCFA buy the arena and pay millions to operate it through 2039. No citywide or countywide vote took place on this controversial action. While many spoke in favor of the arrangement in a hearing before the city council, others opposed it. Residents from the East Side and the Hilltop questioned using city funds in this manner. A Republican candidate for the city council (which was Democratic in its composition), who had not signed up ahead of time to speak before the council, was denied the right to address that body. Shouting "You are all spineless crooks. It's not a public meeting," he left council chambers right before he was to be forcibly ejected.[102]

In 2014 Nationwide Arena boasted revenues of nearly $21 million. Ticket sales and fees accounted for nearly $14.5 million of that income, with concession revenues, facility fees, rental revenues, and the sale of merchandise bringing in smaller amounts. Only the contribution of over $4 million from the FCCFA, much of which came from city taxes on the casino, permitted arena officials to report a small "profit" of $65,000. A loss was forecast for 2015, despite a slightly larger projected contribution from the FCCFA.[103] As casino revenues failed to meet expectations, and thus city taxes from those revenues were below those hoped for, the future of city funds to the arena were in doubt.[104]

---

102. Ibid, 4 October 2011, p. A1.
103. Ibid, 11 June 2014, p. B1, reprints Nationwide Arena's budgets.
104. Ibid, 12 November 2014, p. D1; and 7 June 2015, p. A1.

The construction of a new baseball stadium for the Columbus Clippers just a few blocks southwest of Nationwide Arena seemed to complete the building of Columbus's sports venues. Named Huntington Park after Huntington Bancshares, whose officers agreed to provide $12 million in funding over twenty-three years, the facility replaced the seventy-four-year-old Cooper Stadium to the west. Franklin County officials bought land for the new stadium from private landowners. The total cost for the facility came to about $55 million, paid for mainly with state and county funds, with the city providing infrastructural improvements. Play began in April 2009.[105]

Not all was sports and conventions. Columbus City Center, a large indoor shopping mall, opened with great fanfare in the summer of 1989, just a block south of Statehouse Square, not far from the site of Columbus's third public market in the late nineteenth century. Ohio Governor Richard Celeste, one of the speakers at the opening ceremonies, encountered such thick traffic around City Center that he leaped from his automobile and sprinted two blocks to arrive at the celebration on time. Over 100,000 people jammed the mall on 18 August, buying $20,000 worth of merchandise at Marshall Field's during the first forty-five minutes the store was open.[106] Benefiting from tax abatements, City Center seemed to possess all of the elements needed for success: 144 upscale retail stores, anchored by several major department stores and connected to nearby Lazarus by an enclosed walkway over High Street; trendy restaurants; an attractive atrium, which was used for public concerts and other events; and ample, inexpensive parking in an attached, multilevel garage. In the end, however, City Center, like most other downtown malls, failed to meet the competition of outlying malls and closed its doors in the spring of 2009. (The downtown Lazarus store had closed its doors five years earlier.) The Polaris, Easton, and Tuttle malls were even newer, larger, and more fashionable than City Center. Above all, they were closer to where most middle-class residents of Columbus lived and thus were more accessible to them.[107]

Despite ongoing efforts to revitalize its downtown area, Columbus became something of an "edge city," as residents continued to move ever farther north and west.[108] Significant business centers developed

105. Ibid, 8 February 2006, p. A1; and 18 April 2009, p. A10.

106. Ibid, 18 August 2012, p. B6.

107. Ibid, 16 January 2002, p. A1; 15 September 2002, p. A1; 15 September 2002, pp. A1and D1; 24 April 2004, p. C1; 12 August 2007, p. A7; and 24 May 2014, p. D1.

108. Joel Garreau, *Edge City: Life on the New Frontier* (New York: Anchor Books, 1991), coined the term "edge city." On edge cities nationally, see Jon C. Teaford,

around Interstate 270, especially in northern municipalities such as Dublin, Worthington, and Westerville. People working in those centers often lived in nearby areas, rarely visiting Columbus's downtown. Encouraged by continuing highway construction and the building of accompanying housing subdivisions, people lived far out in what had once been countryside. Of the 60,000 new housing units added to Franklin County during the 1990s, 85 percent were built outside of Interstate 270, which ringed Columbus.[109]

Columbus's outward march raised important issues about who would pay for infrastructural improvements such as roads, schools, parks, and police and fire stations. In late 2003 Mayor Michael Coleman put forth a new city policy on this matter. In a widely publicized memo to Columbus's development director Mark Barbash, Coleman said that private real-estate developers needed to pick up more of the costs of development in a "pay as we grow" manner. "The time has come in our city's history," Coleman stated, "where it is necessary that new neighborhood development better pay for itself and its share of community services." He suggested that developers pay an impact fee for every residence they built. Matt Habash, president of the Columbus city council, agreed, observing that council members had been exploring the imposition of impact fees for some time. There was nothing revolutionary in Coleman's plan. By this time many communities across the United States imposed impact fees, including about forty communities in Ohio, mainly in the central and southwestern parts of the state.[110]

Coleman's ideas generated mixed, but generally positive, responses. The head of the Ohio Sierra Club found Coleman's memo to be "a pleasant surprise," saying that he "like[d] the fact that the mayor is talking about sprawl." Rosemarie Lisko, president of the Northwest Civic Association, representing residents in an area of rapid growth, favored the imposition of hefty impact fees on developers, stating, "They're the ones reaping the rewards of putting Columbus in a hole." On the other hand, Malcolm Porter, the acting director of the Building Industry Association

Post-Suburbia Government and Politics in the Edge Cities (Baltimore: Johns Hopkins University Press, 1997). By the 2000s there was growth as well to the south and east of Columbus, as lower-middle-class residents moved into the suburbs of Groveport and Pickerington. Nonetheless, the most rapid growth took place to the northwest and northeast of Columbus. Some cities and towns around Columbus developed into their own, smaller, edge cities, even as they served as part of Columbus's much larger edge city. See Contosta, *Lancaster*, 230–31, 258–60.

109. *Columbus Dispatch*, 28 May 2006, p. D1.
110. Ibid, 19 November 2003, p. A1.

of Central Ohio, stated that he had "a lot of questions" about Coleman's new policy, for example, "How much does it cost? What are the details?" Robert Schottenstein, the head of M/I Homes, a major real-estate developer, was caught a bit by surprise and opined diplomatically, "The health and welfare of greater Columbus and the longtime vitality of this region requires that these issues be explored."[111]

The first test of Coleman's new approach came in the spring of 2004, when Columbus officials considered rezoning 433 acres annexed in 2002 to the northwest along Hayden Run for the construction of 2,600 homes by three real-estate developers—M/I Homes, Dominion Homes, and Lifestyle Communities. City officials proposed that the developers pay much of the cost of developing wider roads in the areas surrounding their developments—not just the costs of roads, electrical connections, and sewers and water pipes inside their areas, as had been done in the past. Under Coleman's "pay as we grow" plan, developers would pay $8 million for road improvements. The city of Columbus and Franklin County would provide $11 million. Over time an additional $21 million would come from property taxes. In addition, home buyers would pay a yearly fee added to their property taxes to cover the costs of city services such as police and fire protection and garbage pickups. Tom Hart, a vice president of Dominion Homes, noted that these arrangements had been negotiated with city officials, saying, "We can't solve every economic problem the city faces. Nobody's jumping for joy on this. Honestly." Jim Hilz, the executive director of the Building Industry Association of Central Ohio, was more outspoken, claiming that with impact fees, "you start to knock families out of affordable housing."[112]

In part, Mayor Coleman was responding to worries of officials in nearby communities that the proposed housing development would hurt their towns and lands. The Dublin city manager repeatedly called for a reduction in the proposed housing density of the scheme, saying "We're concerned because the impact of the developments ultimately impacts our residents." An administrator for Washington Township emphasized that he wanted road improvements made before, not after, houses were built.[113] The vice president of the Hilliard city council said that his "primary concerns were about traffic" and "density." In a revealing twist, Columbus officials, now backed by real-estate developers,

111. Ibid, 26 October 2003, p. D1; and 22 November 2003, p. C5.

112. Ibid, 27 May 2004, p. A1.

113. Ibid, 16 April 2004, p. A1; 27 May 2004, p. A1; and 28 May 2004, p. D1.

replied, "If they don't want density, they don't want work-force housing, something a teacher, firefighters can afford."[114] In the end, the rezoning was approved unanimously by the Columbus city council, despite vocal opposition from representatives from Hilliard, Dublin, and other nearby communities. Over the next few years, the homes went up.[115]

Not surprisingly, between 2000 and 2006 many of Columbus's inner suburbs declined in population, while the populations of those farther out rose. The populations of Grandview Heights, Marble Cliff, Upper Arlington, Worthington, Bexley, and Whitehall dropped between 6 and 7 percent, and that of Westerville fell 1 percent. Suburbs and towns several miles beyond Interstate 270 gained in population, some dramatically so. To the west and north, Plain City experienced a population jump of 24 percent; Dublin had one of 16 percent; and Powell had a boost of 83 percent. New Albany to the east had a population increase of 73 percent. New Albany's population soared from 414 people in 1980 to over 8,000 in 2014. It is an upscale area northeast of Columbus, where the median price of a house was $460,000 in 2014, compared to the median price of $115,000 for a house in Columbus in that year. Pataskala, a larger, less upscale municipality, saw its population rise 23 percent. To the southwest, Pickerington experienced a population rise of 66 percent, and Canal Winchester had one of 27 percent. For the city of Columbus, the population increase during those six years was 3 percent.[116]

However, even as Columbus and its suburbs, especially the outer ones, sometimes called "exurbs," continued to spread out, political and business leaders renewed efforts to refurbish the downtown. Hubs of activity developed around the convention center and Nationwide Arena, as bars, restaurants, and movie theaters went up. The arena needed city and county support to stay in the black, but it did generate substantial business activity around it. Farther south, the closed City Center was torn down. Columbus Commons, a grassy park, home to numerous musical concerts, soon surrounded by retail shops and upscale apartments and condominiums, took its place in the early 2010s.[117] Even farther to the south, in the northern reaches of German Village, the Brewery District, composed of brew houses, restaurants, and housing, enlivened downtown life.

114. Ibid, 7 June 2004, p. D1.
115. Ibid, 15 June 2004, p. C1; and 16 December 2004, p. A1.
116. Ibid, 28 June 2007, p. A1; and 16 February 2014, p. D1.
117. Ibid, 4 February 2009, p. A1; and 26 May 2011, p. A1.

Getting people to move back downtown from suburbia, not just developing entertainment venues for conventioneers and residents, was increasingly seen as the key to the rebirth of the downtown. In 2002 business and political leaders put forward a "Downtown Plan" to encourage the construction of new housing in Columbus's downtown area. In unveiling the plan at the renovated downtown Southern Theatre in April of that year, Mayor Coleman called for the building of 10,000 new downtown housing units within a decade. Tax abatements lay at the heart of the plan. The city council approved a fifteen-year waiver for city taxes on new commercial and industrial construction downtown, a twelve-year waiver for renovated commercial and industrial buildings, and a fifteen-year waiver for new residential buildings deemed to be "of historical or architectural significance." Some downtown housing projects could even garner 100 percent tax abatements.[118] At the time, the office-building vacancy rate in downtown buildings was one of the highest in the nation, about 21 percent. Coleman also pledged the city to major investments in the downtown area and sought substantial state funding for these projects. Officers of American Electric Power, the leading electric utility in Columbus; Huntington Bank; and The Limited, Leslie Wexner's fashion firm, each pledged $2 million to a housing-loan fund to encourage the construction of downtown housing.[119]

Much of the renovation focused on the downtown waterfront of the Scioto River, along what became known as the "Scioto Mile." In 1994 Mayor Lashutka and the Franklin County commissioners created a nonprofit group, Riverfront Commons, charged with guiding redevelopment along the banks of the Scioto River. Three years later, that group put forward plans for the redevelopment of those riverbanks over a period of fifteen to twenty-five years at an estimated cost of $150 to $300 million.[120] Results appeared, as the city spent about $149 million on new or greatly renovated government structures on or near the east bank of the river between 2010 and 2014: the city hall, a public safety building, a central police headquarters, and a city office building.[121] On the west bank was the Center of Science and Industry, which had moved there from a location on East Broad Street in 1999. Boasting an exhibition space of 320,000 square feet, it was housed in the revamped Central High School, which

118. Ibid, 23 March 2014, p. A1; and 28 March 2014, p. A17.
119. Ibid, 19 March 2002, p. B4; 12 April 202, p. A1; 18 April 2002, p. C1; 21 April 2002, p. G2; 20 October 2002, p. D5; and 28 August 2003, p. C1.
120. Ibid, 26 December 1999, p. 13A.
121. Ibid, 20 October 2014, p. A1.

had closed some years before. Just to the north was Veterans Memorial Hall. Opened on East Broad Street in 1955, the hall moved to the west bank of the Scioto River in 1964, where its auditorium served as a venue for conferences and entertainment. The aged hall was slated for demolition in 2014, to be replaced by a new Ohio Veterans Memorial and Museum. Leslie Wexner and his wife pledged $25 million for the construction of the new facility, with Franklin County and state of Ohio officials expected to put forward most of the rest of the projected cost of about $50 million.[122]

Important cultural establishments remained downtown—the symphony, ballet, opera, and equity acting company—housed in new or recently refurbished theaters in buildings around Statehouse Square. The city's public art museum underwent a major expansion a few blocks to the east on Broad Street. As had been hoped by proponents of Columbus's 1908 plan, the district around the statehouse and river was becoming a center for civic activities. Occasionally there was too much success. In mid-2015 residents of tony downtown condominiums complained of the noise made by children playing in a large public fountain at the south end of the Scioto Mile, leading to restrictions in the use of that fountain.[123]

Was all of the downtown building and renovation enough to create the new, lively downtown that Mayor Coleman and other civic and business leaders fervently desired? New housing went up, and the office vacancy rate went down, to below 10 percent by 2014. In 2013 Hills Market, a grocery firm, announced that it was opening a store in the downtown area to serve people moving there. In late 2014 Brian Ross, the head of Experience Columbus, the city's Convention & Visitors Bureau, trumpeted major increases in the number of visitors to Columbus, including their spending and their overall economic impact.[124] While certainly increasing, downtown housing units did not rise in number and variety as quickly as Coleman had hoped. Much of what was built was upscale, high-end housing, with less middle- and low-income housing made available. Overall, Columbus's downtown population nearly doubled from about 3,500 people in 2000 to about 6,200 residents a decade later. Still, the 10,000 housing units predicted by Coleman had not all been built; they simply were not needed. Then, too, the downtown remained something of a captive to its past. It was long and linear, stretching for several miles along High Street, a legacy of original

---

122. Ibid, 11 June 2003, p. A1; and 21 October 2014, p. A1.
123. Ibid, 4 May 2015, p. B1.
124. Ibid, 15 October, 2014, p. D2.

settlement north along the Scioto River, furthered later on by streetcar construction. Critics thought that, as a result, Columbus's downtown still lacked the "density" and activities at street level needed to make a city not just an enjoyable place in which to live, but also economically and environmentally sustainable over the long term.[125]

Columbus residents faced additional challenges in the early twenty-first century, ones that went well beyond their downtown. Striking a workable balance between downtown revitalization and neighborhood development remained a major issue, especially how best to redevelop the city's East and South sides. Coleman, who began serving as the mayor of Columbus in 2000 and who still acted in that capacity fourteen years later, wanted the city government to reinvigorate neighborhoods as well as the downtown. Between 2010 and 2014 the city spent considerable sums on "neighborhood parks, roads, buildings, and blight."[126] Additional billions, we have seen, went into citywide water and sewer construction and alteration.

There were, as well, questions about relations between Columbus and its neighboring suburbs and towns. The development of a metropolitan park system suggested some ways those relationships might be resolved. City of Columbus parkland covered 280 acres at the close of World War I, and only a few additions took place during the 1920s. During the Great Depression city officials added just one park to their list and cut their recreation department's budget 70 percent. In 1945 voters approved a $775,000 bond issue badly needed for repairs to park and recreational facilities, beginning a long period of improvements and expansion. Parks were opened within Columbus throughout postwar decades: Whetstone Park, formerly the Fuller Farm, in 1950; the Park of Roses, within Whetstone Park, three years later; Antrim Park to the north in 1960; Bicentennial Park on the downtown riverfront in 1976; and Berliner Park, formerly Southview Park, on the Scioto River south of downtown in 1984.[127] By 2010 the city of Columbus possessed 230 parks, 23 recreation centers, and 7 public golf courses.

At the same time, the Columbus and Franklin County Metropolitan Parks District, a separate entity formed in 1945, over six decades came to own seventeen regional parks embracing over 27,000 acres, more

---

125. For a provocative examination of this issue nationally, see Anthony Flint, *This Land: The Battle over Sprawl and the Future of America* (Baltimore: Johns Hopkins University Press, 2006).

126. *Columbus Dispatch*, 20 October 2014, p. A1.

127. Ibid, 25 April 2001, p. G1.

than 42 square miles, in seven counties in central Ohio. All but two of those parks lay outside of Interstate 270. Clear Creek in Hocking Hills is a full hour's drive south of Columbus.[128] Led by Lee Tucker, a newspaper man with "a lifetime interest in conservation," a citizen group in Columbus formed the Metropolitan Park Study Committee during World War II. In May 1945 this committee recommended establishing a park district "to preserve, protect, and restore natural resources of the county," and several months later the Metropolitan Park District was created. Funding became available in 1947, and in that year the first parklands were purchased. By 2014 the district's budget came to $28 million, up from $19 million in 1999.[129]

Although residents of areas taken for parks sometimes resented what they viewed as Columbus "land grabs," cooperation more often prevailed. In exercising their right to eminent domain, Columbus officials paid market prices for parklands they acquired. Towns sometimes contributed to park development. Dublin officials contributed $7.7 million of the $20 million to develop Glacier Ridge Park, which was within their city's limits. Supported by levies passed and paid for by Franklin County voters, the parks are open free of charge to all. In 2013 Metro Parks derived $19.3 million of its $26.9 million in revenues from a ten-year property-tax levy approved by Franklin County voters in 2009. Most of the rest came from local government funds, government grants, and government partnerships.[130] Metro Parks took as its mission statement the somewhat contradictory goals of "to conserve open spaces, while providing places and opportunities that encourage people to discover and experience nature."[131]

Some of the same cooperation, and occasional friction, took place as the Columbus Zoo expanded. Private promoters had established a small zoo at the intersection of Morse Road and High Street in northern Columbus in 1903, but it lasted only a few years. City officials, strongly supported by members of the Wolfe family, set aside land for the first permanent zoo in Columbus at the southeast corner of O'Shaughnessy

---

128. Metro Parks was (is) "a separate political subdivision organized under Ohio revised Code, Section 1545." Its Board of Park Commissioners consists of three citizens of Columbus who serve three-year terms without compensation. They are appointed by the judge of the Probate Court of Franklin County and hold monthly public meetings to decide park matters. See Metro Parks, *Parkscope*, Fall, 2013, p. 3.

129. *Columbus Dispatch*, 26 August 2014, p. B1; and *Parkscope*, Winter, 2014–15, pp. 8–10.

130. *Columbus Dispatch*, 13 November 2006, p. E2; and Metro Parks, "Annual Report, 2013," unpaged.

131. *Columbus Dispatch*, 8 June 2013, p. A8.

Reservoir.[132] Opened in 1927, the zoo experienced rocky times during the Great Depression and World War II but expanded rapidly during post-war decades, especially after Jack Hanna took over as director in 1978, a position he held to 1992, when he became Director Emeritus of the zoo, a position he still holds. Becoming a national celebrity through numerous television appearances, Hanna boosted the zoo with enthusiasm. Franklin County voters responded by passing tax levy after tax levy to support the zoo. By 2010 the Columbus zoo was rated as the most family-friendly zoo in the United States. By that time about 2.4 million people attended the zoo each year, not all from Franklin County.[133]

In 2014 Franklin County voters faced a permanent property-tax levy to increase substantially their support of the zoo, whose officials contemplated building a luxury hotel on their institution's grounds to make it a resort destination for visitors. The *Columbus Dispatch* strongly supported the levy, noting that the zoo contributed "more than $238 million a year to central Ohio's economy." Many Columbus residents, however, doubted the levy's value and questioned its fairness. One letter writer to the *Dispatch* probably expressed the views of a number of Columbus residents when he penned, "I think it is unfair for only Franklin County property owners to pay taxes to support the zoo, which is located in Delaware County." Continuing, he wrote, "This is particularly true given that Delaware County residents have some of the highest incomes in the state and country." Others simply objected that the levy was too high at a time when there were many other calls for peoples' monies. The levy failed, with a resounding 70 percent vote against it.[134] However, in 2015 voters approved a smaller renewal levy by a wide margin.

## Living in Columbus

Columbus and the areas around it continued to change economically and environmentally in the late 1900s and early 2000s, as they had for two centuries. What did it mean to grow up in Columbus, as the city and its

---

132. Lentz, *As It Were*, 172–75.

133. *Columbus Dispatch*, 24 March 2013, p. B5; 9 February 2014, p. E6; and 7 February 2014, p. A19. In 2010 the zoo took over the Wilds, a financially troubled, 9,000-acre conservation area built on reclaimed coal lands in southeastern Ohio. For an introduction to that relationship, see *Columbus Dispatch*, 26 November 2012, p. B1.

134. *Columbus Dispatch*, 29 January 2014, p. A2; 14 February 2014, p. A15; and 5 June 2014, p. A1.

suburbs expanded in the mid-twentieth century? The lives of two young men coming of age in the metropolis shed light on what Columbus was like. James A. Dunn reached maturity as an African American living and going to school on the city's North Side and Central District during the 1920s and 1930s. Bob Greene, a Caucasian youth, came of age in the affluent suburb of Bexley during the 1960s. Their differences in race, time period, and locality meant that the young men had varying experiences growing up. Yet, because they lived in central Ohio, they shared common experiences as well.

Born in a small coal-mining town in West Virginia in 1913, Dunn spent his childhood in Charleston, where his mother worked as a domestic for a white family. When that family moved to Columbus in 1926, Dunn and his mother traveled north with them. At first Dunn and his mother lived in the basement of the house that the white family bought in Clintonville on Columbus's North Side. Dunn attended Clinton Heights Elementary School, finishing sixth grade there, and then went to Crestview Junior High. Dunn later recalled, "I studied hard all the time. I wanted to study and do something for my mother. I wanted to help her, get a home for my mother."[135] Dunn began participating in athletics in junior high. Crestview Junior High was integrated—not all Columbus schools were segregated at that time—and Dunn later remembered that he played speedball (soccer), track, and basketball on integrated school teams. Football was not offered in junior high, but Dunn played Saturday-morning football in an all-black citywide league. He was the captain of "Dobb's Cubs," which won the league championship one year.

After a few years in Columbus, Dunn moved with his mother to a rented house on Buttles Avenue in Flytown. Dunn went to Central High School. At Central High—later closed and renovated as the site for the Center of Science and Industry—Dunn continued his love affair with football, serving as the star quarterback for the school's team, which won city championships in 1930 and 1931. Dunn later recalled that playing the 1931 championship game in the Ohio State University stadium on Thanksgiving Day was the high point of his young life. Dunn was selected for Ohio's all-state team as a sophomore and junior. On Saturdays he enjoyed attending Ohio State University football games and sold "pinks,"

---

135. Interviews by the author with James A. Dunn, 8 April 1995 and 2 June 1995. The tape-recorded interviews, along with transcripts, are in the James A. Dunn Collection in the archives and library of the Ohio Historical Society (Ohio History Connection). See *On Board the* USS Mason: *The World War II Diary of James A. Dunn,* ed. Mansel G. Blackford (Columbus: Ohio State University Press, 1996), xxxi–xxxiii.

newspaper accounts of the games, which he hawked on High Street at the conclusions of the contests. Dunn also went to professional football games at the Ohio State Fairgrounds. Watching the Pittsburgh Steelers play the Philadelphia Eagles was "just like ice cream." There was however, more to high school than football. Dunn continued to study hard and performed well academically. He remembered, "I loved English; I loved to read . . . the *Merchant of Venice*."[136]

The schools Dunn attended were integrated, but much of social life in Columbus was segregated. Dunn later recalled that in downtown movie theaters, such as the RKO Palace and the Ohio Theatre, African Americans "sat upstairs, way in back" in sections known as "nigger heavens." Then, too, coaches for Central High, Dunn remembered, had difficult times finding diners that would serve all members of the football team when they went on the road. The coaches, Dunn recalled, "stood up for them." Dunn admired their actions in doing so, but he also felt that "the coaches used blacks to win, but didn't want too many of them."[137]

Dunn returned to Charleston with his mother in his senior year in high school, when the family for which she worked moved back there. Schools were completely segregated. Dunn again starred in football and graduated from all-black Garnet High School. He attended West Virginia State College, then an African American school in Charleston, married, and went to work at a nearby Carnegie Steel plant. During World War II, he served as a signalman on the *USS Mason*, a destroyer escort shepherding convoys to North Africa and Europe and the only oceangoing warship in the United States Navy with an all-back crew. After the conflict, Dunn sought work in Charleston but could not "get into the union" there. He returned to Columbus with his wife. In Columbus, Dunn and his wife secured jobs they liked—James with the large Defense Supply Center Columbus, his wife in a dress shop downtown. They lived on the East Side, where they raised a family, with their daughter graduating from the Ohio State University. Dunn passed away in 1996, and his wife died a few years later.[138]

Born in Columbus in 1947, Bob Greene drew up in the leafy eastern suburb of Bexley in well-to-do circumstances. His father was vice president of the Bronze Shoe Company in Columbus, a maker of memorabilia such as bronzed baby shoes. His mother was a stay-at-home wife, and his sister was a year or two younger than he. His family had a summer

---

136. Ibid.
137. Ibid.
138. Ibid. My father was captain of the *Mason*.

cottage in the bucolic Hocking Hills south of Columbus. A diary Greene kept when he was seventeen years old as a junior and senior at Bexley High School provides insights into coming of age in Columbus's suburbia. Bexley had about 15,000 residents, "virtually all of them white," and was "the kind of suburb where teenagers generally didn't have to worry about where their allowance money was coming from." Bexley was distinct from Columbus in Greene's mind. "Once you drove over the Bexley line, he observed, "you were in Columbus itself, so when people went 'downtown,' they were going to downtown Columbus." Shopping was still done downtown at the Lazarus Department Store, as well as at numerous neighborhood shops in Bexley, including local drugstores, grocery stores, record shops, ice-cream parlors, and an eatery called the Toddle House. Bexley High School had about eight hundred students, few enough, Green thought, that "everyone tended to know everyone else." Many of Greene's activities, like Dunn's a generation before, revolved around his school.[139]

Sports were important for Greene—basketball and tennis, not football. Not skilled enough to make the high-school basketball team, Green played instead in a high-school fraternity basketball league on a team named the "Epsilons." He earned a high-school varsity letter in tennis, and wearing his letter jacket to school on game days filled him with pride. He was ecstatic when Bexley beat archrival Upper Arlington in tennis one spring. Like Dunn, Greene attended Ohio State University football games and wrote about the university stadium as "the most thrilling thing I had ever seen. My heart started beating faster."[140]

Activities with other teenagers occupied most of Greene's time away from school. He loved listening to music, both folk and rock-and-roll, on his radio and record player, and he tried to copy musicians he heard by playing the guitar. The Beatles first appeared on American television in 1964. Upon seeing them perform, Greene abandoned folk music and television shows such as *Hootenanny*. Joan Baez and the Kingston Trio lost out to the Beatles and the Rolling Stones. After attending a Kingston Trio concert at the Ohio State University's Mershon Auditorium, Greene wrote, "I was bored . . . All I could think of was how cool it would be to see the Beatles live." In a telling aside, Greene noted, "I suppose the Beatles are for the New Yorks and Chicagos and Los Angeleses; the Dave Clark Five are for the Columbuses." Dating and "looking for girls," often

139. Bob Greene, *Be True to Your School: A Diary of 1964* (New York: Ballantine Books, 1988), viii–ix, 6, 94.
140. Ibid, 9, 111, 280 (the source of the quotation).

in other suburbs such Whitehall, were parts of Greene's weekend routine, for he and his friends had the use of automobiles. Road trips took them as far north as Cleveland, especially to the amusement park Cedar Point, and as far south as Cincinnati. More commonly, they cruised their neighborhood and went to high-school and country-club dances. Greene had summer jobs, including a position as a copyboy and copywriter at the *Columbus Citizen-Journal,* made possible in part by his work on the Bexley high-school newspaper.[141]

Greene left Columbus to become a nationally syndicated columnist for the *Chicago Tribune* and the author of numerous books. Unlike Dunn, he never returned to live in Columbus. Greene's social and economic status served him well. He was hardworking and took advantage of all he could learn at the *Citizen-Journal.* Equally hardworking, Dunn found his advance blocked by economic hard times and racism. Although eventually able to carve out a comfortable life for himself and his family in Columbus, Dunn proved unable to succeed beyond that city. Social capital, as always, mattered.

## Land-Use Policies and Realities
## over Two Hundred Years

Columbus's development of land-use policies certainly had controversial moments, as not all residents shared equally in planning or its results. Real-estate developers benefited most from private deed restrictions. Zoning ordinances usually ratified what had already been laid out in private covenants. As the example of the development of Upper Arlington by Ben and King Thompson shows, minorities and less-well-to-do residents in the Columbus area gained little from either zoning or deed covenants and, indeed, were hurt by them. More than that, freeway construction devastated some of their communities. Yet the direction of Columbus's growth was generally set less by zoning officials and real-estate subdividers than by the city's geography and decisions made about water use in the nineteenth century. Like many other midwestern cities, Columbus grew upstream to avoid pollution downstream. That growth, we have repeatedly seen, was to the north. The South Side, as a consequence, long remained less well developed than the rest of the city.

---

141. Ibid, 13, 19, 21, 43, 90, 267, 285, 328 (the last two pages are the sources for the quotations).

# CONCLUSION

# Columbus
# in 2012

In early 2014 humorist Joe Blundo wrote in his column for the *Columbus Dispatch*, "Columbus is at the center of a metropolitan area that has managed to grow to almost 2 million people without anyone on either coast noticing." Continuing, he observed of Columbus residents, "We're a national leader in anonymity." That condition, he noted, had given "rise to a genre of literature: travel stories in which writers from New York and Los Angeles come here and gush about all the restaurants, museums and corporate headquarters they didn't know we had." Blundo concluded, "They've been writing the same story for 30 years."[1] Many Columbus residents were still searching for a sense of identity for their city and still hoping for national recognition. They might have looked a bit more closely at their past. Many of the same types of issues that had run throughout the history of Columbus remained important in 2012.

Matters about environmental change and economic development certainly remained prominent. Some were typical urban "NIMBY" (Not In My Back Yard) ones. For about a decade, residents in northwest Columbus opposed plans by the Ohio State University to increase operations at its airfield located in that region of the city. The city of Columbus had expanded to surround the airport, once far out in the countryside, and newcomers objected to the noise created by airplanes using it. Banded

---

1. *Columbus Dispatch*, 4 January 2014, p. E1.

together as the group WOOSE (We Oppose OSU Airport Expansion), organized in 2002, they fought plans to lengthen the airport's main runway to accommodate more and larger airplanes. They urged the university to close the airport altogether. No resolution to this issue had been reached in 2015.[2]

Controversies of considerably larger regional issues continued to embroil water-use and land-use matters in Columbus into the twenty-first century. These controversies went well beyond local NIMBY concerns to encompass more broadly and more deeply felt quality-of-life issues. One of the most hotly debated matters in the early 2000s was how to preserve Big Darby Creek on the western edge of the Columbus area. This controversy resonated, in turn, with long-term environmental and development matters in the history of Columbus.

Big Darby Creek flowed for 79 miles from its headwaters in a southeasterly direction through relatively undeveloped woods, farmland, and a much-used Columbus metropolitan park to enter the Scioto River at Circleville south of Columbus. Draining 574 square miles of land, the creek lay right in the path of the spread of Columbus to the west.[3] Throughout the late 1900s and early 2000s debates raged about how best to develop lands abutting the creek—or whether to develop them at all. The main fears were that sewage and runoff of lawn fertilizer would pollute Big Darby Creek, endangering its rare flora and fauna. In late 2013 a type of catfish found only in Big Darby Creek, the tiny Scioto madtom, was declared extinct. Opponents of development thought that suburban housing would so radically increase the impacts of people on the creek that all development should be forbidden.[4]

As groups such as the Nature Conservancy bought land along Big Darby Creek to try to preserve it, members of governmental agencies pondered what to do. With a temporary moratorium on growth coming to an end in 2006, representatives of the city of Columbus; the city of Hilliard (an independent municipality to the west of Columbus); Grove City; Franklin County; the town of Harrisburg; and Brown, Norwich, Pleasant, Prairie, and Washington townships agreed to the "The Big

2. This issue received very extensive press coverage. See esp. *Columbus Dispatch*, 11 July 2013, p. B1; and *Worthington News*, 24 April 2008, p. 1.

3. Irene F. Dameron-Hager, "The Contribution of Environmental History to the Development of a Model to Aid Watershed Management: A Comparative Study of Big Darby Creek and Deer Creek Watersheds in Ohio," PhD diss., Ohio State University, 2004.

4. *Columbus Dispatch*, 4 December 2013, p. A2

Darby Accord" on how to proceed. The terms of this complex compact sought to balance suburban development with environmental protection. The building of more houses would be allowed, but only under strict regulations. The Accord envisioned the construction of twenty thousand new houses over thirty years, with a town center built just south of Interstate 70 passing from Columbus westward through the area and across the creek. However, the Big Darby Creek compact required that half of the area be retained as green space, laid out to strict standards to try to prevent any fertilizer or sewage runoffs. One requirement was very deep setback distances with natural buffers for any developments near the creek. The Accord also required that developers pay $2,500 for each house they constructed to help offset conservation costs.[5]

The Accord had teeth. Members of the Accord denied permission for a dairy farm, one proposed for 5,400 milk cows, to begin operations near Big Darby Creek in 2007. They feared that some of the projected 140,000 tons of manure its cows would produce each year would wash into the creek.[6] Five years later the advisory council to members of the Accord rejected plans of a national real-estate developer for nearly seven hundred houses and apartments in a new subdivision near Big Darby Creek, saying that its building density was too high and that the system proposed for the management of storm water was inadequate.[7] Even so, questions remained about just how well the Accord would function in the future. Breaking with precedent, the city of Columbus agreed in 2009 to extend water and sewer connections to several hundred residents in Prairie Township without requiring them to agree to annexation.[8] Taking this step seemed to indicate that Columbus officials had abandoned their imperialistic use of water and sewer systems. Not all suburban residents were convinced of this change, however. To make the Accord fully operational, officials of all of the affected governmental entities had to approve it. As of mid-2015, Hilliard officials were dragging their feet. The development of seven hundred houses and apartments turned down by the Accord's advisory council would have been in Hilliard, greatly increasing that town's tax base. Hilliard's elected councilmen wondered if strict environmental protection of Big Darby Creek was worth the cost

5. Ibid, 8 January 2006, p. D4; 10 March 2006, p. D3; 17 May 2006, p. B3; 14 June 2006, p. C1; 1 August 2006, p. D1; and 11 July 2006, p. B4.

6. Ibid, 30 December 2006, p. B1; and 12 January 2007, p. E1.

7. Ibid, 3 October 2006, p. D2; 6 January 2007, p. C1, p. C2; and 18 November 2011, p. B5.

8. Ibid, 15 August 2009, p. B1.

of the lost taxes. Meanwhile, restoration of the creek began, including the transplantation of 1,500 endangered mussels from streams in Pennsylvania to Big Darby Creek during the summer of 2012.[9]

As questions about the Big Darby Creek Accord suggested, there would be controversies and conflicts on social, economic, and environmental matters in the Columbus region well into the future. They would be settled, if past actions were any guide, by a complex, ever-changing mixture of public and private actions. Both private and public decision making had been important in the past development of Columbus. There was never a time when either was absent. Then, too, the Big Darby Creek controversy highlighted ongoing tensions between economic growth and environmental protection in the Columbus area. Residents wanted both but found themselves having to make hard choices between the two. Such tensions had run throughout the history of Columbus.

In water matters, private actions had been most important in Columbus's early years. There was no public water works until the 1870s. However, even in the antebellum years decisions made by city councilmen to try to rid their town of diseases and prevent fires had been important. Public actions became more significant with the creation of water and sewer systems after 1870, especially from 1904 onward. As part of the optimism of the Progressive era, Columbus residents saw in government actions solutions to water problems and were successful in eliminating waterborne diseases from their city. Those actions greatly shaped Columbus, encouraging, for example, the northward growth of the city. Business and political leaders saw improving their city's water supply as a way to stimulate economic growth in the early 1900s. A century later Columbus residents harbored more nuanced views. They still regarded water and sewer improvements as necessary for business advances. However, they also viewed streams passing through their region as sources of recreational enjoyment and as places of ecological importance. Hence, they worked to preserve Big Darby Creek and to restore free-running waters to the Scioto River by removing low-head dams from the river.

In land-use issues, which were perceived as less life-and-death matters than water ones, private decisions were often more important than public ones. Privately owned electric street railways helped Columbus expand, although they operated under the terms of public franchises. In later decades shopping centers and subdivisions pulled Columbus residents outward. Private deed restrictions proved more significant than public zoning

---

9. Ibid, 15 August 2012, p. B1; and 29 August 2012, p. B2.

ordinances in determining the shape of communities. Nonetheless, public actions were also important. Subdivisions and shopping malls needed
streets, including interstate highways, and water and sewer connections.
Politics and public policies, often embodying the wishes of business leaders, and frequently rubberstamping what they had already done—as in
zoning ordinances that adopted provisions from deed restrictions—made
Columbus the type of city it became.

As a midsize city in the Midwest, Columbus differed from larger
coastal metropolises such as New York and Los Angeles. Columbus
lacked the resources to build long aqueducts tapping distant water supplies. Nor, at first, was that necessary. However, as typhoid fever threated
the development of their city, Columbus residents proved remarkably
open to innovation, proving more innovative in the development of
water-use than land-use policies. The presence of a well-educated corps of
engineers and an enlightened mayor proved crucial in this respect. That
innovation, and that of similar innovations in other midsize American cities, has been too long overlooked by scholars. Conversely, Columbus residents were less innovative in their approaches to land use. In this sphere,
they were more followers than leaders. They trailed residents of New
York City and Los Angeles in the adoption of zoning, for example. As in
most midwestern cities, there was much room for Columbus to spread
out, for there were no natural boundaries to urban sprawl in central
Ohio. Consequently, land policies lacked the immediate urgency of water
policies.

Columbus was not seen as part of the Midwest by most Americans
by the late twentieth and early twenty-first centuries; yet the city's history over two centuries partook of many elements of what some scholars
have labeled the accepted "meta-narrative," or master narrative, of the
development of the Midwest.[10] Early settlers, so the story went, wrested
civilization from the wilderness (including Native Americans) by heroic
actions. Wolves howled in the nearby wilderness during pioneer days.
Economic growth and social equality, the tale continued, came to charac-
terize the growing region and city. A market economy and education for
all were part of this rosy picture of a homogeneous society imbued with
bourgeois values. Markets were open to all. With strong social and economic bases, the story continued, the Midwest and Columbus dominated
the United States well into the twentieth century. Deindustrialization, the
master narrative concluded, resulted from factors beyond the control of

---

10. Cayton and Gray, eds., *The Identity of the American Midwest,* 140–96.

Midwesterners. At the same time, as we have seen, the history of Columbus supported "anti-narratives." Society was not homogeneous. In fact, immigrant groups and African Americans, and the reactions of native whites to them, created numerous conflicts. Those conflicts made agreements on water and land issues difficult. A stratified society, not characterized by equality of opportunity, likewise complicated matters. The very existence and growth of Columbus and other midwestern cities denied the pastoralism so cherished as a defining characteristic of the Midwest by most writers, although many Columbus residents sought it in their plans for parks and their schemes for the use of the Olentangy and Scioto rivers as bucolic play lands.

Water and land issues were played out in the creation and implementation of public policies. Those policies favored some who lived in Columbus over others. As Columbus moved ever northward, following its river system, those living on the South Side, many of whom were immigrants and African Americans, suffered. Odors from the sewer plant and, later, the city's landfill wafted over their district, discouraging development. Similarly, residents living on Columbus's East Side, who were predominantly African Americans, found their community cut up by interstate highways. Columbus became the largest city in Ohio, as measured by area, and the only major Ohio city still growing in population by 2000; but urban expansion came only at social and environmental costs to some of its residents.

# Populations of Ohio
## Columbus and Other Cities, 1800–2010

| YEAR | OHIO | CINCINNATI | CLEVELAND | COLUMBUS |
|------|------|------------|-----------|----------|
| 1800 | 45,000 | N/A | N/A | N/A |
| 1810 | 231,000 | 2,540 | N/A | N/A |
| 1820 | 581,000 | 9,642 | 606 | N/A |
| 1830 | 938,000 | 25,000 | 1,706 | 2,435 |
| 1840 | 1,519,000 | 46,000 | 6,071 | 6,048 |
| 1850 | 1,980,000 | 115,000 | 17,000 | 18,000 |
| 1860 | 2,340,000 | 161,000 | 43,000 | 19,000 |
| 1870 | 2,665,000 | 216,000 | 93,000 | 31,000 |
| 1880 | 3,918,000 | 255,000 | 160,000 | 52,000 |
| 1890 | 3,672,000 | 297,000 | 261,000 | 88,000 |
| 1900 | 4,158,000 | 326,000 | 382,000 | 126,000 |
| 1910 | 4,767,000 | 401,000 | 561,000 | 181,000 |
| 1920 | 5,759,000 | 451,000 | 797,000 | 237,000 |
| 1930 | 6,647,000 | 456,000 | 900,000 | 291,000 |
| 1940 | 6,907,000 | 504,000 | 878,000 | 306,000 |
| 1950 | 7,947,000 | 503,000 | 914,000 | 376,000 |
| 1960 | 9,706,000 | 503,000 | 876,000 | 471,000 |
| 1970 | 10,652,000 | 453,000 | 751,000 | 540,000 |
| 1980 | 10,798,000 | 385,000 | 574,000 | 565,000 |
| 1990 | 10,847,000 | 364,000 | 506,000 | 633,000 |
| 2000 | 11,353,000 | 331,000 | 478,000 | 712,000 |
| 2010 | 11,537,000 | 297,000 | 397,000 | 787,000 |

# BIBLIOGRAPHIC ESSAY

I have indicated the primary and secondary sources upon which I have relied in preparing my history in footnotes in each chapter. What follows in this bibliographic essay is an account of those secondary sources that were of most importance to me, sources that might well be accessed for further information on the history of Columbus.

Ed Lentz, *Columbus: The Story of a City* (Charleston, SC: Arcadia Publishing, 2003), is the most comprehensive recent history of Columbus available and is particularly strong on social and political developments. Betty Garrett and Edward R. Lentz, *Columbus: America's Crossroads* (Tulsa, OK: Continental Heritage Press, 1980), is useful. Ed Lentz, *As It Were: Stories of Old Columbus* (Delaware: Red Mountain Press, 1998), and Bill Arter, *Columbus Vignettes* (Columbus: Nida-Eckstein Printing, 1966–69), four volumes, provides valuable sketches of life in Columbus. For photographs of Columbus's past see George E. Condon, *Yesterday's Columbus: A Pictorial History of Ohio's Capital* (Miami, FL: E. A. Seemann Publishing, 1977), and Richard E. Barrett, *Columbus, 1910–1970* (Charleston, SC: Arcadia Publishing, 2006). Charles C. Cole, Jr., *A Fragile Capital: Identity and the Early Years of Columbus, Ohio* (Columbus: Ohio State University Press, 2000), covers developments before the Civil War. Chester Winter, *A Concise History of Columbus, Ohio and Franklin County* (no place of publication listed: Xlibris Corporation, 2009), is valuable mainly for its account of Columbus's early years. Henry L. Hunker, *Industrial Evolution of Columbus, Ohio* (Columbus: Bureau of Business Research, College of Commerce and

Administration, Ohio State University, 1958), is an institutional account of the industrial development of Columbus. For a case study see Mansel G. Blackford, *A Portrait Cast in Steel: Buckeye International and Columbus, Ohio, 1881–1980* (Westport, CT: Greenwood Press, 1982).

On the development of Columbus's early water system, see Conrade C. Hinds, *The Great Columbus Experiment of 1908* (Charleston, SC: History Press, 2012). Patricia Burgess, *Planning for the Private Interest: Land Use Controls and Residential Patterns in Columbus, Ohio, 1900–1970* (Columbus: Ohio State University Press, 1994), and Douglas Knerr, *Suburban Steel: The Magnificent Failure of the Lustron Corporation, 1945–1951* (Columbus: Ohio State University Press, 2004), are valuable on twentieth-century developments. Henry L. Hunker, *Columbus, Ohio: A Personal Geography* (Columbus: Ohio State University Press, 2000), offers a geographer's view of the expansion of Columbus after World War II. Many of Columbus's developments in the twentieth century may be viewed in WOSU TV's production, "Columbus Neighborhoods." By mid-2014, eight one-hour-long programs, each of which dealt with a different district of Columbus, had been produced. An accompanying book, *Columbus Neighborhoods,* eds. Tom Betti, Ed Lentz, and Doreen Uhas Sauer (Charleston, SC: History Press, 2013), describes buildings in the neighborhoods.

Older histories remain valuable, especially for their reprints of documents now hard to find and for their biographical sketches. The ones I used include, in chronological order of their publication, William T. Martin, *History of Franklin County* (Columbus: Follett, Foster, 1858); Jacob H. Studer, *Columbus, Ohio: Its History, Resources, and Progress* (Columbus: no publisher listed, 1873); Alfred E. Lee, *History of the City of Columbus* (New York and Chicago: Munsell and Company, 1892); William Alexander Taylor, *Centennial History of Columbus and Franklin County* (Chicago and Columbus: S. J. Clark Publishing Company, 1909); Osman C. Hooper, *History of the City of Columbus Ohio: From the Founding of Franklinton in 1797, Through the World War Period, To the Year 1920* (Columbus and Cleveland: Memorial Publishing Company, 1920); and Opha Moore, *History of Franklin County* (Indianapolis: Historical Publishing Company, 1930).

I have relied on numerous works to help place developments in Columbus in their appropriate contexts. Mellior Scott, *American City Planning Since 1890* (Berkeley: University of California Press, 1969), remains valuable, as do the nineteen essays comprising *Planning the Twentieth-Century American City,* eds. Mary Sies and Christopher Silver (Baltimore: Johns Hopkins University Press, 1996). Most recently the *Journal of Urban History* has published thematic issues of special use, including "Technology and the City," vol. 25 (March 1999), and "Technology, Politics, and the Structuring of the City," vol. 30 (July 2004).

Martin V. Melosi, *The Sanitary City: Environmental Services in Urban America from Colonial Times to the Present* (Pittsburgh: University of Pittsburgh Press, 2008), first published by Johns Hopkins University Press in 2000, is crucial on water issues. See also Martin V. Melosi, *Precious Commodity: Providing Water for America's Cities* (Pittsburgh: University of Pittsburgh Press, 2011), a collection of eight essays. Daniel Schneider, *Hybrid Nature: Sewage Treatment and the Contradictions of the Industrial Ecosystem* (Cambridge, MA: MIT Press, 2011), is the place to begin to review the history of sewage matters. Catherine McNeur, *Taming Manhattan: Environmental Battles in the Antebellum City* (Cambridge, MA: Harvard University Press, 2014), deals with water matters and much more. David Stradling and Richard Stradling, *Where the River Burned: Carl Stokes and the Struggle to Save Cleveland* (Ithaca: Cornell University Press, 2015), examines environmental and social issues.

For developments in the state of Ohio, see Andrew R. L. Cayton, *Ohio: The History of a People* (Columbus: Ohio State University Press, 2002); Kevin F. Kern and Gregory S. Wilson, *Ohio: A History of the Buckeye State* (Chichester, UK: Wiley Blackwell, 2014); George W. Knepper, *Ohio and Its People* (Kent, OH: Kent State University Press, 2003); and *The Documentary Heritage of Ohio,* eds. Phillip R. Shriver and Clarence E. Wunderlin, Jr. (Athens: Ohio University Press, 2000). The seven essays in *Ohio and the World, 1753–2053: Essays toward a New History of Ohio,* eds. Geoffrey Parker, Richard Sisson, and William Russell Coil (Columbus: Ohio State University Press, 2005), are valuable, as are the twenty-four biographical essays in *Builders of Ohio,* eds. Warren Van Tine and Michael Pierce (Columbus: Ohio State University Press, 2003). On antebellum Ohio see *The Center of a Great Empire: The Ohio Country in the Early Republic,* eds. Andrew R. L. Cayton and Stuart D. Hobbs (Athens: Ohio University Press, 2005), a collection of nine essays; and R. Douglas Hurt, *The Ohio Frontier: Crucible of the Old Northwest, 1720–1830* (Bloomington: Indiana University Press, 1996).

On midwestern history and studies, see *The Identity of the American Midwest: Essays on Regional History,* eds. Andrew R. L. Cayton and Susan E. Gray (Bloomington: Indiana University Press, 2001), a collection of eleven essays. For a recent survey of historical literature, see Jon K. Lauck, The *Lost Region: Toward a Revival of Midwestern History* (Iowa City: University of Iowa Press, 2012). Now-classic studies include Andrew R. L. Cayton and Peter S. Onuf, *The Midwest and the Nation: Rethinking the History of an American Region* (Bloomington: Indiana University Press, 1990); and James R. Shortridge, *The Middle West: Its Meaning in American Culture* (Lawrence: University Press of Kansas, 1989). Most writers—especially poets and novelists—who have depicted the Midwest in the twentieth century have pictured it as a land of farms and small towns, largely ignoring the region's large cities. On this enduring image of the Midwest in literature, see William Barillas, *The Midwest Pastoral: Place and Landscape in the Literature of the American Heartland* (Athens: Ohio University Press, 2006). For an examination of the realities of the diversity, complexity, and heterogeneity of the Midwest, state-by-state, see the essays by thirteen scholars in *Heartland: Comparative Histories of Midwestern States,* ed. James H. Madison (Bloomington: Indiana University Press, 1988).

# INDEX

*Note: Page numbers in italics refer to figures.*

Abbott, Carl, 14, 22

Abrams, Richard, 91

African Americans, 28–29, 84, 85, 124–25, 178–86, 211; discrimination against based on zoning and covenants, 165–66, 169; disenfranchisement of, 155; Great Migration of, 149, 184n86; middle-class, 185

agriculture, 9–10, 43; commercial vs. subsistence, 10; declining importance of, 30

AIU Citadel, 137

Akron, 10, 112n54; college graduates in, 40; population of, 31; unemployment rate in, 31

Allied Council of Central Civic Associations, 102

Alum Creek, 53, 70, 89, 130–31, 145; pollution of, 71, 74, 101, 102n19; water supply from, 105

Alum Creek Dam/Reservoir, 106

American Electric Power, 11, 197

American Federation of Labor (AFL), 153n96, 182

American Insurance Union, 137

American Rolling Mills, 152

American Water Works Association (AWWA), 93n139; Ohio Chapter of, 93n139

amusement parks, 133–34

Anderson, Sherwood, 10

Anheuser-Busch brewery, 105

Arena District, 46, 191

Arlington Country Club, 37

Arlington Ridge Company, 169

Ashbury Company, 169

Assembly, 37

automobile and automobile parts manufacturing, 28, 30

Automobile Club, 37

automobiles, 137–38, 148, 175, 178; growing importance of, 157–58, 162

Banc One Corporation, 40

Barbash, Mark, 194

Bartholomew, Harland, 164

Battelle Hall / Battelle Grand, 189

Battelle Memorial Institute, 188

Beechwold Community Center, 102

Bellepoint, 109, 110

Berlin (Germany): sewage farming in, 88; slow-sand filtering in, 64

Bexley, 102n19, 107, 128n29, 130–31, 133, 140, 158, 173, 183, 196

Bhutan, refugees from, 171

Big Darby Accord, 208–9

Big Darby Creek, 104, 108, 110; as National Scenic River, 110; pollution of, 207; preservation of, 207–9; as State Scenic River, 110

"Big Dig," 113

Big Walnut Creek, 53, 104, 105

Birkbeck, Morris, 62

Blackberry Patch, 184

Blacklick Creek, 53

Blueprint Columbus, 113

Blundo, Joe, 38, 172, 206

bond issues, 92–93, 105, 112, 159, 185

Borden Company, 39

Boston, 3, 47–48, 113, 114; competition for water in, 104n26; municipal water system in, 55, 64; school desegregation in, 186; urban water development in, 50; water filtration system in, 64

Boston Associates, 28

the Bottoms, 139

Boulder Dam, 100

Brentnell, 183

BrewDog, 42

Brewery District, 196

brewing, 28, 75

Brooklyn, sewer system in, 72

Brown, Kirk, 14n18

Brown, Rowland, 186–87

Brown, Uriah, 13–14

Brown Township, 207

Brown v. Board of Education, 186

Buck, Thompson, 168n31

Buckeye Steel Castings Company, 26, 33–38, 35, 43, 86, 126, 130, 147, 152–53

Building Industry Association of Central Ohio, 194–95

Burgess, Patricia, 11, 164–65, 167

Burnham, Daniel, 123, 136

Bush, Flora, 37–38

Bush, George Herbert Walker, 37n87

Bush, George W., 37n87

Bush, Samuel Prescott, 33–38, 47, 96, 147, 153

business growth, 47–48; tension between environmental change and, 2, 6, 95, 100, 101, 206, 209

Buttles, Joel, 13

California, 44; average daily consumption of water in, 105

Camp Chase, 19

Canal Winchester, 196

Capital University, 128

Cardinal Health, 11

CARE, 45

Carnegie Steel, 152

casino, 134, 191–92

Casto, Don M, 175, 177

Cather, Willa, 5

Cayton, Andrew R. L., 4, 23, 124

Celeste, Richard, 193

Center of Science and Industry, 197

Central Market, 19

Central Reservation, 117

Central States Water Works Association, 93n139

cesspools, 54, 74, 84

Chadwick, Edwin, 55

Champion Avenue Elementary School, 151

Chase, Salmon P., 20

Chicago, 13, 47–48; Columbian Exposition, 129; fire in, 72; sewage research in, 81n106; sewer system in, 72; suburban population of, 170; urban water development in, 50; water-intake cribs in, 67

Children's Hospital, 38

China: sewage treatment in, 88

Chittenden Hotel, destruction of by fire, 72

cholera, 53, 55–56, 58, 64n53, 65, 74, 90

Cincinnati, 8, 10, 13, 16, 22, 26, 33, 48, 90, 128, 147; African Americans in, 149, 184; average daily consumption of water in, 104; chlorination in, 84; college graduates in, 40; destruction of communities by freeways in, 180; employment in, 40; firefighting in, 60; municipal water system in, 63; population of, 14n19, 23, 32, 38, 171, 213; professional sports in, 189; sewer system in, 68, 73n84; suburban population of, 170; tax base of, 107; typhoid fever in, 63, 74; water filtration in, 64, 67

Circleville, 207

Citizens' Sanitary Association, 71

City Beautiful plan (1908), 3, 140, 141–55, 157, 159; and neighborhoods, 149–55

city government, 39, 42, 84, 91, 99, 183, 191

City Planning Commission, 112

civic center, proposed, 145, 146

"civic revival," 147

Civil War, 19–20

Clark, Beth, 149

class, 149; conflict, 153

Clay, Henry, 18

clean air and water laws, 110

Cleveland, 8, 10, 13, 16, 22, 26, 27, 48, 89, 90, 124, 147n79; African Americans in, 149, 184; average daily consumption of water in, 105; board of health in, 65; college graduates in, 40; destruction of communities by freeways in, 180; environmental justice in, 85n114; municipal water system in, 63; population of, 14n19, 23, 31, 32–33, 38–39, 171, 213; professional sports in, 189; rain gardens in, 113; sewer system in, 68; suburban population of, 170; tax base of, 107; traffic lights in, 137; transition of from industrial to service city, 40n92; typhoid fever in, 74; unemployment rate in, 31, 40; water-intake cribs in, 67

Cleveland, Columbus, and Cincinnati Railroad, 16

Cleveland Gatling Gun Regiment, 34

Clintonville, 158; green infrastructure in, 113

"cloud scrapers," 136

Cole, Charles, 117

Coleman, Michael B., 171, 194–95, 197, 199

Columbus: airport, connection to, 178, 180–83; annexation by, 107, 158, 174, 187, 208; anomalous nature of, 170–71; anti-narratives concerning, 211; as "Arch City," 91; Articles of Incorporation of, 57–59; average daily consumption of water in, 104; boundaries of, 118, 129–30, 187; as capital of Ohio, 11, 13–14, 47, 117; city charter for, 154–55, 158; city plan of, 92; and college graduates, 42; as commercial city, 11–23; congestion in, 135–37, 140, 157; as crossroads for United States, 9; as dangerous place to live in antebellum era, 53; design for, 1; diversity of, 124, 171; as "edge city," 193; elements of business success in, 47–48; employed workers in, 40n93; experiences of living in, 201–5; as financial, educational, and service center, 38–43; flushing toilets as rarity in, 85n113; geographic location of, 47; as home to state government, 8; identity of, 42, 172, 206; incorporation of as city, 14, 57; as industrial metropolis, 26–33; as industrial powerhouse, 10; as "Intelligent Community of the Year" (2015), 42; as largest city in Ohio, 211; as major American metropolis, 172; map of new water and sewer system, 77; master plan (1957), 164; and midwestern state capitals, 13; as multifaceted city, 1; naming of, 12–13, 13n14; north-south development of, 134; ordinances concerning fire, 59; ordinances concerning odors from industry, 118; ordinances to clean up, 57–58; original plat of, 121; outward march of, 194; as part of the Midwest, 210; police and traffic direction in, 137–38, 138; population of, 9, 14, 14n19, 31–32, 38–39, 158, 171, 211,

213; relations between neighboring suburbs and towns and, 199; settlers in, 124–25; slow development of, 13; spatial expansion of, 9, 171; story of, as America's story, 2; unemployment rate in, 30–32; young professionals, retention of by, 42

Columbus and Franklin County Metropolitan Parks District, 199–200

Columbus and Xenia railroad, 16, 123

Columbus Auto Club, 148

Columbus Blue Jackets, 191–92

Columbus Board of Health, 58, 65

Columbus Board of Public Service, 78

Columbus Board of Realtors, 182

Columbus Board of Trade, 27, 29–30, 66, 78, 122, 127–28, 139, 141–42; "The City of Columbus," 30

Columbus Brewery District, 125

Columbus Buggy Company, 27

Columbus Chamber of Commerce, 27n66, 31, 99, 106, 182, 186–87

Columbus Chill, 190

Columbus City Center shopping mall, 193

Columbus City Hall, 19, 122, 197; destruction of by fire, 72, 122; inadequacy of, 140

Columbus Clippers, 189, 193

Columbus Club, 37

Columbus Commons, 196

Columbus Coop Foundry, 151

Columbus Crew, 190

Columbus Cultural Arts Center, 126

Columbus Department of Building and Zoning Services, 167

Columbus Department of Engineering, 98

Columbus Department of Public Service, 88

Columbus Division of Water, 108, 110

Columbus Female Benevolent Society, 25

Columbus Forge & Iron, 151

Columbus Gallery of Fine Arts, 38

Columbus Landmarks Foundation, 179

Columbus Public Schools, 187–88

Columbus Railway, Power & Light Company, 133

Columbus School Board, 151

Columbus State Hospital, 122

Columbus Street Railroad, 132

Columbus Water Works, 29, 83, 98, 103

Columbus Zoo, 200–201

Concord Township, 109

Conn, Steve, 171, 180

Cooper Stadium, 193

corn production, 9–10, 21, 23

Cornell, Brownie, 105

covenants. See private covenants

Cox, James A., 97

Cremean, Warren "Hap," 106

Cumberland Ridge, 183

Curtiss-Wright Aviation Company, 33

Cuyahoga River, pollution of, 67, 110

Darby Creek. See Big Darby Creek

Dayton: board of health in, 65; college graduates in, 40; flood relief activities in, 96; Great Miami River, 98; homeownership in, 133

decentralization, urban, 157, 171

deed covenants. See private covenants

Deep Stage aquifer, 104

deindustrialization, 10–11, 32, 39, 179, 210

Delaware County, 109

Dennison, William, 69

Deshler, David W., 52, 52n7, 124

Deshler, Elizabeth ("Betsy") Green, 52, 55, 139

Deshler, Helen, 38

Deshler, William, 139

Detroit, 27; homeownership in, 133; street layout of, 118

Dickens, Charles, 24–25

diphtheria, 56, 58

disease: miasmic vs. bacterial causes of, 50, 55, 58, 63–67; vaccination against, 65. See also infectious disease; waterborne diseases

Dominion Homes, 195

downtown: balance between neighborhood development and revitalization

of, 199; central business district,
159; cultural establishments in, 198;
demise of, 126, 176–77, 193–94;
development of, 3, 32, 134, 155;
"Downtown Plan," 197; high priority
placed on, 185–86; housing projects, 197–98; improvements to, 159,
185–86, 188–93, 196–99; lacking
density, 199; office-building vacancy
rate, 197–98; residential population
of, 184, 198; return to, from suburbs,
197; and sewers, 72; tax abatements
for, 197; waterfront development,
197
Dublin, 187, 194, 196
Dublin Road Water Works, 129
Duncan, Robert M., 186
Dunn, James A., 202–3, 205
Dwight, Margaret, 15
dysentery, 56, 64n53

Eagle Coffee House, 20
East Columbus, 183
Eastern Europe, immigrants from, 29,
84, 151
Eastgate, 183
East Side, 71, 95, 107, 108, 172, 185,
192; African American community
in, 180, 184, 211; as "Bronzeville,"
184n85; intrusion of commercial and
industrial business into, 165; redevelopment of, 199; segregation in, 150
East Side Pumping Station, 70, 76,
84n110
economic development, 9–11, 95, 101,
206
education, 32, 38–43. See also schools
environmental change, tension between
business growth and, 2, 6, 95, 100,
101, 206, 209
environmental issues, 9, 95, 104; and
public policies, 110–14; suburban
development and, 208; urban expansion and, 211
environmental justice, 51–52, 85, 89, 93,
108, 165
epizootic disease, 56, 74
Erie and Kalamazoo railroad, 16

Espy, Ben, 183
ethnicity, 149; conflict in, 153
Euclid, 160
*Euclid v. Ambler,* 160
Evans-Cowley, Jennifer, 42
Experience Columbus. *See* Greater
Columbus Convention and Visitors
Bureau
"exurbs," 196

F. & R. Lazarus department store. *See
under* Lazarus
Farm Bureau Life Insurance Company, 44
Farm Bureau Mutual Fire Insurance Com-
pany, 44
Farm Bureau Mutual Insurance Company,
43
Fashion Department Store, 176
Federal District Courthouse, 32
Federal Glass, 152
federal government, 39–40, 112; funding
by, 17, 32–33, 103, 106, 162, 172,
185
Federal Highway Administration, 181
Federal Housing Authority (FHA), 166–
67, 173–74, 175
Federated Women's Clubs, 129, 142
Federation of Sewage Works Associations,
93n139
finance industries, 32, 38–46
firefighting, 59–60, 72
FirstEnergy, 11
Flakes, Olivia, 182
Flytown, 139, 151; disappearance of, 179
Foos, Joseph, 12
Ford, Henry, 30
Frankfurt (Germany), zoning in, 160–61
Franklin, Peter D.: *On Your Side,* 43n105
Franklin County, 27–28, 32, 106, 158,
162–63, 171, 193–95, 198, 200–201,
207; floods in 98; "free people of
color" in 124; rural nature of, 22–23
Franklin County Convention Facilities
Authority (FCCFA), 189, 192
Franklin County Health Planning Coun-
cil, 182

Franklin County Regional Planning Commission, 162–63

Franklin Park, 128–29, 131, 145

Franklinton, 11–12, 15, 18, 21, 61, 62–63, 71, 95, 118, 126, 130, 133

freeways. *See* highways

Friends of Sawmill Wetlands, 111

Gahanna, 178

garbage-disposal plant, 88–89, 115, 141

German Village, 125, 128, 133, 135, 151, 179, 196; gentrification of, 179

Germany, 44; immigrants from, 28, 47, 125–26, 151

Gibbs, Jack, 190

Gladden, Washington, 148

Goodale, Lincoln, 126–27

Goodale Park, 20, *127*, 127–28

Goodale Redevelopment Project, 179

Goodspeed, Wilbur, 34

Goodyear Tire & Rubber, 11

Grand Coulee Dam, 100

Grand Rapids: homeownership in, 133

Grandview Avenue Shopping Center, 175

Grandview Heights, 133, 173, 184, 196

Gray, Samuel, 78

Great Britain: activated-sludge process in, 100; sprinkling filters in, 87; zoning in, 161

"The Great Columbus Experiment" (1904–08), 76–91, 94, 105

Great Depression, 30–32, 44, 103, 134, 137, 157, 199

Greater Columbus Convention and Visitors Bureau, 172, 198

Greater Columbus Convention Center, 188–89, 196

Great Flood (1913), 95–98, *96*; deaths in, 96

"great mortality transition," 90

"Great White City" conservatory, 128

Greece, immigrants from, 151

Greene, Bob, 202, 203–5

green technologies, 113

Gregory, John H., 74, 76, 80, 82–83, 86, 93, 105, 147

Griggs, Julian, 78–80, 84–85, 87, 92–93

Griggs Dam/Reservoir, 79, *80*, 82, 89, 94, 97, 98, 105, 109, 129, 145

Grove City, 207

Groveport, 193n108

Guthrie, Woody, 100

Habash, Matt, 194

Hamilton: board of health in, 65

Hammond, Jerry, 183

Hanford Village, 180, 184

Hanna, Jack, 201

Hanna, Mark: death of as impetus for action on water and sewage, 51, 75, 116

Hannah Neil Mission and Home for the Friendless, 25

Hap Cremean Plant, 106

Harrisburg, 207

Hart, Tom, 195

Hayden, Daisy, 38

Hayden, Peter, 118

Hayden's Cut, 118, 124, 178

Haygood, Wil, 107, 172, 185

Hazen, Allen, 82

highways, construction of, 172–73, 178–84, 194, 205, 210–11

Hilliard, 195–96, 207, 208

Hilltop, 130, 133, 150, 158, 192

Hilz, Jim, 195

Himes, J. S., Jr., 150

Hinds, Conrade C., 49, 70n73, 76, 80, 89, 106n30

Holly, Birdsill, 69

Holly Manufacturing Company, 69

Holly pumps, 69–70, 82, 84

"home rule," 154

Honda, 40

Hoover, Charles, 81, 83, 93, 105, 106n30, 147; *Hoover's Water Supply and Treatment* ("Lime Book"), 83

Hoover, Clarence, 81, 93, 105–6, 147

Hoover, Herbert, 160

Hoover Dam (Colorado River), 100

Hoover Dam/Reservoir, 105–6

housing, 148, 182, 188, 194–98; in commercial and industrial districts, 160; congestion in, 157; public, 184; redevelopment of, 163–64; segregation in, 186
Howe, Henry, 26
Hungary, immigrants from, 151, 178
Hunt, Lamar, 190
Huntington Bancshares, 193
Huntington Bank, 197
Huntington Center, 25
Huntington Park, 193
Hurst, Anne S., 45
Hurt, R. Douglas, 10

Imhoff, Karl, 101, 102n19
immigrants/immigrant neighborhoods, 85, 125–26, 174n52, 178, 211
impact fees, 194
Indiana, 9; average daily consumption of water in, 105
Indianola Highlands, 133
Indianola Park, 134
industrial districts, 159–60
industrialization, 10–11, 26–33, 43, 64, 129, 140
infectious disease, 52–53
insurance industry, 40, 43–46
Intelligent Community Forum, 42
interstate highways. See highways
Interstate 670, construction of and displacement of African American communities by, 180–84; environmental and budgetary issues, 181–82
Ireland, immigrants from, 28, 47, 125, 151
Ironton: board of health in, 65
ironworks, 29, 30, 47
Italian Village, 151, 183
Italy, immigrants from, 151, 178

Jackson Pike Plant, 103, 113–14
Jacobs, Gregory S., 31, 188
Japan: sanitation and waterborne diseases in, 64n53; sewage treatment in, 88; zoning in, 161

Jeffrey, Joseph A., 141
Jeffrey, Robert, 79, 92, 141–42, 147, 153
Jeffrey Manufacturing Company, 141–42, 153
Jennings-Lawrence Company, 103
Jersey City (New Jersey), chlorination in, 84
Johnson, Charles, 168
Johnston, James, 12
JPMorgan Chase & Company, 40

Karb, George J., 78, 92
Keever Starch, 152
Kelsey, Albert, 143
Kentucky, migrants from, 124, 178
Kerman, Piper, 42
Kern, Kevin, 124
Kerr, John, 12
Kilbourne, James, 60
King Thompson Company, 168
Know-Nothing Party, 125–26
Kolb, Charles B., 140n60
Kroger, 11
Ku Klux Klan, 153

labor organizations, 153n96
Laird, Pamela Walker, 47
Lake Erie, 15, 63, 67, 72; eutrophication of, 110
Lancaster, 17, 19, 20, 58, 107, 118, 124
land use, 1–2, 9, 93, 116–55; controversies in, 207; downtown, neighborhood, and suburban development, 3, 133; policies and realities, 205; and spatial and social layout of Columbus, 51; urban development and, 156–205; urban expansion and, 129–41; variety of, 123
Lashutka, Greg, 189–90, 197
Lattimer, George W., 142
Lauck, Jon K., 4
Lazarus, Fred, 135–36
Lazarus, Ralph, 135–36
Lazarus, Robert, 31
Lazarus, Simon, 135–36

Lazarus Department Store, 39, 97n8, 135–36, 173, 176; branches of in suburban shopping centers, 176–77, 186; closure of, 41, 193

Lechner Mining Machine Company, 141

Lee, Alfred E., 53, 73, 88

Lentz, Andrea, 133

Lentz, Ed, 118, 129–30, 153, 158

LeVeque, Katherine S., 137n55

LeVeque, Leslie, 137

LeVeque (Lincoln) Tower, 137

Lever, William, 161

Lifestyle Communities, 195

The Limited, 40, 182, 197

Lincoln, John, 137

Lincoln, Murray D., 43–46, 47

Lincoln Theatre, refurbishment of, 185

Lindbergh, Charles, 30

Linden Community Center, 102

Linden Heights, 133

Lisko, Rosemarie, 194

London, 131

London (UK): Chelsea water works, 64; sewer system in, 72

Lord, Austin, 142–43

Los Angeles, 3, 210; urban water development in, 50; zoning code in, 160

Lowrie, Charles, 142–43

lunatic asylum, 122, 130; fire at, 122

Lustron Corporation, 33

Lutheran Theological Society, 125

MacNeil, H. A., 143

Madison (Wisconsin), 13; annexation by, 174

Magnetic Springs, 131

Mahoney, Timothy, 8

Main Pumping Station, 86

malaria, 56, 74, 125

manufacturing, 10, 21–22, 27–31, 33, 39, 162

Marathon Petroleum, 11

Marble Cliff, 133, 184, 196

Mark, Mary Louise, 150

market house, 18–19; regulation of, 19

McCabe, Lida Rose, 16, 19

McConnell, John H., 190

McGerr, Michael, 91

McKinley, William, 75

McLaughlin, Alexander, 12

Melosi, Martin, 50, 85; The Sanitary City, 50

Metropolitan Committee, 106, 185

Metropolitan Park District, 200

Metropolitan Park Study Committee, 200

Metropolitan Columbus Schools Committee, 186–87

Michigan, 5, 9; average daily consumption of water in, 105

Mid-Ohio Regional Planning Commission (MORPC), 163, 181, 183; "Insight2050," 163

Midwest: deindustrialization of, 39; distinctiveness of, 4; ethnicity of, 124; homeownership in, 133; meta-narrative of development of, 210; Ohio as part of, 5; population of, 31; as "Rust Belt," 40; suburban growth in, 170; urbanization of, 22

M/I Homes, 195

Mill Creek, 108, 110

Miller, James, 168

Milwaukee: homeownership in, 133; municipal water system in, 64; sewage research in, 81n106

Minerva Park, 134

Mississippi River, 23

Moore, Opha, 53

Morgan, Arthur, 98n10

Mount Vernon, board of health in, 65

Municipal Union, 142

National Hotel, 20

National Road, 15, 17, 19, 20, 24

Nationwide Arena, 189, 191–92, 196

Nationwide Insurance, 11, 39–40, 43–46, 46, 191–92

Nationwide Insurance Enterprise, 46

Native Americans, 100

Nature Conservancy, 207

neighborhoods, 180, 182–83; balance
    between downtown revitalization
    and development of, 199; and City
    Beautiful plan, 149–55; development
    of, 3, 131, 133; immigrant, 125;
    segregation in, 186; working-class vs.
    middle-class, 85

Neil, William, 23–26, 28, 47, 61, 124,
    130

Neil House, 24–25, 25; destruction of by
    fire, 60, 69

Neil House Hotel, 25

Nelson Road water plant, 105

Nepal, refugees from, 171

networking, 24, 37, 47

New Albany, 182, 196

Newark, 131

New Deal projects, 32, 103

New England, migrants from, 124–25

New York City, 3, 47–48, 114, 210;
    board of health in, 58; Central Park,
    127; Engineers Club, 38; homeowner-
    ship in, 133; municipal water system
    in, 55, 64; ordinances for cleaning
    up, 57n25; street layout of, 118;
    urban water development in, 50; zon-
    ing code in, 160

Nichols, J. C., 168

NIMBY (Not In My Back Yard), 206–7

Noble, John, 20

Norfolk & Western Railroad, 78

North American Aviation, 33

North Market, 19

North Side Civic Association, 102

Northside Improvement Association, 102

Northwest Civic Association, 194

Northwest Ordinance (1787), 4, 61n41

Norwich Township, 207

Nye, Russell, 147


Ogle, Maureen, 51

Ohio: average daily consumption of
    water in, 105; decline of city centers
    in, 176n58; deindustrialization of,
    39; disease and mortality in, 53n8;
    economic development in, 9–11;
    industrial output in, 32; leading
    industries of–11; as part of Midwest,
    5, 9n3; municipal water works in,
    66; population of, 14n19, 33, 38n88,
    213; recession in (1970s), 181;
    unemployment rate in, 31–32; urban
    reform in, 147n79

Ohio Agricultural and Mechanical Col-
    lege, 41

Ohio and Erie Canal, 15, 54

Ohio Bell, 39

Ohio Board of County Commissioners, 32

Ohio Club, 37

Ohio Department of Development, 192

Ohio Department of Health, 85

Ohio Department of Highways, 173

Ohio Department of Transportation
    (ODOT), 181, 183

Ohio Environmental Council, 111

Ohio Environmental Protection Agency,
    112

Ohio Farm Bureau Federation, 43–45

OhioHealth, 40

Ohio Historical Society, 14n18

Ohio History Connection, 14n18

Ohio Manufacturers' Association, 153

Ohio Mulch, 114

Ohio National Guard, 126, 153

Ohio River, 15, 16, 60, 63, 114; dumping
    of sewage into, 68, 110

Ohio Sierra Club, 194

Ohio Stage Company, 24

Ohio State Board of Education, 187

Ohio State Department of Health, 79,
    85–87, 101–2

Ohio State Fair, 38, 128

Ohio State University, 8, 24, 36, 39–42,
    48, 130, 133, 135, 149–50, 189–90;
    airfield expansion, 206–7; as booster
    of central Ohio economy, 41; enroll-
    ment at, 41; "incubator" of high-tech
    firms at, 41; Industry Liaison Office,
    41; Schottenstein Center, 189

Ohio Theatre, 32, 122

Ohio Valley Sanitation Compact, 68

Ohio Veterans Memorial and Museum, 198

Olentangy Park, 133–34

Olentangy River, 11, 23, 53, 60–61, 69, 71, 76, 82, 89, 98, 104, 111, 145, 150, 211; pollution of by sewage, 74, 101

Olmsted, Frederick Law, 127

One Nationwide Plaza, 46, 189

Onuf, Peter S., 4, 23, 124

O'Shaughnessy, Jerry, 98

O'Shaughnessy Dam/Reservoir, 98–100, 99, 104, 105, 109

outhouses, 54, 57

Paisley (Scotland): slow-sand filtering in, 64

Palace Theatre, 137n55

Panhandle Route, 37

parks, 3, 92, 99, 111, 126–29, 141–42, 144–45, 148, 199–200, 211

Parsons Avenue Business Men's Association, 102

Parsons Avenue Water Plant, 108–9

Pasteur, Louis, 65

pastoralism, 211

Pataskala, 196

Patterson, John H., 96

Penick v. Columbus Board of Education, 186

penitentiary, 119, 189; fire at, 119

Pennsylvania, 10; average daily consumption of water in, 105

Pennsylvania Railroad, 30

Philadelphia, 3, 33, 48, 114, 118; municipal water system in, 55, 64; street layout of, 118; urban water development in, 50; water filtration system in, 64; Wissahickon Heights, 165

Pickerington, 193n108, 196

Pickerington Ponds, 110; Wildlife Refuge, 111

Pierce, Elijah, 185

Pittsburgh, Cincinnati, and Chicago and St. Louis Railroad, 37

Pizzuti, Ron, 190

Plain City, 196

Pleasant Township, 207

Poindexter Village, 184–85

Poland, immigrants from, 151

politics, 2, 5, 115, 210; and business, 19; and expert knowledge, 51; purification of, 91; reform of, 147

pollution, of water supplies, 2, 55, 64, 70–73, 84, 101, 105, 110, 205, 207

population density, 171; control of, 157

Porter, Malcolm, 194–95

Portsmouth: board of health in, 65

Port Sunlight (Great Britain), 161

Post Office Building, 32

poverty, amelioration of, 55, 91

Powell, 196

Prairie Township, 207, 208

private covenants, 156, 165–67, 169–70, 205, 209–10; power of, 167; and racial discrimination, 165–66, 169

privy vaults, 54, 57, 74, 84

Procter & Gamble, 11

professional sports, 189–91

Progressive Insurance, 11

progressivism, 91, 147; limits to, 93

Providence (Rhode Island), diagnostic laboratory in, 65

public education system, problems with, 186–88

public health, 65, 92

public / private interaction, 2–3, 18, 95, 132, 156, 157–67, 209–10

public schools, 39, 186–87

public zoning, 156, 157–67, 170, 175, 205, 209–10; area commissions on, 162; first ordinance (1923), 158–61; weaknesses of, 164–65, 167

race/racism, 149–50; conflict and violence, 153; discrimination based on, 165–66, 169

railroads, 16–17, 19, 24–25, 29–30, 34, 38, 47

real estate, 23–26, 133, 157, 164, 165, 167, 174, 205

regional planning, 156, 162–63

regional shopping malls, 175–77, 185

retail stores, 174–77. *See also* Lazarus
  Department Store
Review Club, 37
Rhodes, James A., 106, 185
Richards, Erin Swallow, 82
Richmond (Virginia): streetcar electrifica-
  tion in, 130; water filtration system
  in, 64
Riverfront Commons, 197
rivers, attitudes toward, 62, 92
Riverside (California), deed restrictions
  in, 165
RKO Palace Theater, 32
Roberts, Kline, 107
Robinson, Aminah, 185
Robinson, Charles Mulford, 1, 143
Rockefeller, Frank, 34
Roethke, Theodore, 5
Romania, immigrants from, 178
Rose, Mark, 3
Rosen, Christine Meisner, 6n15
Ross, Brian, 198

Salem, 68
Sanders, Heywood T., 189n96
San Francisco, 3; competition for water
  in, 104n26; fire in, 72; urban water
  development in, 50
*The Sanitary City* (Melosi), 50
sanitation, 54, 65
San Margherita, 151
Schiller, Friedrich von, 128
Schiller Park, 128
Schneider, Daniel, 50n3, 91
schools: for blind and deaf, 119, 122;
  desegregation of, 186–88; segregation of, 150–51, 186–88. *See also*
  education
Schottenstein, Robert, 195
Schwing, Hannah, 23, 25
"Scioto Mile," 111, 197
Scioto River, 11, 15, 21, 23, 82, 92, 109,
  118, 207, 211; cleaning of, 111–12;
  damming of, 76–80, 104, 108; disuse
  of, 29; flooding of, 62–63, 94, 95–98;
  improvements to, 98n10; as open

sewer, 61; outlawing of bathing and
  swimming in, 62; pollution of, 101–2,
  114; relocation of stretch of, 181;
  renovation of downtown area of,
  197; use and abuse of, 60–63; water
  levels in, 104
Scioto River Pumping Station, 82
segregation, 150; residential, 185;
  of schools, 150–51, 186–88; social,
  178–79, 184–85
Sellers, Christopher, 6n15
Sensenbrenner, Maynard E. "Jack,"
  106–7
service industries, 32, 38–43
sewage, 54–55, 71, 101; complex nature
  of, 66; dilution of, 101; disease and,
  65; environmental concerns about,
  112–14; farming of, 88; mixture of
  water and, 55, 73, 112; overflows of,
  112–13; pollution of water by, 55,
  101–2, 110, 114; private solutions
  for, 55; remediation of, 112–14;
  research on, 81n106; settling vs.
  purification of, 101; treatment of,
  50n3, 68, 76, 77, 80, 82, 84–88, 91,
  100–102, 115, 141–42
sewage plant, building of, 85, 102–3, 148.
  *See also under* South Side
sewer systems, 50, 54–55, 63, 66–68,
  71–73, 140, 209–10; alterations to,
  94–95; inefficiency of, 101
Shaker Heights, 180; deed restrictions in,
  165
*Shelley v. Kraemer* (1948), 166
Shepard, 183
shopping centers, 175–77, 185, 193,
  209–10
Short Hills (New Jersey), deed restrictions
  in, 165
Simplex Foundry, 151
skyscrapers, 137
slaughterhouses, 57–58, 118
slavery, 124
sludge, 87, 100, 102, 114
slums, 140; elimination of, 157, 185
Smith, Dr. McKendree, 75
Smith, Walter, 181
social capital, 24, 37, 47

Somalia, refugees from, 171

South Campus Gateway Center, 41

Southerly Wastewater Treatment Plant, 113–14

southern Europe, immigrants from, 29, 84, 149, 151

Southern Theatre, 197

South Side of, 33, 35, 88, 93, 102–3, 108, 115, 130–31, 133, 144, 150, 151–53, 211; employment disparities in, 178; industrialized, 154; lack of adequate sewers in, 84–85; as less well developed, 205; multicultural district in, 178–79; redevelopment of, 199; stench, 93, 118, 152–53, 167, 176, 211

South Side Business and Improvement Association, 84

South Side Business Men's Association, 89

South Side Civic and Industrial Association, 102

South Side Protective Association, 102

South Side Settlement House, 178

South Well Field, 108–9

Southwest Advancement League, 102

sprinkling filters, 86–88

stage coaching, 24–25

Standard Oil Company, 34

Standard Zoning Enabling Act, 160

Starling, Lyne, 12, 12n13, 61

state government, 27, 39–40

Statehouse Square, 116–19

State Institution for the Deaf and Dumb, diphtheria and typhoid outbreak at, 56

"State of the Young Professionals" conference (2007), 42

steel production, 30, 33–38

Steelton, 33, 150, 152, 153n95

Stewart's Grove, 128

St. Louis, 13; municipal water system in, 64; population of, 31; suburban population of, 170

St. Mary's, 183

storm water, mixture of with sewage, 73, 112

streetcars, 129–36, 172, 199, 209; electrification of lines, 130–31; public/private planning and, 132; and urban decentralization, 157

streets: improvements to, 138–39, 143–44; layout of, 117–18

suburbs: development of, 3, 39, 133, 157–58, 170, 194–96; and environmental protection, 208; examination of, 3–4; and highway expansion, 173; movement by whites to, 187; and natural environment, 174n53; relations between Columbus and, 199

Sullivant, Lucas, 11, 12n13, 15

taxes: abatements to encourage downtown revitalization, 197; increases in, to pay for arena, 190; levy in support of zoo, 201; tax bases

Taylor, Frederick, 37

Taylor, William, 90

Teaford, Jon, 13, 147

Tennessee Valley Authority, 98n10

Thompson, Benjamin, 167–69, 205

Thompson, King, 167–69, 175, 205

Thompson, William Oxley, 36, 36n86

Thurber, James, 94, 97

Thurber House, 185

Toledo, 10; college graduates in, 40; homeownership in, 133; population of, 31; unemployment rate in, 31

Tomes, Nancy, 65

Town and Country Shopping Center, 175–76, 177

Transcontinental Air Transport Company, 30

transportation, 14–19, 23–26, 30, 47, 60. See also railroads; streetcars

Trevitt Heights, 183

Tucker, Lee, 200

typhoid fever, 29, 51, 53, 56, 58, 64, 65, 67–68, 74–75, 79–80, 84, 90, 115, 116, 210

unemployment, 30–32

Union Department Store, 176

Union Railroad Station, 123, 188, 191
unions, 36; fear of, 31
United Mine Workers of America, 153n96
United States Steel, 36
Upper Arlington, 107, 133, 158, 170,
    173, 176–77, 184, 196; development
    of, 167–70, 205
Upper Arlington Company, 169
Urbana, 23, 131
Urban Arts Space, 41
urban environmentalism, 3
urban growth, 95, 108, 129–41, 156–205;
    and natural environment, 174n53,
    211
urban infrastructures, improvement of, 91
urbanization, 10, 22
urban planning, 93, 140–55
urban problems, 139–40
urban sprawl, 174, 181
Urlin, George C., 129
U.S. Department of Transportation, 183
U.S. Environmental Protection Agency,
    110, 112, 181

Van Brimmer, Barbara, 53
Vance, Joseph, 24, 117
Vanderbilt, William, 26
Veterans Administration, 174
Veterans Memorial Hall, 198
Virginia Military District, 11, 12n13

Wales, immigrants from, 151
Ward, J. Q. A., 127
Waring, F. H., 63n51
Warren: board of health in, 65
Washington Park. See Schiller Park
Washington Township, 195, 207
water: average daily consumption of,
    104–5; chlorination of, 84n110;
    clean, lack of adequate supply of, 9,
    49, 64, 68–76; and development of
    Columbus, 94–115, 134; expendi-
    tures on, 70–71; filtration of, 63–64,
    66–67, 69–70, 78–79, 82–85, 103;
    hard vs. soft, 50, 78; and importance

of public policy, 91–93; local frag-
    mented systems of, 52–60; manage-
    ment plan, 98; mixture of sewage
    with, 55, 73; municipal systems of,
    55, 63–68; private and public contri-
    butions to development of, 95; pri-
    vate solutions for, 55; proper use of,
    111; purification of, 80, 83, 90, 115;
    quality of, 110; quest for in Colum-
    bus, 68–76, 95, 104–9; recreational
    and environmental uses for, 95, 104;
    role of in shaping Columbus, 49–93,
    114–15; shortage of, 103–4; softening
    of, 78, 82–83
waterborne diseases, 49–50, 53, 55–57,
    63, 74, 115, 140, 147, 209; affecting
    animals, 54–55; miasmic vs. bacterial
    causes of, 50, 55, 63, 64–67; vanish-
    ing of, 90
Water Environment Federation, 93n139
Water Pollution Control Federation,
    93n139
water supply, 29, 76; copious, 53; disease
    and, 66; inadequacy of, 49; pollution
    of by sewage, 55
water system/water-treatment system,
    69, 76, 77, 78–80, 82–83, 103, 115,
    140, 141–42, 209–10; alterations to,
    94–95, 98–100, 147–48; between
    wars, 98–104; cost of, 84
water use, 1–2, 9; in American cities,
    63–64; controversies in, 207; envi-
    ronmental changes in, 52; in industry,
    problematic nature of, 49–50; inno-
    vation in, 210; and spatial and social
    layout of Columbus, 51
Weisenburger, Francis, 22
Wells, Christopher, 137, 165, 174
Western Electric, 39
Westerville, 187, 194, 196
Westminster-Thurber, 179
West Side Board of Trade, 102
West Side Pumping Station, 70, 76,
    78–79, 82, 84n110, 95, 98
West Virginia, 124; migrants from, 178
wetlands, 95, 110–11
Wexner, Leslie, 182, 188, 197–98
wheat production, 9–10

Whetstone River. *See* Olentangy River

white Appalachians, migration of, 29, 84, 151–52, 179n65

Whitehall, 173, 175–76, 196

Whitten, Robert, 158

the Wilds, 201n133

Wilson, Gregory, 124

Wolfe, John F., 190–91

Wolfe, Robert, 97

Wolfe Enterprises, 190

Wolfe family, 106, 200

Wood, Jethro, 21

Wooley, Charles, 53

WOOSE (We Oppose OSU Airport Expansion), 207

World War I, 28, 36; and City Beautiful plan, 148; and Great Migration, 149

World War II, 32, 39, 41, 44, 45; deindustrialization after, 10, 32–33; industrial and population growth during, 103; railroad industry after, 38; search for water after, 104–9; suburbanization after, 39, 158

Worthington, 21, 60–61, 70, 107, 124, 131, 173, 178, 187, 194, 196; green infrastructure in, 113

Worthington Industries, 38, 190

Worthington Manufacturing Company, 61, 123

Wright, Joel, 117–18; map by, *120*

Wright, Orville, 90

Wright, Wilbur, 90

Wyandotte Building, 136

Xenia: board of health in, 65

Yoakum, Dwight, 179

Young Ladies Playground Association, 129, 142

Young Professionals Commission, 42

Youngstown, 10; board of health in, 65; college graduates in, 40; population of, 31; unemployment rate in, 31

Yugoslavia, immigrants from, 178

Zanesville, 131

zoning. *See* public zoning